Sleepy Hollow
as American Myth

ALSO BY STEVE A. WIGGINS

Holy Horror: The Bible and Fear in Movies (McFarland, 2019)

Sleepy Hollow as American Myth

Irving's Story Retold, Adapted and Cemented in Popular Culture

STEVE A. WIGGINS

McFarland & Company, Inc., Publishers
Jefferson, North Carolina

LIBRARY OF CONGRESS CATALOGING-IN-PUBLICATION DATA

Names: Wiggins, Steve A. author
Title: Sleepy Hollow as American myth : Irving's story retold, adapted and cemented in popular culture / Steve A. Wiggins.
Description: Jefferson, North Carolina : McFarland & Company, Inc., Publishers, 2025. | Includes bibliographical references and index.
Identifiers: LCCN 2025009004 | ISBN 9781476697574 paperback ∞
    ISBN 9781476655512 ebook
Subjects: LCSH: Irving, Washington, 1783-1859—Film and video adaptations | Irving, Washington, 1783-1859. Legend of Sleepy Hollow—Influence | Headless Horseman (Fictitious character)—In popular culture | BISAC: LITERARY CRITICISM / American / General | SOCIAL SCIENCE / Folklore & Mythology | LCGFT: Literary criticism | Film criticism
Classification: LCC PS2092.F55 W54 2025 | DDC 813/.2—dc23/eng/20250318
LC record available at https://lccn.loc.gov/2025009004

ISBN (print) 978-1-4766-9757-4
ISBN (ebook) 978-1-4766-5551-2

© 2025 Steve A. Wiggins. All rights reserved

No part of this book may be reproduced or transmitted in any form or by any means, electronic or mechanical, including photocopying or recording, or by any information storage and retrieval system, without permission in writing from the publisher.

Front cover image: © deendesign/Shutterstock

Printed in the United States of America

McFarland & Company, Inc., Publishers
  Box 611, Jefferson, North Carolina 28640
    www.mcfarlandpub.com

To Kay, Kietra, and Neal.

In memory of Doris and Homer.

Table of Contents

Preface   1
Introduction   6

1. The Basic Story   17
2. Headless: The Lost Character   25
3. The Old Dutch Church   38
4. Sleepy Hollow's Early Afterlives   54
5. Sleepy Hollow Animated   70
6. How Halloween Met Sleepy Hollow   82
7. Xennial Developments   94
8. Moving Toward the Millennium   111
9. Tim Burton's *Sleepy Hollow*   124
10. Burton's Aftermath   139
11. Fox and Friends   157
12. Novel Mythologies   171
13. The Haunted Hudson   181
14. Unseen Ghostly Characters   192

Final Thoughts   201
Useful Reading   215
Index   221

Preface

What draws you to Sleepy Hollow? How did you first learn about it? Sleepy Hollow has become one of America's best-recognized myths, but how did it become one? I hope you like mazes. Here's one:

July 2015. Early morning Manhattan. I find myself having breakfast with novelist Neal Stephenson. I'm working in New York City and he's there on a book tour. We met at the W Hotel in Union Square. I wondered at the name. New York City has no shortage of individualized properties, of course. A lunchtime walk through Midtown reveals many such wonders. Still, the "W" had to stand for something. I checked the website; nothing about the name. The first W was at 49th and Lexington. This one was on Park and 17th, in Union Square.

Washington Irving was born in Manhattan. Of course, Manhattan in 1783 was a much smaller city. The population of about 20,000 squeezed into a square mile in the area of the Financial District in Lower Manhattan. Even what would become 17th would've been a bit of a hike.

But Irving was on my mind. After a scholarly hibernation of more than a decade, I'd begun work on an article on the then-popular Fox hit, *Sleepy Hollow*. Neal has always been indulgent of my writing aspirations—he'd acknowledged my work on Asherah in *Snow Crash*—and politely asked what I was working on. This led to too much information on my part about "Sleepy Hollow." It was then that I noticed the painting by Marcus Pierce above Neal's head.

In cartoon style you see a naked woman sitting up in bed. She's saying in a speech bubble, "Of course I don't think you're inadequate; I love you." Then your eye is drawn to her lover standing in the doorway. He's fully dressed in colonial-era military garb, his cloak tattered as if he's been in battle. He has no head. You then make the connection. This is in the Irvington Restaurant at the W. Irvington. Irving. Although New York wasn't then the major metropolis that it is today, it was already showing importance in Irving's day and he had conjured the name "Knickerbocker" in his description of Dutch

New Yorkers. The town of Irvington is named for Washington Irving. What better symbol of Irving is there than the Headless Horseman?

And that Headless Horseman would keep reappearing in unexpected places. A cameo, for instance, in *Shrek 2*. He's one of the fairy tale creatures sitting in the Poison Apple with his chums, drinking through his headless mouth. (Then taking a sobriety test.) Everyone in New York knows the story. Indeed, across the country people know the story. It's America's ghost myth. And it's had quite an afterlife. Quite a few afterlives.

While it may have nothing to do with the name Washington, the combination W and Irvington spurred me on to write a book about horror movies, beginning with *Sleepy Hollow*. Religion frequently plays into horror. Consider Sleepy Hollow, the home of the Old Dutch Church—the oldest surviving church in New York—fertile ground for mythology. What was really going on, however, was deeper: the discovery of what it meant to be an American under the enchantment of Tarrytown. I was falling under the spell of Sleepy Hollow.

This is not a book about Washington Irving. Rather, it is a book about the one story that broke loose from its original framing and has, alone among the writer's voluminous works, become an American myth.

This book is for horror fans, among others. Horror fans who wonder how a scary story can ever grow to the level of a national myth. "Sleepy Hollow" has done just that. It has a history of slowly developing from a funny story to a unique horror film that has sparked more horror films. As time goes on, the story becomes more and more part of the horror genre even as religious elements increase. By the way, "horror" as used in this book refers to the genre, generally in cinematic or literary contexts. Each of us followed some path in this maze to get here. Otherwise I presume you wouldn't be reading this book.

A huge question hangs over this tale of ghosts and love: how exactly did it become an American myth? Many of us first encountered it as a cartoon. It appears now and again in our lives, often around Halloween. Somehow, without ever reading it, we know how the story goes. This book explores what it means to become mythic. It's a tricky path. It involves horror movies and cartoons. Old books and new. Television channels flipping past.

This book is a puzzle. A labyrinth. Like Theseus, I'm not sure that I know the way out of it and there's a monster in here, too. It's fueled by that unrelenting sense that something's after you. You don't know what it is. You don't even know if it's real or not. Nevertheless, you know, just know, it's pursuing you. And you know that you're not the first person it's been after. Other heads have also been lost in this maze. It starts when we're young.

Kids love pretend danger games. Chase, hide-and-seek, even peek-a-boo, if Robert Eggers is in the room. And childhoods are fragments.

Preface

Have you ever met a child specialist? Theirs is a world of short attention spans. Fragments. One of those fragments is "The Legend of Sleepy Hollow," particularly if you're an American who was allowed scary things as a kid. A short story written by Washington Irving—he started building this maze—and published in 1820, this particular tale became deeply enmeshed in the American psyche. Those of a certain age were likely introduced to the story through Disney's somewhat incongruous mash-up, *The Adventures of Ichabod and Mr. Toad*. Well, it's not so much of a mash-up as it is a strange editorial decision to publish two utterly dissimilar stories in the same animated feature. I remembered nothing of Toad, but Ichabod gave me much to ponder.

This book follows Sleepy Hollow through the ages. It's a fool's errand to attempt to document every popular rendition of "The Legend of Sleepy Hollow." No definitive database lists everything, and even if one did, some have been lost and more will keep coming. This book is an attempt to document as much as possible about this myth in non-interactive media. In addition to this puzzle there are games. Countless asides and references in other television shows and movies. What I'm offering instead is a guided tour through a cross-section, a map, if you will, highlighting what you might find if you spend far too much time with the headless. There will be surprises—Easter eggs—along the way.

Another branch of this labyrinth: very few books on Sleepy Hollow exist apart from derivative works of Irving's original. In these days of easy self-publication some have made an effort to put the town of Sleepy Hollow back on the map via that route, but Johnny Depp and Tom Mison did more in that department via fictional representations. Sleepy Hollow is small-town America. Those of us who grew up in such settings know they are worthy of consideration simply for being what they are: places ordinary Americans live. And the strange things that happen in them. A few tourists may shell out a shilling or two to read travel books about such a place, but when the hunger strikes, something more is required. That's why I wrote this book.

You see, once a story is told it's open to retelling. If it survives long enough it'll end up with multiple afterlives. It may even become a myth in its own right. Sleepy Hollow has come to mean whatever we need it to. It reflects the age in which it's retold.

At each new telling, new elements are added. Even the original story seems to have been based on an older tradition of Brom Bones racing the Headless Horseman for a bowl of punch. While historians have sought the real-life people who inspired Crane, Bones, Katrina Van Tassel, and the Headless Horseman, any writer of fiction has the license to take liberties. I'll likely be taking one or two here myself. It's like a road trip.

The Hudson Valley is a storied, strange place. At one time a haunted hollow and at another a hotspot for UFO sightings. Even Henry Hudson himself disappeared after "discovering" it. The proximity to New York City makes it seem more tame than it is. Sleepy Hollow has appeared in paintings, postage stamps, video games, and audio recordings; it has been referenced as Americana in songs and theatrical productions. Further west, other towns were named after it. It's fair to say that the story is a major part of American culture.

Many times as I was following the paths that would lead to this book, I found fascinating and forgotten bits of gothic Americana. Some of it is hardly gothic at all, as befits a labyrinth. Many people are part of this story, some famous and some who barely merit a Wikipedia article. We'll follow many of them a short time—we'll meet the nearly-forgotten co-creator of Mickey Mouse. We'll find out why Gaston is such a brute in *Beauty and the Beast*. We'll see how Christmas and Halloween aren't all that different. We'll even learn where Smurfs come from. But these paths keep coming back to Sleepy Hollow.

After wandering this labyrinth for many years I realized nobody had published a book trying to trace, in some measure, the twists, turns, and dead ends along the path to where romantic leads could face off with a demonic Headless Horseman in the present day.

This book resulted from the reading of a wide variety of books over many years. In the "Useful Reading" section at the end I've tried to reconstruct the formative sources (I wasn't taking notes!), most of which I've read quite through.

I do want to single out two modern authors after my own heart: Gary Denis and Joe Nazare. Denis undertook to self-publish the nonfiction *Sleepy Hollow: Birth of the Legend*. It gathers an impressive amount of data about "The Legend." I raise it here because I'm not doing what Denis does. He's looking back to find the origins of the story. I'm primarily looking ahead to see how that story has moved into its multiple afterlives. That's where Nazare enters the picture. As part of his book *The Legend of Sleepy Hollow: Ultimate Annotated Edition* is the essay "Eerie Rider: The Headless Horseman's Forays into Pop Culture."* That essay, which I discovered only after this book was written, explores eerily similar territory to this one, completely independently.

---

* Prior to finishing this book I was unaware of Joe Nazare's essay. My sense of just how maze-like this myth is bloomed when I did read it and found many of my observations foreshadowed there. We both dug out some of the same obscure references. I tend to think this confirms part of what I conclude as well. Much of what Nazare touches on, I linger over; I wish I'd found his essay sooner! I had read and relied on Gary Denis' *Sleepy Hollow* before starting this book. Both Denis and Nazare consult more literary scholars than I do here. I have no desire to replicate their work.

Preface

Although this book was written during the isolation of the Covid-19 pandemic, it benefited profoundly from my usual supporters: Kelly Murphy of Central Michigan University, who supplies me with materials I otherwise can't access and who read this book in draft form, pointing out some areas for improvement; Jeff Hora, who comments on my blog without condemning my strange tastes; David Koslow, who follows up my blog posts with frequent suggestions; John Morehead, who likes to talk about my books and all things scary and religious; Robin Mitchell Stroud and Debra Levy Martinelli of *The Incarcerated Christian* podcast, who liked to talk about religion and horror; Dawn Keetley of Lehigh University, who publishes my musings on *Horror Homeroom*; Claire Donner, director of the New York office of Miskatonic Institute for Horror Studies, who arranged a course on the topic; Rhiannon Graybill of the University of Richmond, who not only says nice things about my work, but also suggested I explore the girl with a green ribbon theme; Doug Cowan of the University of Waterloo, who takes the time to exchange the wisdom of religion and horror; and Brandon Grafius, who has shown that people will buy such books. Layla Milholen at McFarland showed enthusiasm for the project from the start. And I thank Lee Sobel and an anonymous reviewer who saw potential here, and although neither brought it to fruition, both helped to shape it. Kay and Kietra, the constants in my life, put up with my excessively early rising to write books before starting work for the day. And, of course, Kay's brother Neal. Whether they know it or not, the encouragement of all these friends keeps me writing. The ideas and their expressions, however, should be blamed entirely on me.

Let's now explore how the dreamy brain vs. brawn, outsider vs. insider, self-important sophisticate vs. self-made worker story became an American myth. Never forget there's a monster here, too. Other stories would eventually come, of course, blending with that of Irving. The story will be disguised, blended, shaken, and stirred. And this has happened so many times that nobody can cover all the forms and formats it takes over time. So I'll be your Ariadne through this labyrinth. This is a myth of many afterlives. There will be others. There'll always be others.

Introduction

What do Will Rogers; Bing Crosby; Jeff Goldblum; Ed Begley, Jr.; and Johnny Depp have in common? Why do we think of the joyous time of harvest as spooky? Why do we consider Halloween as the time for ghost stories, and not Christmas? How did the instructions for avoiding the apocalypse end up in George Washington's Bible? How can a fairly simple short story everybody already knows still support new editions, new books, new movies, new television series, new adaptations of all kinds? The map out of this labyrinth isn't at all clear—Daedalus is long dead but King Minos' Minotaur is still in here.

Everyone's heard of Sleepy Hollow. You wouldn't be reading this book if you hadn't. Maybe your introduction was a Halloween party. Or a major theatrical release on film. Most likely, however, it was a cartoon seen in childhood. Many people familiar with the story will know little of Washington Irving, its author.* Most won't realize that this story is a modern myth. It never disappears for long in American culture.

This history, like any history, isn't comprehensive. Especially when it comes to television episodes and recent novels based on Sleepy Hollow. I have, however, tried to find and analyze all feature-length movies based, however loosely, on Irving. The path through this labyrinth is mostly chronological. Since it is a maze, this history is a good place to get lost. And like any good labyrinth, there's a monster involved.

The purpose of this exploration is to consider the many paths—thus the labyrinth metaphor—that "The Legend of Sleepy Hollow" has taken from being a short tale written by Irving to earn some money to become a major American myth. These trails are snapshots of where we are as a nation and raise questions of who is considered an outsider at any given moment. The track sometimes shifts unexpectedly, making this a most unpredictable maze. The slow move from a comic, yet gothic, tale to a

---

* All quotes from "The Legend of Sleepy Hollow" are from the original 1820 publication, found in *The Sketch Book of Geoffrey Crayon, Gent.* (A.L. Burt Company).

full-blown horror movie and on to American myth takes many twists and turns.

The story is written as a folksy tale with Irving's trademark humor, and the ghost in the story becomes a ghost in the machinery. It took the better part of two centuries before "The Legend..." was adapted into a horror film that inspired a renaissance of interest in this humble tale. After 1999 new films and novels—both graphic and text-based—laid new paths for the labyrinth. Our Daedalus was an unlikely writer named after the first president of the United States.

Irving's Star

Washington Irving (1783–1859) is an author whose star has risen and fallen more than once. Born just as the Revolutionary War was ending, he had a front-row seat to much of America's early history of independence. This means that "The Legend of Sleepy Hollow" was among the earliest American ghost stories. We've been retelling it for our entire history as a nation.

Irving's first book, what we might call a sleeper hit, ushered him into fame. A satirical look at life in Manhattan, *A History of New York* "by Diedrich Knickerbocker" (1809) established Irving's literary reputation. "Knickerbocker" would go on to become his preferred pseudonym for a select few of his works. Despite the success of his first book, it would be a decade before he published another. He, in the meanwhile, had moved to Europe. He stayed for 17 years. It was there that *The Sketch Book of Geoffrey Crayon, Gent.* (1819–1820), his second and most famous book, was published. Since writing books to make a living wasn't really a thing at the time, *The Sketch Book* came out in seven small volumes that were a true miscellany. It contained essays and stories, and it sold well, partially because of the success of his *History of New York*.

Irving wasn't a novelist. For fiction, Irving preferred short stories. Although some classify *A History of New York* as a novel, it was really a satire that was part history and part fiction. Irving would later try his hand at actual history, but he had no formal education in the field. "Geoffrey Crayon" was Irving's usual pen-name for his short story—"sketch" was his word—collections. He would end up as the author of several books—normally numbered 16—including six sketch collections and six biographies, but his fame was sealed in his earlier work. He wrote to keep income flowing, and much of his output is forgotten today. Feted and praised in his lifetime, Irving attained political office and lived to see himself become a local celebrity even as he settled in Tarrytown for his final years. His fame was largely because of Sleepy Hollow, one of his early sketches.

Irving started out strong and went down from there. The slow decline of his literary achievements didn't hurt him much. Irving died still remembered and much loved. After his death his star reascended as others began to write about the Hudson Valley, the region with which he was closely associated. Then literary criticism kicked in. Irving was considered a not very original talent. He'd written satire and sketches. He tried an amateur hand at writing history and biography. He never wrote a novel. He never even went to college. Today Irving remains primarily known for his two early short stories: "The Legend of Sleepy Hollow" and "Rip Van Winkle." It's clear he adapted both American and European tales and legends into these stories, both buried in the otherwise English-flavored *Sketch Book*.

Over time "Sleepy Hollow" and "Rip" began to be read as mere children's stories. Ghost tales and sophistication are a tricky mix. Then M.R. James and Henry James (not related), a generation later, showed that there could be substance in such things and yet later Shirley Jackson made ghost stories high art. Irving was assigned to a lower tier in America's literary heaven. Others wrote clearly defined, deep short stories and novels or poems. The American literary tradition was still finding its way. Washington Irving's mythic potential remained unrecognized.

During the time of James (either Henry or M.R., take your pick), cinema began to develop. In the late nineteenth century early versions of Irving tales were filmed. Irving's star rose again with America's adoration of silver-screen fame. Then adaptations began to appear on television. What was quietly happening in the background is that Sleepy Hollow was becoming a myth.

In fact, perhaps movies are a form of modern myth in themselves. Meanwhile, Irving was continually mined for source material by popular culture. Sleepy Hollow won out in cinema. This story has been reclaimed anew for each generation. "The Legend of Sleepy Hollow" was so well known that throw-away references to it could immediately be caught. George Costanza (Jason Alexander) could riff his way to popularity in the season nine episode of *Seinfeld*, "The Burning," partially by suggesting the crew of Kruger Industrial Smoothing grind the head of a statue down to nothing and rename it Washington Irving. The Headless Horseman, only implied, is so well known that everyone gets the joke.

The first large pop cultural undertaking based on the story was a silent film starring Will Rogers in 1922, just about a century after the story was published.* Some 37 years later a major animated version joined the

---

* Throughout the book I will name only the actors portraying Ichabod Crane, Katrina Van Tassel, and Abraham Van Brunt/Brom Bones. If another character plays a major role, they may also be named as well. (In other words, I will not be naming every single actor whose character is mentioned.) Movies will generally be referenced by directors' names, unless a more convenient reference is evident.

parade. Capitalizing on the popularity of Bing Crosby, Disney produced a big-screen cartoon rendition that would be the first giant step in the myth of Sleepy Hollow. Irving's risen star was holding steady. Some television versions, family friendly, began to appear a couple decades later, just as Halloween was becoming a holiday worth noting in America. People were paying money to be scared. Then at the turn of the millennium Irving's star shot high into the nighttime sky when Tim Burton and Johnny Depp teamed up on *Sleepy Hollow*, making it a true horror story for the first time.

Other writers, producers, and directors noticed. More and more revisionist versions appeared as autumn grew scarier and Halloween dominated October. Films, television shows, and even musicals appeared. Then, in 2013, Fox Television aired the unexpected hit, titled, like Burton's film, *Sleepy Hollow*. Pairing a patrician white man with a young, Black, female police officer, complete with a monster-of-the-week format that had worked so well for other supernatural television, such as *Buffy the Vampire Slayer* and *The X-Files*, *Sleepy Hollow* rapidly grew, and then lost, an audience. Irving was nevertheless becoming a fixed constellation in the pop culture firmament, his legend a myth. Paramount has announced that Lindsey Beer will direct a new big-screen version of Irving's classic. The myth lives on, but Irving didn't work alone.

Writing Early America

Washington Irving had been dead for only two years when it happened. The classic American card game, *Authors*, was published. In 1861, appropriately in Salem, Massachusetts, G.M. Whipple and A.A. Smith devised the game, which has remained available ever since.* Of course, Irving was represented. The object of the game, an early form of "Go Fish," is to collect sets of four cards for each author. The earliest form of the game listed three works and one author card. Irving was, of course, one of the authors and *The Sketch Book* was one of the works. But the game evolved.

By the middle of the nineteenth century, when Sleepy Hollow had once again captured public imagination, it broke free of *The Sketch Book*. You see, each game card lists a different work. Poets are represented by poems, of course, but prose authors mostly by books. Now each author had four works listed. Ironically, Washington Irving's four cards eventually

---

* For information on the game *Authors*, see Kaplan and Miller, *The Game of Authors Compendium*.

became *Tales of a Traveler*, *The Alhambra*, "Rip Van Winkle," and "Legend of Sleepy Hollow." America's first famous author, it was recognized, was most known for two of his earliest stories.

Published just over two centuries ago, "The Legend of Sleepy Hollow" soon became America's founding ghost story. It continues to hold that place by adapting to the demands of its time. Stories become legendary, or even mythical, through adaptation. There's a period, said to be about a century,* during which the base text is treated as "the way the story goes." After that it begins to take on a life of its own. This is one of the signs that a story has started to become a myth. People keep telling it and retelling it.†

What is a myth, really? You're probably thinking Greek gods—maybe even mediated by Disney's *Hercules*. If so, you're not wrong, but that's only part of the story. Myths are more than that—they're stories we tell to make sense of life. There's often a religious element to them, even if you have to dig to find it. Many stories are meaningful, but only a few are so meaningful that the merest hint can bring them to mind. If someone says "Sleepy Hollow," images immediately pop up in your mind. You know the basic outline of how the story goes. You've stepped into the world of myth.

Let's compare this to our perfectly fine companion, Rip Van Winkle. We all know how it goes. A guy falls asleep for 20 years while the world changes around him. It's a good story. Although there are ghosts in it, there's nothing scary about it, really. We tell it to kids and forget about it. We don't forget about Sleepy Hollow. There's a lesson there because there's danger. You may not believe in ghosts. You may never visit the Hudson Valley. If you do, however, you'll certainly be keeping an eye out for a Headless Horseman. You won't be looking for an old guy sleeping.

Washington Irving grew up in Manhattan. Supported by his family, he grew up wanting to be a writer—technically not an available American profession at the time. Although New York City in that period was small compared to today, it rapidly expanded to have a population of about a million and a half during Irving's lifetime. Then, as now, it was easier to get a start as a writer with ready financial resources and a Manhattan location. "The Legend of Sleepy Hollow," however, was written in Europe as Irving tried to figure out what to do with his life. He decided to become a myth-maker.

Irving led a remarkable life that included having been sent to live

---

* Ball, *Modern Myths*, 352–53.
† A few useful websites have been https://ultimatepopculture.fandom.com/wiki/Headless_Horseman [and] https://assets.scriptslug.com/live/pdf/scripts/sleepy-hollow-1999.pdf, and https://joenazare.com/ (all last accessed 2 February 2024), and, of course, IMDb.

in Tarrytown (adjacent to Sleepy Hollow) in his youth to avoid an outbreak of yellow fever, then spending years overseas hanging out with well-known writers of his day such as Sir Walter Scott, attaining literary fame, hobnobbing with presidents, and becoming the U.S. minister to Spain, among other things. Granted, the pond of American writers was small at the time, but Irving, unlike his younger contemporary Edgar Allan Poe, achieved real acclaim during his lifetime. We'll check in on Poe here and there since his influence in what would become the American gothic tradition that would develop into horror was truly foundational. Mythic, even. Other writers have noted the Irving–Poe connection. It's not generally noted, however, that both Irving and Poe moved to England in the summer of 1815, a quarter-century apart in age. And they both wrote for life.

James Fenimore Cooper, Nathaniel Hawthorne, Henry Wadsworth Longfellow, Herman Melville, Emily Dickinson, Ralph Waldo Emerson, Henry David Thoreau, Walt Whitman, and Louisa May Alcott were all also younger contemporaries of Irving. Charles Brockden Brown, while not as well known today, was about ten years older and was likely the first American gothic writer. It was a heady time to be an American reader. A few years older than Cooper, Irving was an early member of this literary set and the first to achieve fame. The grandfather of Americans who ply the pen.

First known for satire, Irving also participated in that myth-making Romantic Movement that brought the world its first gothic novel, Horace Walpole's *The Castle of Otranto*. It appeared in 1764, less than two decades before Irving was born. In Philadelphia, Charles Brockden Brown, after writing seven extant gothic novels, died in 1810, a decade before the publication of "Sleepy Hollow." Mary Shelley's *Frankenstein* appeared two years before Irving's story. Both "The Legend of Sleepy Hollow" and "Rip Van Winkle," cast in a folksy, humorous vein, nevertheless suggested some of the darker elements that were brewing with the Brontë sisters in England and Poe closer to home. Ghosts, past secrets, and haunted locations occur in both of Irving's early Knickerbocker stories. They're humorous but they're also curiously gothic, appropriate for a labyrinth of mythic fame.

The Myth of Sleepy Hollow

Two next-generation chroniclers, Charles Montgomery Skinner and Edgar Mayhew Bacon, were already considering Sleepy Hollow mythic before the twentieth century awoke. Skinner and Bacon are both writers that appear mostly as footnotes in history. Both born in Irving's latter years, they had an idea of the power of folklore. Skinner was a gatherer of American myths and legends. He anticipated that over time few American legends would survive, but they would become our great national myths. Befitting his origins in upstate New York, his most famous work, *Myths and Legends of Our Own Land* (1896), opens with tales from the Hudson Valley. The book covers the whole of the United States in the early twentieth century, but foregrounds those of this particular, peculiar region of his home state. Skinner didn't predict which of the many legends included would indeed become mythic, but even at the turn of the last century he saw Irving as a potential myth-maker. Tucked under Skinner's "The Hudson and Its Hills" section, "The Galloping Hessian" eventually broke through.

Bacon was born in the Bahamas and made his small literary reputation by writing period books about places he'd lived. Having come to settle in the Hudson Valley, he wrote *Chronicles of Tarrytown and Sleepy Hollow* (1897), a miscellany that remains in print. He too saw the lasting potential of Irving's Sleepy Hollow worth noting. Those who'd encountered Irving's work knew he'd shaped the region.

When we think of myths today, once we get past the "untrue" part, we tend to go for the Classics. The Greek myths, mentioned above, for example. And we tend to do it through movies such as *Clash of the Titans*, or rewritten versions, like those of Madeline Miller or Natalie Haynes. The point of mythology is to provide a culture the meaning it requires. It functions like a religion—myths are not literally true, but that doesn't mean they're unimportant. They give our lives structure. They explain the unexplainable. Religion may be on the decline, but belief is still alive and well. We still believe in myths.

Think about *Clash of the Titans* for a moment. Or even Disney's *Hercules*. Movies do more than entertain. They also instruct. Both of these films have lessons to teach. It may be helpful to think of movies as a whole as vehicles for modern myths. Some last, but most don't. Myths give us labyrinths, and they also provide meaning to people as history unfolds. And the characters don't have to be wearing togas. We'll explore the movie tradition of Sleepy Hollow and the Headless Horseman in coming chapters. They're part of the myth building.

Washington Irving was conscious of the need for American myths. Throughout this book the various mythic components of labyrinths, legends, mazes, and folklore will be ways of exploring this particular myth. It changes over time and becomes what's needed at any one historical moment. While remaining flexible it retains characters and situations that continue to appeal, whether the cultural mood is for humor or horror.

Introduction

By itself, "The Legend of Sleepy Hollow" isn't that scary. A supposed headless ghost on his horse throws a pumpkin at a credulous school teacher. It's the build-up that makes it frightening. The prior knowledge that there is such a ghost. And the aftermath. Indeed, the knowledge that this land is haunted. And that the motives of Ichabod Crane aren't pure. All of this takes time. The existential threat of the revenant is almost a religious threat. Otherwise we expect the dead to stay dead. The fear comes in that classic, primal, nighttime chase and not knowing if the Headless Horseman is real or not. We'll need to keep an eye on the Horseman especially.

I'm not suggesting here that "Sleepy Hollow" is the *only* American myth. There are many, of course. "The Legend," however, has often been somehow devalued as the work of Washington Irving. His star ascends and descends, and this middling performance somehow implicates his most famous story. This maze, which is a mythic idea in its own right, will demonstrate how this short story has become its own myth, one of Skinner's few.

This ever-growing labyrinth contains some recurring themes: the Old Dutch Church will show up like the occasional navigational landmark in the maze. The historical and continuing nightmares of America—our issues with diversity and equity, and our relationship with American Indians—our ghosts—will also appear at many turns. We'll periodically bump into Edgar Allan Poe wandering around in here. America's many ghosts will jump out at us from many blind corners. There will even be some dead ends. Perhaps a bit of shine will help us make it out alive. And, of course, the Headless Horseman is in here with us. Irving's story was simple, but not so simple as it seems.

Indeed, trying to follow Irving as a writer quickly leads to a maze. While we won't be spending time with his other collections of sketches, we'll have occasion to note some of them below. Briefly, Irving followed his *Sketch Book* with *Bracebridge Hall* and *Tales of a Traveller*, two more books of short stories. He then turned to trying history and biography before penning *Tales of the Alhambra* and *The Crayon Miscellany*. Then it was back to history and biography before his final sketch book, *Wolfert's Roost*, which, appropriate for a maze, includes repurposed pieces from a magazine started by a friend that went by the title of *Knickerbocker*. Yes, this is a labyrinth.

Irving began sketching out this maze but it had earlier contributors. "The Legend of Sleepy Hollow" is attributed to Diedrich Knickerbocker, and yet it was published in a book by Geoffrey Crayon, Gent.—Crayon was Irving's pen name for his books of sketches. Sleepy Hollow was written under a pseudonym wrapped within a pseudonym. These layers form a vertical maze. *The Sketch Book of Geoffrey Crayon* was actually authored by Washington Irving who was borrowing characters, such as the Headless Horseman, from a blend of American and European folktales and stories. Whenever "Crayon" reaches Sleepy Hollow, or the Hudson Valley, he adds the layer of "Knickerbocker." In other words, the published story is two pseudonyms removed from its own author and that author didn't make it up. This is the nature of myth. Others have tried to sort out the past history of the story, so here we're trying to move forward through the maze. Biographers puzzle over these layers of deception Irving laid. He gave us a story with no sex or violence, which is as funny as it is frightening, a nightmare of a labyrinth. And mazes always exist in some kind of space.

A Sense of Place

What makes Irving's story so appealing, at least in part, is the sense of place. Without having ever been to the Hudson Valley the reader can conjure it in her or his head. There's something homelike to it into which Knickerbocker introduces the uncanny. The Dutch folk fear the Headless Horseman, introduced in the story even before Ichabod Crane. Indeed, the scene painted is dreamy, drowsy, and mystical. There are many ghosts, these nightmare-prone people believe, that roam this isolated valley. But this is American gothic with a smile. The people are content, even with their ghosts. No matter whether the reader supposes the phantom that chases Ichabod away is Brom Bones or not, the Horseman preceded Crane and will linger after he has fled town. Readers will find themselves in the maze laid down in America's early gothic myth and the Headless Horseman is the key to understanding this place.

"Sleepy Hollow" is set in a Dutch world. Already by Irving's time the Dutch colony that launched New York's European American identity was ancient history. The Dutch had founded and then surrendered Manhattan, along with considerable holdings in the Mid–Atlantic states. In 1664, over a century before Irving came along, the English had simply claimed the New Netherlands and threatened to take it by military force. And it seems the English had no desire to record the Dutch claims or rehearse their history in what was being taken, thus laying groundwork for historical mazes as well. Just because the colony changed hands, however, doesn't mean the Dutch left. They were under new management, but this was still home. And that sense of place remains.

Ironically, one of the few chronicles of Dutch New York was the satire by a young Washington Irving. *A History of New York* was his first formal book and it was published under the name Diedrich Knickerbocker. It helped launch Christmas just as the *Sketch Book* would help launch Halloween. Certain it is, this place is a maze.

So it was that Dutch enclaves continued to exist in the region formerly administered by the West India Company. One of those regions was Tarrytown. It was an area with which Irving was well acquainted. It's also a region still associated with the uncanny, as we'll see. The journey through this maze will keep bringing us back to the haunted Hudson Valley. This spooky region will be the focus of the Chapter 13. Yet Irving tells the story with a smile. It's a story of a real place. And Sleepy Hollow is a haunted location within a labyrinth.

Roadmap to a Labyrinth

Dealing with a maze is much easier with a map. Since I'll be your guide, I should give you a sense of the direction we'll be moving. We'll be starting close to Washington Irving and moving further from him as we go on. We'll look at the legend as Knickerbocker told it, and then consider the characters, scenes, and setting. These are the basic building blocks of any myth. They require some level of belief, even if it's fiction. Once we've done that long enough to orient ourselves, we'll move into the twentieth century and the pathways by which the legend became a myth. The story changes over time, moving from a fun folk story to horror and beyond. The Headless Horseman will make it mythic and requires particular attention.

For those interested in the prehistory of the tale, Irving, writing as Knickerbocker, laid out quite a few of the themes and even some of the early ideas in his much longer *History of New York*. It will pop up here and again in the maze. That book, however, isn't a ghost story. Nor is it an American myth. It's a small key in the legend of the ghostly map we're examining.

This book offers one way through the maze. That doesn't mean there aren't other ways. In fact, for many mazes we pay our money in hopes of getting a little lost. Our labyrinth is "The Legend of Sleepy Hollow."

While not scary, yet it is. And it has become more so over time through its association with Halloween and religion. Being chased at night is a real enough terror, even from the relative safety of an enclosed car. What if you were exposed in the open air, on a slow horse? What if a monster covets the very head that's atop your own neck? And what if you were to make this into a proper horror film? Ah, but we're getting ahead of the story. To begin with, we need to consider "The Legend" as it was laid out by Washington Irving, writing as Geoffrey Crayon, Gent., who collected the story from Diedrich Knickerbocker.* Here's how the story goes.

---

* A list of all the pieces attributed to Diedrich Knickerbocker by Washington Irving seems not to exist. The list would include these pieces: *A History of New York*, "The Legend of Sleepy Hollow" and "Rip Van Winkle," both from the *Sketch Book*, "Dolph Heyliger" from *Bracebridge Hall*, from *Tales of a Traveller*, the Money Diggers (part four), which includes "Hell-Gate," "Kidd the Pirate," "The Devil and Tom Walker," "Wolfert Webber; or, Golden Dreams," and "The Adventure of the Black Fisherman," and finally the sketch "Guests From Gibbet-Island: A Legend of Communipaw," which, like other writings in *Wolfert's Roost*, was originally published in *Knickerbocker* (see Final Thoughts). This itself is a labyrinth.

1

The Basic Story

You can read this book without reading "The Legend of Sleepy Hollow" in Washington Irving's own words. It's widely available for free on the internet and also in countless printed editions. In case the slow-paced, descriptive style of the era isn't enticing to you, I'll start out by giving a bit of a detailed description of Knickerbocker's narrative here, along with some further consideration of the cast of characters. This will be a fairly bare-bones retelling of Irving that I'll do my best not to embellish. At least not too much. But first, what kind of "book" did Irving write?

The Short Story

Although sometimes called a novel, "The Legend of Sleepy Hollow" is actually a short story. At about 12,000 words, Sleepy Hollow falls into that nebulous category of novelette, a piece between story and novella. As originally published, remember, it was part of a series of stories and sketches, themselves as part of a series of booklets. There are mazes everywhere. Although it's the longest "sketch" in the *Sketch Book*, it was never written as a stand-alone book. It wasn't long enough for that.

Sleepy Hollow was one "sketch" from Irving's second book. Literarily speaking, he was starting from a fairly high bar. His satirical first book, *A History of New York* (1809), made a splash when it was published. Since pen names were a fashion at the time, it was attributed to Diedrich Knickerbocker. It could be that his later Knickerbocker tales, "Sleepy" and "Rip," were intended as a kind of continuation of his "brand." His brand had humor and satire laced through it. "The Legend of Sleepy Hollow" isn't presented as particularly scary, although it scares in a gothic kind of way.

Many Americans, particularly in recent decades, know the story without ever having read it. Myths are like that. Even short stories might feel like long-form fiction to those of us with internet-length attention spans. Taking a close look, however, we can see just how much media control this narrative. It's a movie or a cartoon. Painting a literary picture, Irving's story takes its sweet mythic time. Still, it's short.

Sometimes published separately, "Sleepy Hollow" is often bound together with the only other sketch in Geoffrey Crayon's first book attributed to Diedrich Knickerbocker, "Rip Van Winkle." Even modern editions of the *Sketch Book of Geoffrey Crayon, Gent.* are retitled *The Legend of Sleepy Hollow and Other Stories*, or something like that.

Diedrich Knickerbocker had established Irving's fame as a satirical writer, and classifying these two stories as Knickerbocker tales set them apart from the rest of the *Sketch Book*. Doubtless he had his reasons for this. *A History of New York* set expectations for Knickerbocker's style. It's worth pausing over just a moment, since *A History* influences "Sleepy Hollow" quite a bit.

Irving was trained to be a lawyer without ever attending college—things have changed since then—but he never officially practiced law. Instead, with his chums he began publishing satirical stories in a magazine they called *Salmagundi*. "Salmagundi," by the way, was a cold salad of the time with unusual ingredients that we would consider strange. The periodical has been called a precursor of *Mad* magazine. Irving fell in love, but his intended died at the age of 17. His first book, what we might call a sleeper hit, ushered him into fame. A satirical look at life in Manhattan, *A History of New-York from the Beginning of the World to the End of the Dutch Dynasty, by Diedrich Knickerbocker* foreshadows the lack of clear genre for much of Irving's work.

A History of New York will appear from time to time in this maze. Some of the stock ideas associated with Knickerbocker's "Sleepy Hollow" find foreshadowing in *A History*. Although it was published 11 years later, you can sometimes almost see the story taking shape in Irving's earlier work. *A History* was fun and funny, but Irving tried to stretch his range as a writer over time. His other sketches were often witty and sometimes informative. After his gothic "Sleepy Hollow," however, Irving's other output is usually only discussed by specialists and true Irving fans. We'll turn to a few of those other sketches here and there. As fate has it, Irving's still best known for "Sleepy Hollow" and "Rip" and not his more serious work. It's now time to head to Sleepy Hollow.

The Story

The tale begins with a folksy introduction to Tarrytown. Appropriate for a ghost story, from the first paragraph the remote location of the setting is emphasized. Not only is Tarrytown an isolated rural port on the wide Tappan Zee, but Sleepy Hollow lies still further a couple of miles into the high hills. In this remote hamlet, the schoolhouse is yet even more isolated from where the people live. Irving's introduction famously emphasizes the mystical, bewitched nature of the place—perhaps cursed by an ancient German or by residue of American Indian ceremonies—that drapes a special drowsiness over the inhabitants. It's a haunted place and all denizens eventually experience it as such.

Overall, the tone is comic. Hearkening back to his *History of New York*, Irving teases the Dutch with their credulous nature, and their drowsy existence in the Hudson Valley. The characters are generally humorous representations as well.

Of the four main characters the Headless Horseman is the first introduced and is the least funny. He's presented as part of the haunted history of the area. He has no active role yet, and when he does have such a role we're not certain if it's him or an imposter. Over time he'll become essential for the making of a myth. The second main character to be introduced is a school teacher from out of state, often considered the protagonist.

Ichabod Crane, while originally an outsider from Connecticut, has been in Sleepy Hollow for some time. His first name, drawn from the Bible—and there's some debate over whether Irving knew a man actually named Ichabod Crane—means something like "where has the glory gone?" (or "absent glory" as a later rendition has it). This comes from the biblical story where the Philistines steal the Ark of the Covenant from Israel, prompting the Israelites to ask that very question. Irving had earlier used the name "Ichabod" to comic effect in *Salmagundi* (Ichabod Fungus), so reading too much significance into an actual individual behind the name is ill advised.

Crane may be viewed as either protagonist or antagonist in subsequent treatments. In Knickerbocker's view his character isn't always admirable, but teachers tend to be good people, working for the benefit of society. As a Connecticut Yankee in the days when states' identities were still stereotypically accepted, his intruding on a neighboring state to show them how to do things speaks of arrogance. The English mansplaining to the Dutch. Crane's loud singing, even if of peculiar quality, reinforces his high self-regard. He's difficult to take seriously with his cartoonish looks and obviously inflated self-opinion. And gullibility.

A hard but judicious task-master, he keeps on good terms with the locals since they provide his room and board. Indeed, Crane makes himself useful on the farm, herding animals, repairing fences, and tending children. Movie renditions tend to show him just arriving in Sleepy

Hollow, and being flighty to the point of utter uselessness. Irving's story finds him settled and accepted among the families with school-aged children, especially among the mothers. He picks up some additional money from teaching singing lessons, but the farmers consider his profession a soft one, compared to their own.

To the rustics, particularly the women, he was learned and sophisticated, second in these qualities only to the parson. He was a master of "Cotton Mather's *History of New England Witchcraft*." Cotton Mather never wrote a book by that title, but his *Wonders of the Invisible World* dealt with witchcraft and the Salem trials. Published in 1693, it was century-old material by the time of the story. Cotton's father, Increase Mather, wrote *Remarkable Providences*, also about witchcraft. These two Harvard-associated, New England Puritan clergy believed in the reality of witches for theological reasons. Crane's belief is of a much more credulous sort. And outdated.

In describing Crane's credulousness and self-comfort by singing Psalms in the woods, his nasal tones heard by the locals just as dark was settling in, Irving makes Ichabod ghostly in his own right. A disembodied, distinctive part of him lingers in the air. His pleasure at trading ghost tales with the women on winter evenings characterizes him as accepted in their society. Still, he has to walk home alone at night.

The Conflict

Despite his late-night walks home through creepy woods, Crane's contented tenure near Sleepy Hollow was truly disturbed by his meeting of Katrina Van Tassel. She's from a family with no school-aged children, so they were unacquainted. She attended his psalmody lessons and, like all the local men, Ichabod was smitten with her. The Van Tassel farm, situated on the Hudson, was well watered and prosperous. Given Crane's aggressive appetite, this prosperity further burnished the appeal of Baltus Van Tassel's flirting daughter. Crane's desire for her wealth again shows him in a less-than-noble light.

Katrina is only 18, but we're not told Crane's age (nor that of Brom, when he's introduced). As Baltus' only child she's set to inherit his large estate. She's a "coquette" who enjoys the rivalry her station creates among the men. This also makes her a comic character; we don't have to worry about her feelings being hurt. All the men want her so it's the lady's choice. Knickerbocker doesn't provide much insight into her outlook, but then again, he confesses not to know much about women. Beyond her stirring the competition, we learn nothing of Katrina's motives. In some later tellings she becomes a woman with agency, but here she's simply a prize over which knights errant joust.

One truth of Ichabod's nature is revealed in his daydreams of marrying Katrina—cashing in the farm, and moving away from the Hudson for the unexplored frontier. He's not a local, and doesn't feel the connection to the land that the Van Tassels, and the others, so obviously do. He's as much a mercenary as the Headless Hessian (Hessians were German mercenaries) is, or was. This characterization of Yankees from Connecticut was foreshadowed by Irving in his *History of New York*.* It describes how, to Knickerbocker's eyes, immigrants from Connecticut settle in a new place only to move on, never satisfied. Crane is such a Connecticut outsider, not exactly a hero. Won over by dreams of wealth—the locals seem to have the same idea, and are also naturally attracted to Katrina—Crane uses his education and cultivation, such as it is, to compete. Finally Brom Bones, the fourth main character, is introduced.

Roughish and rowdy, Brom has a good sense of humor and is well liked despite his capers. Fun and fun-loving, he completes the cast with a smile. Abraham Van Brunt—aka Brom Bones—is afforded a little more character than Katrina. The fact that "Bones" is used in place of his surname suggests he is not to be trifled with. His physicality is stressed in contrast to Ichabod's ghostliness. We're not told that Brom's a farmer, but just about everyone else here is, except the parson and pedagogue. He has a small band of young mischief-makers who look to him as a leader, but, Irving informs us, he's not wicked. A rantipole—wild or reckless—character, he too is liked by everyone. Rough, strong, and uncouth, he stands out among the locals and he seems to have caught Kristina's eye. If, in the end, he is the Headless Horseman—Irving gives plenty of hints that he is—he's smarter than he's given credit for being. He's an excellent horseman, a brash storyteller, and a knowing laugher.

Thus the love triangle at the heart of the story is set. Locals know to back off when Brom sets his eyes on Katrina, and she doesn't discourage him much. Willowy, ghostly Ichabod considers himself more than a match for the stronger, and possibly younger, Bones. Pliable yet perseverant, Crane continues wooing Brom's intended furtively, under his guise as singing-master. Their warfare is covert with Brom focusing on Crane's credulousness and questionable singing talent.

As we'll see portrayed in Disney's famous retelling, there's no dialogue at all in the tale. What the love triangle shows, and means, is demonstrated

---

* See book three, chapter seven (reiterated in book seven, chapter two). This is perhaps complicated by our current association of the Yankees with New York, a foreign idea in Irving's day.

through narration either of the characters' actions or their intent as told by the narrator. Irving's tall-tale style doesn't really lend itself to dialogue, but it means any reinterpretation will be open to considerable development. The characters don't speak for themselves.

The Party

When a fateful quilting-frolic invitation arrives, Crane rushes his students through their lessons to prepare for his ill-conceived fantasies. This night, he has decided, he will make his intentions known to Katrina. Interestingly, although Brom is described as the best horseman around, the description of Ichabod's borrowed horse Gunpowder makes reference twice to the devil in him. Not only that, the horse's one spectral eye echoes Ichabod's own ghostliness. Indeed, as he leaves Van Ripper's farm, Ichabod on Gunpowder is compared to an apparition. The autumnal scene is set on his ride. Nearing the farm the wild birds give way to cultivated produce, but even the sloop on the Tappan Zee is like a floating ghost "suspended in the air."

Amid the description of the elderly farmers and their rusticated offspring, Brom Bones stands out. Not least because of his spirited horse Daredevil. The horse's name brings the prince of darkness back into equine description, but he is named here for the first time. In his reverie at the party fare, Ichabod's dissatisfaction with his lot in life again comes to the fore. When he inherits all this he'll foreswear his past as a teacher. Far better to be a wealthy landowner. We're allowed a glimpse at Crane's resentment about his life, and Katrina is his way out of it.

Ichabod fancies himself as good a dancer as a singer, and Irving notes that he might rival St. Vitus. The reference here is perhaps to Sydenham's chorea, an autoimmune disorder that causes uncontrolled jerking, somewhat insensitively known as the "St. Vitus dance." St. Vitus was indeed the patron saint of dancing due to the wild revels that took place before his statue on his saints' day in Germanic settings. Irving had found dancing a particularly rich activity for commentary in his earlier comic writing. Here, Ichabod wins the dance over Brom. When the evening dies down, the old men begin telling war stories, and they eventually lapse into ghost tales. Ghosts are plagued by the fact that those they knew have moved on, an itineracy that once again connects the outsider pedagogue with the concerns of spirits. There's a lack of permanence.

Tales of the Headless Horseman spell out that he can't cross the bridge behind the church. This is repeated in Bones' account of his race with the Horseman, which he won. Instead of paying his debt, the Headless

1. The Basic Story

Horseman vanished at the bridge. Ichabod lingers after the others have left only to leave abruptly after a short interview with Katrina.

The Chase

Ichabod's trek home contrasts with his anticipatory afternoon jaunt. The doleful ride evokes mention of Major André, whose massive tulip tree stands among the favorite lurking places of the Galloping Hessian. Then again the haunted brook, also associated with André's capture, affords only a rude log bridge. When Gunpowder balks at the bridge, Ichabod spies the Horseman.

Not aware that the Horseman is headless at first, due to the dark, Ichabod worries as the rider paces him instead of either passing or falling behind. When he can finally see his silhouette and notices his headlessness, Ichabod thumps Gunpowder into a run. The Horseman's head is on his pommel. Gunpowder, as if possessed by a demon, makes a wrong turn, toward the bridge by the church. Crossing the bridge, Ichabod supposes himself safe, only to have the Horseman hurl his head, which crashes into Ichabod's, knocking him off Gunpowder.

Later, while searching for his saddle, and perhaps Crane, Hans Van Ripper finds the saddle, Ichabod's hat, and a shattered pumpkin. Ichabod had been boarding with Van Ripper, who therefore accounts for Ichabod's possessions. He burns his books and attempts at poetry for Katrina. The locals wonder at what happened to Crane but soon forget him and move the school to a new location and hire a new teacher. Rumors come back that Ichabod has survived, and soon Brom marries Katrina. He has a knowing look when anyone brings up Ichabod's pumpkin. The road to the church was reconfigured to avoid the bridge, and the abandoned schoolhouse was said to be haunted by Ichabod Crane.

Ghost Story

The one remaining character, left ambiguous by Knickerbocker, is the Headless Horseman, or Galloping Hessian. Irving gives strong hints that in his only actual appearance in the story he is Brom Bones. However, he also leaves the question of the reality of the Horseman open. Some unfortunate Hessian lost his head and is buried in the churchyard. Locals claim to have encountered him before. Brom seems to have taken this ghost as a means of ridding Sleepy Hollow of his rival. Indeed, the idea seems to occur to him only when Ichabod dominates Katrina at the dance. Brom's not presented as the kind of character who plots out long-term strategies with their consequences. He is an American free spirit.

Ghostly characters will hereafter dominate this story, but the Headless Horseman opens the door to "The Legend of Sleepy Hollow" becoming a myth. If you read literary analysts on the story, the Horseman is decidedly downplayed. Here we'll make him central. He's responsible for the tale's becoming both horror and mythic. Indeed, without the Headless Hessian "Sleepy Hollow" would have remained a tale discussed only by literary scholars and ignored by everybody else. Instead it grew into a myth.

This basic retelling, which has a few of its own interpretations, demonstrates that any reader takes her or his own ideas from the tale. It's pretty obvious that the story is funny, although also eerie. The real ghostly character in all this seems to be Ichabod Crane. He appears, intrudes, and vanishes like a phantom. Don't take this literally—he's physically present, eating a ton and courting Katrina. But his singing is said to linger like a ghost. Then, at the very end, the locals claim Crane haunts the schoolhouse. Such is the magical atmosphere of Sleepy Hollow. The story in Irving's own words is paced slowly and reading it is one way to interpret it as you see fit while wandering around this labyrinth. I encourage you to do so.

Notice a few other things about Knickerbocker's ghost tale: Halloween is never mentioned. The Headless Horseman is brought up even before Ichabod. Brom is introduced fairly late in the story and, along with the Horseman, is the character whose motives are most plain. A postscript notes that rumors of Ichabod's survival filter back to Sleepy Hollow. He's married and now into law and politics. Or, the old Dutch wives insist, he was really spirited away by the Headless Horseman.

America's headless ghost entered national folklore, tied together with Crane. The tale would become mythology. More recent versions exist where only the Headless Horseman remains of the four principal characters—as a ghost he doesn't die. Most of the retellings feature Ichabod Crane as the protagonist and Brom Bones as some kind of lout. But not all, as we'll see. Some have Brom as the hero. And many focus on Katrina only as a love interest. Sometimes she's given agency, but many storytellers follow Irving's lead here. But that nameless, headless fourth character: He survives to become America's ghost, a reflection of who we are as a country.

"Sleepy Hollow" engages gothic sensibilities and has a ghost as (perhaps) one of the characters. The style, however, isn't that of Poe, or even Hawthorne, where threat is real and there's no doubt that something untoward is happening. The tale is, however, more mythic than those of Hawthorne or Poe. This humorous folktale with its ghosts will become horror only over time and it seems that this could happen only in the labyrinth known as America. And what is a labyrinth without a Minotaur?

2

Headless: The Lost Character

It's late on a spooky night. A lone rider on horseback in a region everyone knows is haunted. Suddenly he sees another rider. Headless. As he kicks his horse into a gallop he shouts a challenge—this will be a race. The terms: a bowl of punch for the winner. Brom Bones crosses the finish line first, but the Horseman disappears, leaving the debt unpaid.

Although intended to terrify the credulous Ichabod Crane, Brom's story is hardly a scary ghost tale, let alone any kind of horror. Sure, it showcases Brom's bravery, but a horserace with a monster seems unconventional when the terms are a mere bowl of punch. We don't know much about the Headless Horseman, despite his constant presence.

Did Headless agree to Brom's challenge? How would he even know? You can't nod or shake a head you haven't got. Or speak without a mouth. Ichabod Crane, literally described as a cartoon, is riding home from a disappointing autumnal party on a sleepy Gunpowder. Everything suggests this should be funny. It is, but it also isn't when he encounters the Headless Horseman. There's something akin to horror afoot. And it has to do with headlessness.

The Lost Character

The Headless Horseman is, as noted above, the first character introduced in Washington Irving's "The Legend of Sleepy Hollow." If Brom, as seems likely, is the "Horseman" of the chase, Headless has no active role at all. Except to frighten. He has no name. Later re-tellers of this story will come to understand that to make it scary you need to make the Horseman real. So real that even as a stand-alone character out of place everyone will recognize him. Although anonymous, we would all recognize a living headless ghost. He's essential to the story becoming myth. What is a labyrinth without a monster?

The fate of monsters always involves people trying to kill them off. Then again, they come at us with mouths open wide, and full of sharp, piercing teeth. Or they fix us with a malevolent stare that bodes something even worse. If you live in *A Quiet Place*, they hear your every word and sigh. They know how to find you. But what if your monster has no head? No mouth. Neither eyes nor ears. Not even a nose to sniff out your fear. The headless wear the perfect mask, but also possess an unusual level of monstrosity. They can't be alive, but are. This monster's threat comes in the form of your loss. You will lose your head, becoming like him, only you won't come back like a vampire or zombie victim. Since he's already dead, nobody's able to kill him. Being dead and yet still after you is the ultimate threat—he can't be stopped. He's the perfect Minotaur for this labyrinth. And this is a myth we're building here.

Ambiguous and Headless

The Galloping Hessian's headlessness is said to have been the result of a cannonball. Like much in "Sleepy Hollow," Knickerbocker anticipated this in his *History of New York*.* There he describes how the Dutch fled when the English came to claim New Amsterdam as their own, everyone afraid "lest he should have his head carried off by a cannon ball." This was precisely the fate of our unnamed Horseman of Sleepy Hollow. The Dutch fears became his reality. As the myth grows he will lose his head through various devices, some of them intentional. There are many ways to be headless.

Strangely, as we'll see in many adaptations ahead, this embodiment of America's nightmare is somewhat likable. Brom challenges him to a friendly contest. In Burton's version (more in Chapter 9), he's almost friendly to those he's not sent to kill. He wounds Brom as a warning when Bones attacks him but he's clearly wanting to be left alone. He only kills him because Brom won't relent. In further renditions he'll be either somewhat justified in his actions or he'll be just a bad seed from the beginning. In the internet sensation *Headless*, she'll be an affable roommate. This Horseman, however, crosses the mythical/religious divide of death. He reaches over and is able to harm the living. Don't trifle with this monster. He's deadly.

The people of Sleepy Hollow need their monster. Their ghosts help

---

* See chapter six of book seven.

2. Headless: The Lost Character

make them who they are. Define them, even. The Headless Horseman is really the star of the show with no spoken lines. There would be no legend of Sleepy Hollow without him. He's necessary for this myth, and he, like all the characters of this story, remains ambiguous.

As we'll see, movies will demonstrate a sharp difference of opinion regarding our national ghost. Sometimes he's a mercenary fighting against American freedom. At other times he's a mercenary turned supporter of the patriots. Sometimes jealousy leads to his decapitation. At least in war it's nobody's fault if their head is shot off. It's one of the quotidian results of people's hurling chunks of metal and stone at one another. You run with those scissors and somebody's going to get hurt. Nevertheless, decapitation is still a horror we particularly abhor. It renders the victims unrecognizable.

The guillotine was, after all, used during the Reign of Terror in France as the main engine of, well, terror. Those coded as America's enemies—our irrational nightmare often contains those of the Islamic faith—still claim to use beheading on American prisoners from time to time. To move in the direction of more comfortable fiction, Richard Donner's *The Omen*, and Ari Aster's *Hereditary* (2018), and many other movies make effective use of decapitation. It's become quite common, but it still causes horror. Headless and angry is even more frightening. A special Minotaur for a special maze.

Sleepy Hollow's Minotaur

The myth of the Minotaur, told in many versions, is really adult fare. Here's the basic story. Minos was the king of Crete, and he maintained his power with the help of a fierce white bull sent to him by Poseidon. Minos' wife, with the bevoweled name Pasiphaë, fell in love with the bull (here's the adult part). The fruit of their union was the monstrous Minotaur, part bull, part man. To contain this dangerous beast, Minos hired Daedalus to construct a labyrinth. The Minotaur, however, being partially divine, required sacrifices. Minos imported young people each year to get lost in the maze and to be eaten by the monster. The Headless Horseman is a distant echo of that story. It all has to do with the wrong head. Or the complete lack of one.

Notice that Irving gives no vivid description of the Horseman beyond its being of tremendous size and misshapen. Much is left to the imagination here. The monster not shown is the most frightening kind, as any horror fan knows. Not seeing a face is similar to not showing the monster at all. Even when he is shown, America's ghost is still not seen. We know he's dangerous. Movie versions love to make him scary. Even Disney will play up the famous chase scene, making it frightening via its black-clad fiend. The Horseman is the horror. Or at least a major part of it. Without him we have only a love triangle—the Horseman makes this a myth. But he's so much more than a ghost.

The Headless Horseman is the past that encompasses a bold American declaration of separation followed by a punishing war. He includes Major André (he'll be properly introduced further in the maze) who was hanged instead of beheaded, but even so, fraught with regret, head cut off from body by rope. The Horseman is the constant pull between two sides that covet the same thing. Land that has been taken from someone else. Here in Sleepy Hollow the Dutch, the English, the American, and the German are all involved in the dispute while the indigenous populations have been forced pretty much out of the story. The mercenary Hessians provide the unnamed and unknown ghost. Like the first Americans he's unknown but still present.

Although in Irving's story Headless is never seen clearly, movies, beginning at least with Edward Venturini's *Headless Horseman* (1922), give him a definite image. We all know he wears a cape and carries something to lop heads with. Whether sword or axe, he's always armed. He tends to prefer black, although some recent revisions vest him with the red coat of the British. Over time the Horseman's clothes have become tattered, probably to make him scary or reflecting ghostly wear and tear. And this raises the main question about him—is he a physical monster or just a ghost? He's Sleepy Hollow's Minotaur.

Like the Minotaur, he's not satisfied unless he has victims. So where does this idea come from? Perhaps unbelievably, it began with Disney. The first rendition of a story we see tends to become our version of reference. Not only did Disney add the horseman's slashing sword, it made him a real ghost and gave him his own song. Don Raye and Gene de Paul wrote the song "The Headless Horseman" that contains the famous line, "The headless horseman needs a head." The animation shows that he's deadly serious about it. On Halloween night, the one night a year he rides, he is sincerely trying to kill Ichabod Crane.

This particular song spells out the Horseman's motives and character. He's first of all, a Halloween monster. He's so scary that demons take flight before him. His head is a jack-o'-lantern—"flaming top," in the song's words. What he wants is your head. Although Disney's characters are all white, the lyrics make clear that color doesn't matter to the Horseman. He's a true monster. We'll talk Disney in Chapter 5.

His horse, we know, is large. Headless is, in a sense, part animal. Size matters when it comes to horses. "Monster" is often a term for "extra

2. Headless: The Lost Character

large." In a day of single-shot muzzle-loaders the advantage of a larger horse for dominating in battle was everything. Movie versions play this aspect up, especially Burton's telling. The horse is part of the monster. Since we're in a labyrinth, the blending of human and animal has to be added to the monstrous aspect. Recall that the Minotaur was a blurring of bull and man. Unlike those in Burton's and subsequent retellings, Knickerbocker's Horseman is always referred to on horseback. He's a *Galloping* Hessian, or Headless *Horse*man.

Can we watch the Headless Horseman without thinking of the surprise of indigenous peoples seeing this odd combination of human and horse for the first time? What kind of monster is this with the bottom portion of an animal and top portion of a human? It has two heads. In "Sleepy Hollow," however, it has only one. The animal head. It's no surprise, then, that later treatments work to make the horse head monstrous with red, glowing eyes. The horse is unnamed. "Daredevil," taken by Burton, is

An early visual representation of the Headless Horseman chasing Ichabod Crane. John Quidor, *The Headless Horseman Pursuing Ichabod Crane*, 1858, oil on canvas, 68.3 × 86.1 cm (Smithsonian American Art Museum, Museum purchase made possible in part by the Catherine Walden Myer Endowment, the Julia D. Strong Endowment, and the Director's Discretionary Fund, 1994.120).

Irving's name for Brom's horse. Burton gives it to Headless's horse. Is the horse also a ghost? The combination is threatening, and mythic.

Different versions of the Minotaur present him in different ways—a man with the head of a bull or a bull with the head of a man. The former is closer kin to the monster in our labyrinth. The bull-headed man has a brain, we know, and yet functions with a brutal lack of regard for mere humans. As spawn of divine activity, he's nearly a god but not quite. And even gods are never entirely safe. We like to believe "God is great, God is good…" Or at least we try to convince ourselves that that's the case. We'll explore this more in Chapter 3. The Headless Horseman has some further depths to plumb.

The Horseman's Nature

The question of the Headless Horseman's nature remains unanswered by Irving since we never find out if the pumpkin-hurler is Brom or not. If the Galloping Hessian can't reach into this world and harm late-night riders and walkers, he's simply another ghost that frightens with unspoken threats. None of Irving's other ghost stories, however, packed this kind of power. Like the new country he roams, nobody knows the Headless Horseman's true intensions.

It keeps coming back to the Headless Horseman's lack of identity. In what seems to be an intentionally lighthearted moment, in Fox's television *Sleepy Hollow* pilot, two heavily armed policemen of the present day demand the Headless Horseman drop his weapons. One turns to the other and says "Do you think he can hear us?" How do you reason with the headless? You can talk to the dead but can they hear you? If they talk back you'll be accused of being superstitious. Or insane. We have nothing to bargain with, apart from our heads.

Not only is his lack of a head an identification issue, it means he lacks empathy. He can't hear your pleas and he regards you merely as that which he lacks—you have a head and that is what he needs (from Disney on). You know you can't live without your head, but this revenant seeks precisely that and maintains an incomplete "life" in the meantime, returning to his grave before dawn. Indeed, his headlessness makes him a monster. You can't see his face to know his emotions. It's horror's ultimate mask.

Still, it's more than just not being able to reason with him that makes his headlessness so frightening. His lack of a head removes his humanity, just like a frightening divinity. We know one thing for certain regarding other people—if they have no head they can't be alive. Four of our five recognized senses are housed in our heads. Without a functioning brain we can't live. To be human is to have a head. This lack on the Horseman's part, along with his murderous intentions and functions, brings him to a new level of mythic monstrosity. But as we'll see in the later chapters, some modern authors have taken his side, making him empathetic. Perhaps there's no getting out of this maze.

As a monster the Galloping Hessian works because not only is he a revenant, but he's a headless man. We can't come to terms with blank eyes that broadcast an empty soul. What then of the headless? Is he real? Media adaptations of the tale really took off in the mythic direction only after the ghost became a reality. Irving's ambiguous ending doesn't satisfy. We fear that which we know can't be, but we fear might be. At the same time, this Headless Horseman isn't completely alone.

Other Headless Horsemen

The Headless Horseman isn't an Irving invention. Nor is "The Legend of Sleepy Hollow" the only American literary rendition of such a figure. In that nightmare period known as the Civil War, an Irish-American novelist who'd fought in the Mexican-American War—Thomas Mayne Reid—began a serialized novel that became *The Headless Horseman: A Strange Tale of Texas*. Published some four decades after Irving's story, in 1865, Reid's tale was reputedly based on a real event. Lest you get the wrong idea, his headless horseman isn't a ghost, but an effort to frighten belligerents during the Texas Revolution. A dead man was decapitated, his head affixed to his saddle pommel, and sent out riding to deter horse thieves near present-day Uvalde (American ghosts abound). Unrelated to Irving's tale, this novel rather surprisingly led to a Russian western released in 1973 and directed by Vladimir Vajnshtok. Titled *Vsadnik bez golovy*, or *The Headless Horseman*, it enters into the expanded labyrinth of headless horse-riders. It has nothing to do with Ichabod Crane or the Hudson Valley. And yet, Reid, chronologically, could have read Irving. He likely did. He knew Poe, and as a novelist overlapped America's first-generation fiction writers.

This is America, however, where the writer of more than 75 novels doesn't merit a biography. But Reid, at least, had drinks with Poe. Poe said that Reid was "a colossal but most picturesque liar. He fibs on a surprising scale but with the finish of an artist, and that is why I listen to him attentively."* Praise to which we all might aspire, considering the source. Nevertheless, Reid demonstrates what becomes of those who spend too much time with the headless.

---

* Howard Paul, "Recollections of Edgar Allen [sic] Poe," p. 556.

Poe himself explored the decapitation trope in his pair of stories, "How to Write a Blackwood Article," and "A Predicament." Originally published together in 1838, and parodic in nature, they seem influenced by Irving's villain as well. Poe could write satire, just as Knickerbocker could. Being Poe, the headless corpse of Signora Psyche Zenobia continues to move and contemplate after losing her head, as instructed by Blackwood.

Headless ghosts were a staple of nineteenth-century lore not only in the Hudson Valley, but also in Scotland and Germany, as well as in many other locations. Irving may well have run into these ideas during his European travels. How a spirit became decapitated is generally part of the draw to such ghoulish stories, and Sleepy Hollow storyteller Jonathan Kruk convincingly points to the European tradition of the Wild Hunt as another element in Ichabod Crane's famous ride.* The point is that stories often contain truths that facts can't match. As proof, the legend of Sleepy Hollow is alive and well. There have been periods, and will likely be more periods, when interest wanes, but we keep coming back to the story because it teaches us something about ourselves, as myths always do. Empiricism is all fine and good until you find yourself facing a headless phantom on a nighttime highway. Experience all of a sudden takes the reins.

There's an incipient fear about headlessness itself. Without our heads we lose everything. And that includes our horses. That leads to yet another path in this headless labyrinth, one that stretches all the way back beyond John the Baptist and Goliath, back to forgotten ages. What's more, headlessness plagues women as well as men, as Signora Psyche Zenobia demonstrated. It has to do with the difficulties of keeping one's head attached.

The Green Ribbon

Although Irving's many other short stories never reached the level of "Sleepy" and "Rip," he also treated headlessness in his "The Adventure of the German Student." This turns out to be a version of the incredibly long-lived tale now generally known as "The Girl with the Green Ribbon."† This story can be traced only so far back on the way to its unknown origins. The basics are that a beautiful girl falls in love and marries. The one thing her husband can never do is remove the green, or black, or velvet, ribbon around her neck. As we come to expect in folktales like this, he eventually does what he's not permitted to do and her head falls off.

---

* Kruk, *Legends and Lore of Sleepy Hollow*, p. 24.
† A particularly helpful webpage on the "green ribbon" theme was https://bookriot.com/the-girl-with-the-green-ribbon/, "'The Girl with the Green Ribbon': A Tale of Many Lives," by Kelly Jensen, accessed 20 November 2022.

2. Headless: The Lost Character

Like "The Legend of Sleepy Hollow," many different versions of the tale exist in published form, including Irving's "German Student." It's found in his book *Tales of a Traveller*. Published in 1824, this collection continued Geoffrey Crayon's predilection for short sketches retold from European legends—he didn't make up the story. His version is spare, compared to "Sleepy Hollow." It's set in France where the guillotine was still used and proudly displayed.

Gottfried Wolfgang, the eponymous German student, dreams of an unknown girl while in Paris. He then meets that same dream girl hanging around the guillotine while he's out for a walk. The guillotine had only been invented in 1792, some 32 years earlier than the story's publication. Alone and homeless, the girl is helpless and Wolfgang takes her to his rented room. The only bit of luxury about her is a black band "clasped by diamonds" around her neck. Deciding that marriage is but a social convention, they wed themselves that night. The next day, as the German student returns from looking for better accommodations, he finds the girl dead in his bed. He brings the police who, astonished, asked how the girl got there as she was guillotined the day before. The black band removed, her head falls to the floor, and the student goes insane. Almost a Lovecraftian ending, no?

About a quarter-century later (1850) the French writer Alexandre Dumas, known for *The Count of Monte Cristo* and *The Three Musketeers*, wrote *The Woman with the Velvet Necklace*. One of his lesser known works, it employs the same basic plot. It seems almost certain that Dumas had read Irving. Irving was quite popular in Europe, and Dumas sets the story in Paris with a visiting German student (E.T.A. Hoffman!), who finds the girl of his dreams (Arsène) at the guillotine. The prolix Dumas has made the short story into pretty much a novel. The first publication translated to English was in 1897 as one of the stories in a book published by Little, Brown under the rather wordy title *Chauvelin's will, a romance of the last days of Louis XV, and stories of the French Revolution: The woman with the velvet necklace and Blanche de Beaulieu*. The book is a collection of novellas. In *Velvet Necklace* the ribbon shifted from black to velvet but the diamonds from Irving remain. Arsène's head was kept on by the ribbon, although, in this version it didn't start out that way, as the plot is more developed. Hoffman meets the girl before she's guillotined and only when he is courting her afterward does her head fall off. Kind of like a nineteenth-century *Twilight Zone* episode. Then, as will happened with Sleepy Hollow, the story was recast for children.

The move to a children's story, much abbreviated and age appropriate, seems to have been Ann McGovern's idea. In a one-page recap called "The Velvet Ribbon," she included it in her Scholastic book *Ghostly Fun* in 1970. Scary stories for children were controversial at the time, but that didn't stop McGovern's adaptation of the story being retold. J.B. (Judith Bauer) Stamper used a version in her initial collection of scary children's stories, *Tales for the Midnight Hour*, also published by Scholastic. This book appeared in 1977 and the story title combines the color and fabric as "The Black Velvet Ribbon." Interestingly enough, these two female authors opened the door for the controversial children's retelling that gave the story the status of an urban legend. Stamper, it should be noted, began her collection with another decapitation story, "The Furry Collar." Note the headless theme here is used by women authors with female victims.

Harried parents objected (and still object) to scary tales for the young. This led to banning efforts for children's author Alvin Schwartz's *Scary Stories To Tell in the Dark* series. The first volume was published by Scholastic in 1981. (Only much later would André Øvredal make a horror movie titled after the book.) Kids, however, are naturally drawn to such fare. Over time the ribbon becomes green. In Schwartz's follow-up to the *Scary Stories* series, his *In a Dark, Dark Room and Other Scary Stories*, a version of the tale called "The Green Ribbon" appeared. This established the popular color for Gen Xers. First published in 1984, this tale led to a revival of the legend in the way that only making a ghost story children's fare can do. We'll see this again with how cartoons will bring Sleepy Hollow back to public interest. The green ribbon narrative has been retold for children countless times since, always ending with the horror of decapitation. And it's always a headless girl, reminding America of its ghosts.

This particular folktale undergoes occasional recurrences of interest, like Sleepy Hollow, for both young and old. Carmen Maria Machado, for instance, brings the story back to adult consciousness in "The Husband Stitch"—a prime example of body horror. The premise remains the same; the husband must not remove, or even ask about the green ribbon. Machado makes clear the female perspective of the story, as if forcing the words out of silent Katrina Van Tassel's mouth. The other women in her story also have ribbons—whether around an ankle or a finger—and men, while not wicked, insist in having all of a woman's body. The horror is the headlessness, both literal and metaphorical. Yes, this is part of America's nightmare too. Machado's story leads off her award-winning collection *Her Body and Other Parties*.

If we turn our gaze toward Christmas, as we'll do in Chapter 6, we may find haunting echoes of such headlessness in the song "White Winter Hymnal," written by Robin Pecknold (a Millennial) of The Fleet Foxes. While not really a Christmas song, it was rebranded as such when other

2. Headless: The Lost Character

artists included it in their Christmas albums. The evocative lyrics, if taken literally, indicate that scarves keep heads from falling off children in the wintertime. The use of the word "throats" instead of "necks" introduces that element of vulnerability that a backbone lacks. The point isn't to be aghast at this set of hauntingly beautiful lyrics, but simply to compare how a piece of cloth or ribbon mythically keeps heads attached, whether red, black, or green. And how this unexpected turn in the maze keeps bringing us back to the same place.

This tale, adapted for children, has a more obscure counterpoint in Arthur Yorinks' *It Happened in Pinsk*, a children's book from about the same period as "The Green Ribbon." In it Irv Irving—surely the name isn't coincidence—awakens one morning to discover that his head has disappeared. Of course, he's only magically decapitated, as can happen in children's books, but by 1983 Irving seems to be acknowledged behind the missing head. The name could be a coincidence, of course, but the association with "Irving" and headlessness suggests a continuing echo of the myth. This time without a ribbon, and with a husband as "victim."

Usually the protagonist of the green ribbon story is female, the counterpart to the generally male Headless Horseman. She, however, is always a victim. Although the Horseman took his chances as a mercenary in wartime—his beheading is always explained as the results of violence—the girl simply has the ribbon. The girl with the green ribbon comes prepackaged that way (unless you research the history). The story is about her body as much as it is about her head. There's every reason to suspect that Irving heard the tale during his travels, but instead of transferring it to America via Knickerbocker, he left the poor girl in Paris where she was guillotined. The story is likely much older than that.

Even Irving's telling is disturbing in its own way. The German student sleeps with the girl—he dreamed of her face, but it's her whole body he wants. Machado understands this. Whose body is it, anyway? Maybe headlessness implies more than is obvious at first.

What makes headlessness such a disturbing concept? Beyond the obvious, of course. When you're in a labyrinth with a monster the primary thing is to get out as quickly as you can. Before the Minotaur gets you. But what do you truly learn if you do that? Isn't the point to find the monster and discover something about yourself and the world you're both fated to inhabit? Why does the headlessness of our monster bother us so much? Is there more to it than a headless ghost?

Time and space don't afford the opportunity for considering all headless characters in literature as we move toward Sleepy Hollow's becoming a myth. But the function of headlessness is clearly to make someone an outsider.

Knowing the Horseman

How well do we know the Horseman? Nobody knows his name and they cower in fear of merely meeting him. He's telling us something of who we are. Over time he'll acquire weapons and the motive of taking somebody else's head, courtesy of Disney. He's holding up a mirror, inviting us to look. Does a Headless Horseman grow bored with no quest? What does he see when he looks into a mirror?

So many questions attend this unnamed rider on an unnamed horse. When he's real he's deadly serious. An outsider. He's mercenary and as a revenant he doesn't know when to quit. We hear various accounts of when he rides. Sometimes it's nightly. Others say that it's as Halloween approaches. Some will counter that something else triggers him—the return of a foe—while still others claim it's every seven years. He rises when someone steals his head, or, as we'll see, when the apocalypse is about to begin.

Tim Burton's *Sleepy Hollow* is really the first major version of the story that pays much attention to the Headless Horseman's character. Instead of a nameless, identity-challenged ghost, he starts off with a head that we see (Shane Williams's animated version will do this as well—see Chapter 8). He's wicked on the battlefield and unstoppable. His wickedness and cruelty dispatch him to Hell but he is able to return when summoned by one means or another. Fox's *Sleepy Hollow* will take it even further. A jilted Brom Bones sells his soul to avenge himself on his former ally Ichabod Crane. Moloch, the buyer of said soul, is a famous demon and the series portrays Hell a few times in various ways.

Taken together this undead rider and unknown massive horse are scary enough on their own. As the story ages two characters stand out—the Headless Horseman and Ichabod Crane. They participate in the famous chase scene on that first scary autumn night, forever bound by a story that simply won't die. It seems the mortal combat of Ichabod and Headless is essential. The eternal struggle in the maze.

Some say, and this seems to be enough to establish fact, that he was a Hessian—a German mercenary—whose head was blown off by a cannonball. He rides out nightly from the churchyard where he's buried back to the battleground in search of his head. Indeed, he seems quite cozy with the Old Dutch Church. Almost as if he haunts that sacred structure. He's always "in a hurry to get back to the churchyard before day-break," Irving tells us. The Galloping Hessian comes back on Ichabod's final night in Sleepy Hollow. Even before the famous chase, he lives on in the stories told about him. The Headless Horseman had been seen many times as of late, Knickerbocker asserts. The specter "tethered his horse nightly among the graves in the churchyard." It's almost as if he can't leave the church but can't enter it either. His interactions with others are ambiguous.

Ichabod encounters a large, misshapen monster on his spooky ride home. He's not said to be armed. All he has as a weapon is his head, which seems, like Cinderella's coach, to turn into a pumpkin in the light of dawn. Headless is difficult to get to know. Being dead, he's the ultimate outsider and he lurks about the church where he's not welcome. That church is essential to the myth of Sleepy Hollow.

3

The Old Dutch Church

Even as a young man I doubted its authenticity, but it was clearly revered in a way that must be similar to how the Shroud of Turin is in Italy. The old guide, a priest if I recall, showed us an actual lantern hung for Paul Revere's ride. This was the Old North Church in Boston, of course. Its history is so storied that children across the country used to learn about it religiously in school. In a day when their social relevance is diminishing, churches reach back to history to demonstrate their importance. An odd feeling comes from sulking about the Old North and other mythic churches, whether or not their lanterns are authentic. Churches have been part of European America from the beginning. The myth of Sleepy Hollow has its own historic church that represents safety from the headless.

The oldest surviving church in New York is a title claimed by the Old Dutch Church of Sleepy Hollow. This church's fame isn't so much historical, however, as it is the result of the imagination of Washington Irving. It features in "The Legend of Sleep Hollow." Well, "features in" may be a bit generous, but it's mentioned in the story several times. Enough to draw in the tourists seeking to connect with the myth. It's an essential piece of the setting. A place where we can touch myth. In the present day the bridge from the chase is reconstructed, but the church is original.

The church and its bridge are the only human-made artifacts in Knickerbocker's tale that can still be touched. And the bridge is a reconstruction. The Old Dutch Church alone survives in Sleepy Hollow.

Facts spin their own stories and create their own mazes. Churches—many now sad and empty—are an inescapable part of our landscape. Our national fabric and our national mythology. They're an essential part of the American myth. And they often incorporate actual labyrinths within their very walls or on their grounds.

This particular church will take us a few strange places as we explore the setting for "The Legend." We'll consider the wider setting of the

The Old Dutch Church in Sleepy Hollow (photograph by author).

Hudson Valley in Chapter 13, but the Old Dutch Church specifically is ingrained in the setting of story. And that setting, as Tim Burton will reassert, has its origins in religion.

The Nature of Myths

Many educated, sophisticated individuals prefer not to discuss religion since the prevailing winds are those of materialism. Still it's there. If something affects you every day, in all areas of life, isn't it best to know about it? Think of the political furor over *Roe v. Wade*. No matter which side you're on, the debate is based purely on religion. The same is true of the teaching of revisionist history. Or evolution. Many of our headline issues are based squarely on religion disguised. It's a crucial element of this labyrinth as well. In many respects, the power of Sleepy Hollow's myth evaporates without it. As "Sleepy Hollow" becomes mythic, religion will be one of the determining factors. It's an integral part of the setting.

As noted above, myth is important for finding meaning. What is myth? Shortened from "mythology," it has become shorthand for "not factual." In a materialist world, "not factual" too easily equates to "not true." But facts aren't the only truths. "Myth," in origin, means "story."* Stories are how we make sense of facts.

First used pejoratively to describe non–Christian accounts of the world and the gods, the word "myth" was coopted by early Christians as a device to claim superiority. Saint Paul, so the myth goes, contrasts myths with true faith for his young friend Timothy in the New Testament: what Christians believe is true; the rest is myth. Myth as "untrue" came into popular usage around 1840, after Irving published "The Legend." Nevertheless, "myth" still has the basic meaning of "story"—something told for a purpose. In ancient times such stories were about gods and heroes. Such tales weren't historical, but they were true.

These days myth and religion are frequent roommates. They are studied together. Both work with the supernatural. Think of Greek mythology with all those unbelievable gods. Nobody thinks that's literal history, but there's truth there nevertheless. And myths never stop being written. These days they're not recognized for about at least a century or two after they're penned. Or circulated. George Washington did not chop down a cherry tree as a child and then confess. It's a myth in more than one way. Now it's Sleepy Hollow's time.

Knickerbocker gave us a story with an Old Dutch Church. As a fixture in Tarrytown, it was a known quantity. As an integral part of the setting it's the goal of the nighttime chase—Ichabod Crane must reach the church bridge. But Knickerbocker also gave us a ghost, a kind of religious monster. And he gave us Crane with his psalm singing. Later on Tim Burton will give us a loaded Bible. Yet further on, Fox's *Sleepy Hollow* will make the Good Book central to its story. Sleepy Hollow really only becomes horror when religion gets introduced to the story. From there it grows into myth. How can that be? Read on.

In the Seventeenth Century

Built in 1685, the Old Dutch Church was already a venerable building by the time Washington Irving had settled in Tarrytown in 1835, a century and a half later.† This is early for a surviving church, but there was nothing noteworthy about it. Until Irving.

Being early enough in America's history, Irving had immense

---

* The origin of the word "myth" is easily found in the *Oxford English Dictionary*.
† For an introduction to the Old Dutch Church see Allen and Griffith, *The Old Dutch Church of Sleepy Hollow*.

3. The Old Dutch Church 41

influence on the culture of his young country. Born in New York City, although he lived for many years overseas, he came to represent the voice of the emerging American literary tradition. America has been home to many writers since then, some successful, many not. Although this chapter explores the church Irving employed, and not Irving himself, he still plays a significant part in its story. Irving was never a member of the Old Dutch Church. Sleepy Hollow shows how influential a single story can become—a small, otherwise obscure, Dutch Reformed Church can benefit greatly from one tale. Even popular books on the religious edifice inevitably turn to the Headless Horseman a time or two. He's still said to be buried in the churchyard, to tempt tourists into the maze.

Although most towns can't claim such a mythic structure, American churches have had an outsized influence on who we are as a people. They're a part of all American Sleepy Hollows. They play a role in our mythology. Anyone who's sat through church board meetings lamenting the lack of funds for the operating budget as money grows tighter even as the worldview of ancient Palestine shrinks in influence, knows the dilemma. Churches invite us to look back. Some insist that that's not enough—churches should remain the engines of empire just as Constantine determined during the Roman Empire. There's nothing wrong with taking a good lazy look back, however. After all, we are in Sleepy Hollow's myth too. It's a place where there's magic in the air. It starts in the seventeenth century.

Sixteen eighty-five. The Salem Witch Trials wouldn't begin for another seven years or so, up in Massachusetts. George Washington wouldn't even be born for nearly half a century yet. Henry Hudson had sailed up this river some 76 years—a lifetime—earlier, and the Dutch had by now already surrendered New York City to the English. A small church was built.

Clearly a building preserved from 1685 was a valued piece of community history—think of Old World cathedrals in a secularized Europe. Ancient churches are often preserved, even when the people around them have moved on in their religious or secular views. And for other, more practical reasons. But they tend to bring in tourist money. Remember the Old North Church where this chapter began.

In the case of the Old Dutch Church, inadequate heating makes it unusable in the colder months, but it's nevertheless preserved in cold storage. Mindsets are what's changed. A single wood-burning stove provides heat to the poorly insulated building. Redesigning the interior loses the historical appeal but modern worshipers expect better temperature control. Back in the day a couple of related ideas about the human place in the world would've made an enormous difference.

One was simply that God did not intend for the comfort of sinners. This was a church in the Dutch Reformed tradition, and Reformed theology isn't exactly accommodating to human comfort. In the past, church-goers would've likely had that reinforced from the pulpit. The second idea is that when it's cold you bundle up. How many people would take throw-blankets to church these days? Or even put on extra layers to keep themselves warm? Instead we expect coziness at the hand of the divine thermostat. The Old Dutch Church is a reminder of a past quite removed from modern ideas of personal comfort or pleasure. There were theological reasons for shivering. Remember, one could even freeze to death in the Overlook's labyrinth.

A more modern solution is to build another church that is better suited to present ideas of reasonable discomfort. And a less punishing theology. That's what the Reformed Church of Tarrytown did. Knickerbocker's Old Dutch Church is still used, but only during the warmer months. Originally, however, the question was if sinners deserved such special treatment.

The Dutch Reformed Church belongs to a branch of Calvinism, the ideology behind Presbyterianism as well. Calvinism is extremely influential in American thought and plays into our nightmare maze in many ways. Large doses of it fueled Congregationalism and Puritanism. John Calvin, the early main thinker of the movement, viewed humans as totally depraved and undeserving of God's mercy or salvation. When these graces were offered—and you could never be sure if they would be—they were a divine gift. Horror fans can get a good sense of this by watching Robert Eggers' *The Witch* (2015). It's a rather unforgiving faith that denigrates comfort. And that's the religion that most frequently inspires religious revivals. And reigns in American politics. It's a crucial part of our national mythology in this labyrinth.

Calvinism was so popular that it branched off into many Christian denominations. The largest one is Presbyterianism but it also includes Congregationalism, the aforementioned Puritans, Evangelical Anglicanism, Reformed Baptists, and, of course the various other churches with "Reformed" in their titles. Historically, the Dutch Reformed tradition, under Frederick Philipse's oversight, became established in Tarrytown. Philipse was a wealthy Dutchman who acquired large tracts of Hudson Valley land starting in 1672. In Europe specific churches dominated different nations. The Netherlands fell under sway of Reformed Calvinism. Philipse's own morals weren't above question, but it was his decision to build a church on his land in his own Dutch Reformed tradition. So the legend begins.

3. The Old Dutch Church

America the Religious

Religion is a dangerous and necessary part of life, kind of like an automobile on a highway. Irving's America was a religious place.* It goes without comment or remark that Ichabod Crane teaches Psalm-singing to supplement his income. The Old Dutch Church plays a role, somewhat prominent, in the tale. Although Irving himself wasn't particularly religious, it was the sea in which he swam. Humans tend to be a religious lot, overall. If it makes you feel better you can substitute the word "supernatural" for "religion." Either way, it's a necessary part of the maze and it's part of the story of how Sleepy Hollow became myth.

Long before African American vernacular English popularized the use of "woke" to point to the necessity of remaining vigilant to systemic racial prejudice, the United States had experienced two or three early religious "Great Awakenings." There were two periods—before and during Irving's lifetime—of intense religious growth. Even the choice of the title "Great Awakening" points to the historians' assumption that religion, in the Christian tradition, is authentic in some way. Think about this—awakening to anything other than "the Truth" is to be caught in a dream within a dream. I said that Poe was in here.

This is important because religion has defined American culture, whether directly or by reaction against it. It's our setting. Like a ghost it's there whether we admit it or not. Historians generally agree there was a third Great Awakening after Irving's death, and perhaps even a fourth during the lifetime of many people alive today. These "Awakenings" have made religion a prominent part of American culture. So what was going on here?

The First Great Awakening took place even before the Declaration of Independence. Still a part of the British Empire, the people of the 13 original colonies tended to be independently minded. Many lived in frontier areas (for Europeans), and there was concern among evangelical leaders that souls were being lost so far from churches. The first national entertainment superstar in American history was an evangelical preacher named George Whitefield. He was a priest of the Church of England, which was Protestant by this point, and an early figure in what would become Methodism. "Evangelical" in this period meant that someone really felt their religion and didn't just go through the motions of attending church. They took it very seriously. Life or death seriously.

Whitefield toured America, bringing in huge crowds of people. It's

---

*Religion in early America in general is discussed by Butler in *Awash in a Sea of Faith* and *New World Faiths*.

estimated that he preached to about ten million people in total—at the time a phenomenal number, it's a respectable social media following even today.* He used drama and rhetoric to encourage commitment to a literalist kind of Christianity. Perhaps the most interesting admirer he had was Benjamin Franklin, who was impressed by his speaking ability and intellect, even if he didn't buy the religion part.† Franklin appreciated the social good that followed from his sermons. These preaching events, each involving thousands, came to be called "revivals."

A second key figure of this "Awakening" was Jonathan Edwards. Unlike Whitefield, Edwards was born in America, but like Whitefield he was concerned that religion wasn't taken seriously enough. He was a Congregationalist minister and may have led the earliest revivals in New England. Most famous for his sermon "Sinners in the Hands of an Angry God," Edwards was nevertheless also an intellectual. He was an Enlightenment thinker who believed in science. A bit older than Whitefield, he also overlapped with America's scientist, again, Benjamin Franklin. Edwards eventually became the president of what was then Princeton College. As a believer in inoculation, had himself vaccinated against smallpox to encourage students to do the same. Not in good health, he died from this attempt to mix science and religion. This is a maze we're still blundering around in.

Along with a number of other preachers, Edwards and Whitefield helped form America's self-image, whether we like it or not. The period from about 1730 through 1755 saw a great number of people taking religion extremely seriously, having been "revived." But the First Great Awakening was over before Irving was born.

The Second Great Awakening (about 1790 to 1840), during the time period in which Irving was alive, was even bigger and more influential. Religion and spirituality once again became important aspects of American life. This was just after the War of Independence, and religion simply exploded in the new nation. Although much of it was evangelical, it also included new belief systems such as Spiritualism—focused on ghosts—and Mormonism, as well as many sects looking for the end of the world. Not only did this sustained religious effort last for about half a century, it was very keenly felt especially in upstate New York.

Washington Irving was not himself persuaded by this religious fervor as far as we can tell, and the Hudson Valley wasn't a particular hot spot for it. It's nevertheless very important context for understanding how religion would come to be integrated in the myth. Even into Irving's famous scary

---

* On George Whitefield as superstar see Davis, *A Nation Rising*.
† Petersen, *The Printer and the Preacher*.

tale. You can't get out of the maze without considering it. It does make sense, in an unusual way.

There's a strange mutual effect at work here. "The Legend of Sleepy Hollow" has spread through American culture in unexpected ways. It was an early example of American literature, written by perhaps the first American to make a living primarily as a writer. Both serious but also humorous, it's a story that gets repeated in many different forms. It evolves. The same is true of religion. The two of them reach out their tendrils and they eventually intertwine. It's a uniquely American myth.

Knickerbocker Goes to Church

Likely the Old Dutch Church would've remained nothing but a quaint curiosity by managing to survive this long, had it not been for Irving's story. Without that story it might've been torn down long ago. As we've already seen, we're both influenced by and uncomfortable with religion. Irving's own memories of this church—recall that he wrote the story while living overseas—play a part in giving the narrative an air of realism. Even the soporific Dutch knew better than to stay abed of a Sunday morning.

The church is mentioned in 11 separate passages in "Sleepy Hollow," giving it a somewhat prominent place in setting the story. The first churchy passage contains three references during the initial description of the Headless Horseman, mainly because his body is buried in the churchyard. The ghost and the church are already inextricably connected.

The second passage regards Crane's teaching of psalmody and his loud singing in the church gallery. His own warbled notes, it is said, still haunt the church—remember his ghostly nature. Crane, after being compared to the parson, amuses the girls between Sunday services by reading the tombstones in the churchyard. The tethering of the Headless Hessian's horse in that same yard in ghost stories reintroduces the church to the tale as the men spin their yarns at the quilting-frolic. A long paragraph description of the church and its grounds ties in a mention of a bridge over which the Horseman won't cross. In Knickerbocker's own words:

> The sequestered situation of this church seems always to have made it a favorite haunt of troubled spirits. It stands on a knoll, surrounded by locust-trees and lofty elms, from among which its decent, whitewashed walls shine modestly forth, like Christian purity beaming through the shades of retirement. A gentle slope descends from it to a silver sheet of water, bordered by high trees, between which, peeps may be caught at the blue hills of the Hudson. To look upon its grass-grown yard, where the sunbeams seem to sleep so quietly, one would think that there at least the dead might rest in peace. On one side of

the church extends a wide woody dell, along which raves a large brook among broken rocks and trunks of fallen trees. Over a deep black part of the stream, not far from the church, was formerly thrown a wooden bridge; the road that led to it, and the bridge itself, were thickly shaded by overhanging trees, which cast a gloom about it, even in the daytime; but occasioned a fearful darkness at night. Such was one of the favorite haunts of the Headless Horseman, and the place where he was most frequently encountered. The tale was told of old Brouwer, a most heretical disbeliever in ghosts, how he met the Horseman returning from his foray into Sleepy Hollow, and was obliged to get up behind him; how they galloped over bush and brake, over hill and swamp, until they reached the bridge; when the Horseman suddenly turned into a skeleton, threw old Brouwer into the brook, and sprang away over the tree-tops with a clap of thunder.

Notice again the close connection between the Headless Horseman and the ground around the church.

In Brom's story the bridge itself, not said to be covered, is called the church bridge. In the chase scene, Gunpowder takes a wrong turn toward the bridge, beyond which lies the church. Spying the church and knowing the bridge is safety, Ichabod crosses, only to be unhorsed by the Galloping Hessian's hurled head. Is his turning back on the church at that moment important? Read on. Hans Van Ripper, seeking his saddle, finds it—along with Ichabod's hat and a shattered pumpkin—on part of the church road. The following Sunday, there was gossip and speculation at the church about what happened to Ichabod. Finally, the road to the church was altered because of the haunted nature of the bridge.

Even if my counting is off, this is a fairly impressive number of references to the church in a short story. It clearly serves as an important landmark in the maze. In Irving's day there was only so much that could be said about horror and religion. We may now write more freely about that mythic connection, but the seeds are there in America's most famous early ghost story. Knickerbocker's was a light touch, however, even when, or especially because, a church was involved.

Irving's Churches

Irving wasn't a particularly religious man. He wasn't a member of the Old Dutch Church, but in his day to be respectable it helped to be a member somewhere. He was part of the Episcopal Church which, especially when compared with Calvinism, had a much more relaxed outlook on matters of enjoying life. As a branch of the Church of England, the Episcopal Church was still a little suspect of English sympathies after the revolution. Irving, as an Anglophile, eventually joined Christ Episcopal Church in Tarrytown, built just two years after he settled in the area. Interestingly enough, the impact of his story led to other strange ecclesiastical developments.

In 1868, some nine years after Irving's death, "The Memorial Church of Washington Irving" was built. This was St. Mark's Episcopal Church at the time, interestingly known as an Irving church although Irving was neither especially religious nor especially alive at the time. Obviously, he was never a member. In an unexpected turn in the Knickerbocker maze this particular church has been Roman Catholic since 1957. The Irving designation was even attested on a historical marker, although a carved memorial plague was also affixed at Christ Church (Episcopal) in 1914, indicating that Irving was a communicant and warden of that particular congregation. It appears that there's a labyrinth here, too. All the churches want to claim a largely irreligious man, it seems. Such is the power of myth.

Biographers note that Irving wasn't a notably active church attender. To be a church warden requires no real theological commitment. The work is essentially to be a part-time overseer of church property and to ensure the peace is kept during services. It can be a largely honorary role. When Episcopalians meet, the rancor and aggression are well hidden; the knives don't come out until after church. In other words, reading religiosity into a warden position is unwarranted. Irving—worldly, somewhat wealthy, and even serving in political office—knew that church membership was respectable. In small towns, especially. Those who don't attend are known. There's a mythic aspect to this self-policing in God's name. But there's a horror to it also.

Religion and Horror

Horror actually has a history that stretches way back before the Bible. Ghosts and monsters have always been with us. As a literary genre, horror's usually traced to gothic novels, starting with Horace Walpole's 1764 *The Castle of Otranto*. It was part of the same Romantic movement that included both Washington Irving and Edgar Allan Poe (as well as many others). The mix included religion from the beginning. Consider Walpole's initial (long) title for his book: *The Castle of Otranto, A Story. Translated by William Marshal, Gent. From the Original Italian of Onuphrio Muralto, Canon of the Church of St. Nicholas at Otranto*. Not only is "Gent." in the title, but the "original" author is said to be a priest. One of the characters is the questionable Friar Jerome. The gothic movement would go on to give us Frankenstein, the Headless Horseman, and Roderick and Madeline

Usher. Horror spread its wings from there, becoming the genre we know today. Even Stephen King regularly mixes religion with horror. When horror translated to film it took religion with it.

Received wisdom, even if not entirely accurate, traces the advent of the horror film to the two 1931 Universal releases, *Dracula* (directed by Tod Browning) and *Frankenstein* (James Whale). Many horror-themed movies preceded them, but these two films were the first named by movie executives as "horror" films. Modern analysis of the genre has grown more sophisticated, but it remains common to see horror defined as movies with monsters. The monsters may be human, or psychological, or even good old-fashioned creatures, but some kind of monster is involved.

Certain it is that viewers in the context of the Universal audience from 1931 on knew religion was part of the very mythic fabric of their society. Dracula was frightened off by a crucifix, after all. You can get used to wandering about in mazes after a while. Since becoming more a secular society beginning in the sixties, many have forgotten that religion permeated classic early horror. It still continues to appear, but it has become somewhat more sophisticated. Dracula made do with just a crucifix and other monsters fell in line. The first feature length Sleepy Hollow movie also shares this trait, as we'll see. The myth of Sleepy Hollow is also part of horror's rise.

Into more recent times, after horror shifted more towards science fiction in the 1950s, religion became less obvious. It was never entirely absent, and when it appeared it was often subtle and maintained the distance between religion and the actual horror. The late sixties, however, represent the birth of the modern horror genre. Horror came of age with 1968's dual releases of George Romero's *Night of the Living Dead* and Roman Polanski's *Rosemary's Baby*, the latter based on a novel by Ira Levin. The influence of that novel would be difficult to overestimate. In written horror Satan now popped up as an indispensable character and he hasn't disappeared since. *Rosemary's Baby* was successful, but was it a fluke? Just five years later William Friedkin's *The Exorcist* proved that *Rosemary* wasn't an outlier, it was the vanguard. Religion had breeched the walls of modern horror.

Many successful religion-based horror films followed, *The Omen* (1976) notable among them. Prior to the sixties it would've been unthinkable to implicate religion directly in horror, although it had already been subtly done, as the Universal monsters showed. What was different now was that instead of being incidental, religion was central to the story. Satan raping a woman is pretty blatant. This is what made Levin's move shocking: traditional religion was shown to be ineffectual against horror.

During this same time the Church of Satan was being launched by

Anton LaVey and the Vietnam War was raging. The movie even shows the cover of a contemporary *Time* magazine asking if God is dead. Political instability was afoot even as Nixon invited Billy Graham to support the Republican cause. In other words, Christianity was no longer the sacred cow that it had been since the Great Awakenings—it was deeply tangled within the labyrinth.

By 1999, when Tim Burton's *Sleepy Hollow* appeared, religion was one of the many effective tools in a writer/director's potential repertoire. *The Amityville Horror* (Stuart Rosenberg, 1979) showcased a priest chased from a house and blinded by a demon only to be disbelieved by his ecclesiastical superiors. More occult, *Poltergeist* (Tobe Hooper, 1982) had a Spiritualist slant, but religion still played strongly in it. Rupert Wainwright's *Stigmata* was released the same year as *Sleepy Hollow* and was based on a completely religious premise of a suppressed gospel. We'll come back to it further into the maze. The list could go on but it's clear that by the time Burton decided to shoot *Sleepy Hollow*, religion had proved itself valuable for inclusion in horror. And it would help make a myth out of Knickerbocker's legend.

Churches can be spooky places at night. This puts us in an odd place because many churches teach there are no such things as ghosts. Well, apart from the Holy Ghost, that is. Still, not a few religious buildings are purportedly haunted. And these unholy ghosts conjure some questions about the supernatural, the ambience that Sleepy Hollow's drowsy atmosphere constantly evokes.

Religion in Sleepy Hollow

Burton's game-changing adaptation, which we'll consider more fully in Chapter 9, took the bold step of adding religion substantially to the story. Becoming myth often requires a dose of religion. The Great Awakening was going on around Washington Irving, and his visits to Sleepy Hollow had impressed him with the Old Dutch Church as one of the pillars of the community. He doesn't, however, make a fuss over religion. Crane teaches Psalm singing because that's what people sang. It's true to the period among a Reformed Christian community. Crane himself sings Psalms to calm his nervous breast at night. He reads Cotton Mather, who was a Congregational minister, and fears witches—a religious monster—in his schoolhouse. The bridge by the church leads to safety from the Horseman. All of these, however, are merely incidental references to the religious culture in which Crane lives and Irving lived, even as they're building blocks of myth.

Ichabod isn't particularly devout. He's not "woke" to the Great Awakening, convincing his students that God created the world in six days six thousand years ago, or any such thing. Religion is one of the minor hues Irving uses to paint this picture. Tim Burton changed all that, foregrounding both religion and the ghost.

Religion and Ghosts

Any discussion of ghosts involves religion because any afterlife is, by definition, well, supernatural. In general, everyone's okay with the fictional supernatural. We see it frequently enough on horror-themed television and in movies. Even in horror novels. Horror thrives on the supernatural. If we squeeze that word slightly, however, we get religion. We live in a world understood by science and where religion always seems to get us into trouble. Talk of ghosts is fine, but the typical understanding of ghosts is that they're spirits. That dumps us right back into the world of religion. America's culture is deeply steeped in religion, even if we don't recognize it. We avoid talking about it. We don't mind demon-talk, and can even tolerate angel-talk. A couple of decades back America was enchanted by angels, then ghosts took over. Ghosts put us in an uncomfortable place. Among the many conservatively religious in America there's a belief that horror, in any form, is satanic. Best stay with the funny version. The myth of Sleepy Hollow has staying power in both respects.

Sleepy Hollow, according to Washington Irving, was a haunted place. Or at least the locals believed it to be so. Chief among their revenants was the Headless Horseman. He's not the only one—remember that Rip Van Winkle also encountered ghosts, including that of "Hendrik Hudson." Hudson may have died in the spectral Arctic, but his ship *Half Moon* had sailed this river, giving a haunted sense to it that even reached as far as the twilight zone. We'll return to the haunted Hudson in Chapter 13. "Sleepy Hollow" also tells of the woman in white of Raven Rock and Major André, both haunting figures.

A standard assumption is that ghosts are the "spirits" of those who have died that, for some reason, remain here. If there's a "here" there's got to be a "there" as well. That "there," whether Heaven, Hell, Purgatory, Hades, or the Otherworld, suggests God or gods. And here's the problem. Americans are becoming less religious, but they retain their belief in something else. It's a maze.

Science can't measure things like spirits. Scientists in general find no evidence that people even have souls. In other words, there's nothing empirically measurable to remain after the brain dies. What could a ghost

3. The Old Dutch Church

be, then? Instead of trying to solve this here, my point is simply that once ghosts are in the picture the supernatural, no matter how muted, is also present. It doesn't matter whether it's fact or fiction, Irving gave us ghosts as part of America's labyrinth and we can't understand Sleepy Hollow without them.

Ghosts haunt that strange place between what might seem like polar opposites—religion and horror. Our current view of "religion" is much less gritty than how the whole thing started out. There were angry gods and bloody sacrifices. Over time, religion evolved into a respectable, sanitized part of civilized life. Sacrifices became historical rather than current. Angry gods became one loving deity.

But even early American gentlemen clergy didn't appreciate the challenges from theater, and later, cinema. Even more, especially scary movies. Conveniently forgetting their own history, eventually their god was about positive things. Horror, though, isn't that just plain negative? What could it possibly have to do with religion?

The door that was forced open by *Rosemary's Baby* made religion available to horror movies. By 1999 when Tim Burton's *Sleepy Hollow* appeared, three decades of religious horror had established a recognized path through the labyrinth, a kind of key to the puzzle. It also helped Sleepy Hollow take on a mythic quality that is lacking without some kind of religious support. Ancient myths were religious stories.

This might seem quite far from ghosts, let alone Sleepy Hollow and its Old Dutch Church. They're all interconnected, however. Ghosts are never really very far off when religion's involved. And the Old Dutch Church is the setting for Sleepy Hollow's horror story. Supernatural entities in a world that discounts religion, ghosts sometimes clash with religion and sometimes ignore it. Ghosts as the souls, spirits, psyches—whatever—of the dead contained religious overtones either way. Figuring out how to handle it is required in the maze.

Once ghosts take on a life of their own, they prove most malleable. As symbols they can charge in, headless, on a horse, or they can give a glimpse of what's behind a nation's deepest fears of getting lost. And the ghosts in this maze may not always be what they appear to be, as we'll see. And they must stop at the church.

Back to Church

It may be of significance that Ichabod Crane is attacked only when he turns his back on the Old Dutch Church to look at his pursuer. Is this symbolic action important? It depends on how the reader interprets the story,

I suppose. If the Horseman is really Brom that night, there's no supernatural threat at all. The church is irrelevant except regarding what Ichabod believes about it. Finding no safety, if he survives, he flees never to return. Let's consider how this changes if the ghost is real.

The tales told by Brom and others that fateful night indicated that the Horseman couldn't cross the bridge, often disappearing in spectacular fashion at that location. This is why Ichabod looks back. If Brom is planning this escapade, then having Ichabod stop at this point would perhaps be important for getting the pumpkin to his cranium. If Crane is looking back at the actual Headless Horseman, however, his turn to look is rather like Lot's wife turning to a pillar of salt for looking back, as in the book of Genesis. Irving knew his Bible. In other words, if the ghost is real, Crane turning his back on the church is a potentially fatal error. All we hear of Ichabod's survival, then, is rumor.

Irving left much unsaid regarding the Horseman, but new elements will cling to his description with influential adaptations such as Disney's and Burton's. For example, in Burton's movie the backstory to the Hessian includes his burial outside the churchyard and the fact that he resides in Hell. This may seem normal since it has been picked up by Burton's followers, such as the Fox television rendition and novels such as Alyssa Palombo's, as we'll see down the road. The Horseman comes from Hell. This changes his character from Knickerbocker's vision considerably. In Burton's version he can't even throw his axe into the churchyard.

Think about it. If the Horseman is a denizen of Hell he's more demon than ghost. Not only does he chop heads, but he also drags souls to Hell. The technical term for someone who leads another to the afterlife is "psychopomp" or "soul guide." Such guides aren't necessarily angels or demons, but they can take many forms. The newly dead, so the thinking goes, may be confused about where to go after this. A psychopomp guides them, usually to Hades—this is where all the dead go in Greek mythology—and this isn't the same as the Christian Hell. Making the Horseman both a psychopomp and a denizen of Hell gives him a demonic quality. Good thing there's a church nearby! The Old Dutch Church plays an important role in making the Horseman what he is. Irving's references to the church demonstrate that it was central to the Dutch folk of Sleepy Hollow.

So churches remain in American society. Our national identity—and sometimes the national register of historic places—includes the inescapable church, whether it's something to which we aspire or we strive to avoid. Since Calvinism condemns secular society the result will always inevitably be a nightmare. Religion takes no prisoners. Many Americans view the church as safety from the ghosts that haunt them. But it can also

3. The Old Dutch Church

condemn its own members. It all comes down to how you interpret the stories you've been told. The labyrinth, remember, was originally built as a prison.

Cinema would prove to be another labyrinth since movies project the makers' vision and version of a story. It's also the maker of myths. Although the first photographic image appeared four years before "Sleepy Hollow" was published, the idea of making moving pictures based on books would still have many decades to wait. But when movies began to appear, among their early offerings was "The Legend of Sleepy Hollow." The story's mythic afterlife was about to begin. But religion would never be too far away.

Now it's time to think about the afterlife. The afterlife of "The Legend of Sleepy Hollow," that is.

4

Sleepy Hollow's Early Afterlives

A large pot of tar boils over an open fire. The local villagers may not have murder in their eyes, but it's not far off. They want to take that boiling, thick, and flammable concoction and coat their new village teacher with it. And then cover him with feathers. They will run him out of town on a rail for being a witch. They have no desire to await the Headless Horseman to take care of Ichabod Crane.

Writers, filmmakers, and other creatives borrow and adapt from one another all the time. While the idea isn't entirely new, the reboot or sequel to a published story wasn't as pronounced in the nineteenth century as it presently is with our endless remakes. Early American authors strove for some measure of originality as well as for profound things to say. Consider those writers who overlapped with Washington Irving—Herman Melville and Edgar Allan Poe, among others—they were developing a new national literary tradition that involved considerable originality. They borrowed, of course, but they altered, often from available lore. They knew the classics, the Bible, and the work of other contemporary writers. They had no idea, however, how motion pictures would eventually change, and redefine, their work. In the case of "The Legend of Sleepy Hollow," such reuse would make it mythic.

Scenes like the one that opens this chapter, from Edward Venturini's *The Headless Horseman* (1922), entered as part of the transition from written story to motion picture. Movie making developed slowly from the still photograph to the computer-generated spectacles of the present. The moving picture was only devised after Washington Irving went to his final rest in Sleepy Hollow Cemetery.

Pictures in Motion

The idea of movies predates the successful commercial implementation of film technology.* As any kid who's doodled a series of slightly different images on the corner of a school tablet or notebook knows, rapidly flipping the pages creates the illusion of movement. The result when using actual photographs has the haunting effect of creating ghosts of the living. Photographs, however, had to get to the point where motion of the subject wasn't a problem. Get beyond the period when sitting still for many seconds at a time was required for a sharp exposure.

The daguerreotype, the earliest stable and successful form of photograph, is generally dated to 1839. Let's take a look at where Washington Irving was then. He was still alive and would be for another two decades. Now returned from Europe for the final time, he was famous and quite settled in Tarrytown. He sat for a daguerreotype around 1849, in his mid-sixties.

Among contemporary writers Edgar Allan Poe has a daguerreotype perhaps more famous than any other. Comparing the two is a study in how writers in the labyrinth of American nightmares viewed the world. Although serious, the smile just beneath the surface can be seen in Irving's image. Poe's life left deeper scars. His photo bears the truth of that. Both writers lost lovers young. They

Daguerreotype of Washington Irving by John Plumbe (the Miriam and Ira D. Wallach Division of Art, Prints and Photographs: Print Collection, The New York Public Library).

---

* For basic background on early cinema, see Kornhaber, *Silent Film: A Very Short Introduction*, and Popple and Kember, *Early Cinema*.

corresponded with one another, as surviving letters attest. Early photography, although it emerged during Irving's lifetime, reveals more than is frequently assumed. Irving gave Poe advice. Poe felt Irving was overrated. Both had a role to play in American horror and both are in this labyrinth.

As the attempt to create the illusion of motion in photographs continued to occupy early inventors, about 30 years after Irving's death, cinema became a reality. Thomas Edison came up with the basic machine capable of displaying pictures in motion around 1888. The Edison Company's kinetoscope appeared in 1891, but the movie industry wasn't born overnight. The kinetoscope was a "peep hole" viewing experience. The idea of a film projector would come about when the concept of the magic lantern (essentially a very early slide projector) was combined with what a kinetoscope could do. The idea of cinema as a business emerged in France. The Lumière brothers, Auguste and Louis, created the cinematograph. In 1895, their father Antoine, in Paris, realized you could project films on a screen for paying audiences. Before that, theaters were for live performances. Early cinema first thrived in Europe, but with the devastation of the First World War, the focus shifted to America.

One main challenge was to find content—movies of most of our lives would be quite dull. Pre-written stories could be adapted. Afterlives of novels and short stories began. Not all of them would become mythic. Most didn't. Sleepy Hollow doesn't hold any kind of record for being the most filmed story, but it was clearly in mind as a candidate for a well-known story that would be fit for film.

Before long photographers and filmmakers began to realize that scary images would attract customers with cash. There was something uncanny about photography itself. In the silent era, "haunted house" films showed off the potential for special effects. Even in the initial days of cinema some horror themes crept in. A rendition of *Frankenstein* even lurked among Edison's early efforts. Budding experiments in cinema included attempts to shock as well as delight. Elements of what would come to be called horror captivated filmmakers from the beginning. Given the prevalence of Spiritualism at the time, ghosts were a popular subject. Indeed, Spiritualism used ghost photography as one of its pieces of supporting evidence.

It wasn't difficult to scare Americans in the early days of the twentieth century. A set of dancing skeletons in a cartoon could be considered macabre and grotesque. Too much for children. Although wildly popular, the first horror films were treated with distaste among "society." From the beginning experts have implied that fear is a negative emotion, to be avoided at all costs. Horror would nevertheless prove immensely popular in movies.

Still healing from the wounds of being forced out of isolation by the First World War, America in the 1920s was suspicious of German products. Early explorations into horror themes such as *The Cabinet of Dr. Caligari* and *Nosferatu*, being German films, didn't take off right away, but they inspired similar efforts. One of the first American feature-length horror-themed films was based on Washington Irving and it too was released in 1922, just like *Nosferatu*.

Taking the Reins from Irving

Irving's "Legend of Sleepy Hollow" is compelling because of what it doesn't say. Its brevity allows for reader interpretation. Is the ghost real? What actually happened to Ichabod Crane? And what of the backstory to these characters—who was Brom Bones, really? Or Katrina Van Tassel? Does that pumpkin prove anything? Brom's reaction to it suggests as much but remains ambiguous. All of these questions have left open countless avenues for adaptation.

Retellings of "The Legend of Sleepy Hollow," like the fragments of a shattered pumpkin, lie strewn here and there. Sleepy Hollow and Headless Horseman iterations would become quite numerous. Several movies and television versions have been produced, spanning the entire history of motion pictures. We'll explore many of these in our story of how Sleepy Hollow became an American myth. In addition to being an American entry into the literary realm of the ghost story, "The Legend of Sleepy Hollow" is also an early American entry into cinema. The first adaptations of the legend generally aren't discussed in the history of horror. Sleepy Hollow's a subject not often taken seriously, and honestly, early movies based on the tale just weren't that scary. They followed Irving's smile. For the impact the story has had, however, it's received surprisingly little sustained attention overall. This is true although the Headless Horseman, like any good monster, keeps coming back.

Literature is never perfectly adapted to other media, of course. A movie reflects the vision of a director, screenwriter, and countless others. The results bear the imprint of those cast as actors. Words are translated into images. Sometimes story elements are altered to become something new. And films frequently stick in our minds more vividly than the exact wording of an author's written expression. We've all seen a movie without reading the book, if we're honest about it. Among its many afterlives, the cinematic efforts to retell Sleepy Hollow continue to influence the tradition with many labyrinthian innovations. Traditions grow until we're unsure of how the story originally went, if we even care to know. One way cinema changed Sleepy Hollow was bringing an already popular story to the level of myth.

When it comes to a short story there are obvious issues adapting it to a feature-length film. First of all there's the length disparity. This didn't apply to early movies, which tended to be what we'd now classify as "shorts," but over time feature films grew to expected formats of over an hour—the main feature of the entertainment. A story a few pages long can require filler to reach the present 90-minute target of the feature-length movie, even if it's an attempt to be faithful to the written version. For an author like Irving, born before the motion picture was invented, writing for the screen wasn't even a consideration. Some Stephen King shorts have been made into feature films but King is a child of the cinema era and that brings with it an awareness of cinematic possibilities, intentional or not. Irving's short story is too compelling to leave alone despite its lack of cinema-ready content.

Please note—although there is a canonical version of "The Legend of Sleepy Hollow" in Washington Irving's own words, any published story becomes only one possible rendition once it leaves the press. Readers are interpreters. Irving himself borrowed ideas that gave us this classic tale. Others will change it until, in some cases, it's almost unrecognizable, with only its mythic skeleton remaining. Irving gets the credit, but this is *our* story. Sleepy Hollow is what we need it to be. And these days, that's horror. But it started out much as much more comedic. It never really loses Irving's smile.

Many of us were likely introduced to the Headless Horseman and company through media first. A Disney Halloween airing, for example, when we were kids gathered around the television like 101 Dalmatian puppies. Visual presentations leave their hooks in us, and many will find their first introduction to Irving's descriptive, avuncular literary style a chore to read. We already know how the story goes, thank you.

A comprehensive list of adaptions would perhaps be quite useful and would demonstrate just how pervasive a tale this is. While this book isn't such a comprehensive treatment, it will hopefully be a useful starting point for wandering the maze of America's ghost story as it becomes myth. Sleepy Hollow is in many ways the start of the American horror tradition. Although intended as a folksy tall-tale, it's worth considering that America's earliest literary tradition included at least a couple of ghost stories. Soon others would add to the number. Poe would transform the horror genre forever, and he took advice from Irving. Washington Irving had a fondness for ghost stories.

In addition to the *Sketch Book*, Irving wrote five other books of short stories in this vein—"sketches" was his preferred term—some of which feature ghosts. Irving wasn't a genre writer. Some of his sketches are more essays than stories. Although these other tales failed to capture the popular imagination like "The Legend," they shouldn't be forgotten. Like most writers, Irving had to earn a living and all his life he collected material that could be worked into stories and essays. The *Sketch Book* was his earliest such collection.

"Rip Van Winkle" was published in 1819, the year before "The Legend of Sleepy Hollow." It too is set in the Catskills along the Hudson River. The village in the story is unnamed. After Rip drinks the liquor of the ghosts of Henry Hudson's crew—not knowing who they are—he sleeps for 20 years. As in Sleepy Hollow, an eerie air pervades the story. These two longest-lasting Knickerbocker tales helped blaze the trail for other American writers, and many followed down the path that would lead to the horror genre as we recognize it today in Shirley Jackson and Stephen King. When Irving began to be translated to film, the first story in movie form was "Rip."

From Story to Film

Some of the earliest cinematic renditions of "The Legend" are, unfortunately, lost. The first using Sleepy Hollow in its title seems to have been "Rip Leaving Sleepy Hollow," from 1896. Certain it is, these were the early days of film—even before attending a theater was part of the experience. Nevertheless, the art form had only been around for about a year when Washington Irving (who'd died about 37 years earlier) was being adapted to it. The film *Rip Van Winkle*, the parent film to "Rip Leaving Sleepy Hollow," was actually a series of shorts focused on Irving's other best known story. In fact, the two tales intertwine throughout time. Although "Rip Van Winkle" wasn't explicitly set in Sleepy Hollow by Irving, the Hollow's name power (or "brand") suggested its use as a setting here. The "Rip Leaving Sleepy Hollow" segment of the movie is one of eight episodes. It was produced by B.A. Rolfe Photoplays, Inc. The episode is very brief and too early to have intertitles with dialogue. The film still exists and can be found in a variety of media but it's not directly about our myth.

Eventually "Sleepy Hollow" would surpass "Rip Van Winkle" on celluloid. None of Irving's other ghost stories made it to film. The myth of Sleepy Hollow kept gaining ground. Many adaptations of "Sleepy Hollow" appeared after 1999, and many more again after 2013. The first year was pivotal because of Tim Burton's film and the latter because of Fox's four-season wonder, *Sleepy Hollow*. Both were surprisingly successful. A curious public couldn't get enough of a two-hundred-year-old story. Not that there had necessarily been a lull before that. A rather steady number of renditions had been produced in the early years of cinema, generally amusing in tone.

Remember, early cinematographers showcased a new technology but that medium required content. A recognized story, no matter how loose or padded, served especially well. Far better, however, was a story that had already acquired enough fame that customers would pay to see it acted out. Irving's star held steady into the cinematographic era when seriously scary material was still considered to be in bad taste. Early versions of Sleepy Hollow were funny. The story has been evolving as America's maze keeps shifting its path. Movies reveal how a funny story turned into horror. Although this is a labyrinth, it's not one without considerable popularity. We'll follow a few of these paths through time, making our way toward the present.

Already by the mid-nineteenth century, "The Legend of Sleepy Hollow" was perhaps America's most famous ghost story. It's fiction, of course, and Irving strongly implies that Crane is the victim of a prank by Brom Bones. It's a ghost story, yes, but one told with a wink and a nod. Filmmakers have had to figure out and sell their own interpretations. Be faithful to Irving, or enlarge the maze with new ideas?

Early Cinema

Our first surviving feature-length movie of Ichabod and company appeared in 1922, an important year for what would become the horror genre. But it wasn't the first version filmed. A group called the Kalem Company (named for its founders, George Kleine, Samuel Long, and Frank J. Marion) produced a short called *The Legend of Sleepy Hollow* in 1908. Little is known of the actual film other than that it existed. The Kalem Company was an innovative film studio that produced some early hits. It was eventually sold to Vitagraph Studios. Early on, Sleepy Hollow had obviously captured the cinematic imagination.*

Even the title Sleepy Hollow alone had some currency, as we just saw with Rolfe's *Rip Van Winkle*. A director named Milton J. Fahrney produced a short titled simply *Sleepy Hollow* in 1911, but it had nothing to do with Irving's story beyond being about a jealous man. Perhaps it was an attempt to capitalize on public interest in Irving's legend. Interestingly, this film ended with an "it was all a dream" resolution, which will reappear later in this maze. It wouldn't be the last time "Sleepy Hollow" would

---

* *The Moving Picture World* (1907–1927) was the source for most of the information on specific early films.

appear in a title unrelated to Knickerbocker's story, counting on its selling power.

Also lost, another film called *The Legend of Sleepy Hollow* was directed by Étienne Arnaud and released in 1912. Tagged as both a short and a comedy, this version left a bit more of a paper trail. Arnaud was a French director and screenwriter, considered one of the pioneers of French film. Between 1905 and 1914 he directed about 60 movies, mostly shorts. Eclair American and American Standard Films are listed as the production companies for Arnaud's *Sleepy Hollow*.

Alec B. Francis was cast as Ichabod Crane. A former London lawyer, Francis gave up law to pursue a theatrical career, even as Irving gave up law to write. Francis moved to America and worked in Vaudeville. "The Legend of Sleepy Hollow" was among his first film roles. He would eventually appear in over 240 films, generally of the silent variety. He's our first named actor in the role of Ichabod.

The Moving Picture World, an early trade journal that ran through 1927, summarized Arnaud's film as follows: "Here is the heart-rending narrative of Ichabod Crane, the schoolmaster of Sleepy Hollow, and his strenuous courtship, the quilting bee, the village dance, the bragging of Ichabod and the true love of Katrina and Brown [sic] Bones, and finally the merry prank by which Ichabod is pursued by the Headless Horseman with a pumpkin lantern in his hand."*

There are several things to notice here. One is that the plot is "heart-rending," presumably for Ichabod. This implies that early on he's shifted from Irving's interloper to protagonist. The description presumes that the reader already knows the story and that the ghost is really Brom. And consider that last descriptive bit: "pumpkin lantern." We can't determine for sure if this was a jack-o'-lantern, but it sounds like it might've been. If it was, this began the association of "Sleepy Hollow" with Halloween. We'll peer more closely at how Halloween helps grow the story to myth in Chapter 6.

There was also a review of the film in *Moving Picture World*:

> A pleasing picture made from Washington Irving's famous story of the school teacher of Sleepy Hollow. There's a schoolhouse scene, with little Dutch-American children that was much liked, as was the quilting bee where the older young folks are having a jollification. It isn't an exciting picture, and the headless horseman won't fool even the children, naturally. Yet we call the release a fair feature; it represents a famous and widely popular story. The little stone church of the picture looks very much like the Sleepy Hollow church at Tarrytown. It is well photographed.†

---

* Vol. 12, No. 3, April 20, 1912, p. 270.
† Vol. 12, No. 5, May 4, 1912, p. 427.

From this we can surmise that the Horseman's a "merry prank," and not really a ghost. Also, the story follows Irving fairly closely. Except the telling is sympathetic to Crane. Movies tend to make Crane the hero of this myth. As Irving wrote him he's perhaps likable, but to anyone who knew his *History of New York*, the Yankee interloper is a kind of anti-hero. We can also see that the story is well known and the movie isn't scary. That will come later. Note that the church is singled out in the review; that church remains central and gains additional significance in Burton's version, as we'll see.

Since copies of this cinematic portrayal haven't survived, and since we have no way of knowing what those responsible for the Disney cartoon had watched, any direct line of causation regarding Halloween would be speculative. It may be that much of the Halloween innovation attributed to Disney may actually reside in movies earlier in the history of the medium. I tend to give Disney credit for the Halloweening of the story—for convenience—but there was likely a more obscure path hidden in this maze.

The year 1921 saw yet another short titled *Sleepy Hollow*, this one in the Post Nature series. Listed as a documentary, it is one of only 36 listings for the production company, which was distributed by Paramount. This one is lost as well, leaving no real trail to follow. A large majority of early films were lost since the medium was considered an ephemeral form of entertainment.

So in the first quarter-century of cinema's life, at least four movies focused on the Irving stories set in the Hudson Valley. Hunger for content in general, however, shouldn't be underestimated. A glance through an early film journal or two will demonstrate that hundreds of films were being made, and Sleepy Hollow wasn't unique in the attention it was receiving. In fact other well-known stories were filmed with greater frequency. Nevertheless, Irving's tale was becoming an American myth nestled just north of New York City. The *Sketch Book* brought attention to the region that easily translated to cinema. The draw would prove irresistible as the story grew into myth.

These short films apparently exist only in the trace fossils they've left, and although they may well have influenced the first feature-length film of "The Legend" and later renditions. They also helped to garner widespread attention even though they haven't survived. They're lost in the maze, and have become, in a sense, ghosts themselves. They demonstrate, however, that interest in Irving's stories early on caught the imagination of filmmakers. By the time the first feature film based on the story was released, engaging a major star of the period, short cinematographic efforts had already been underway with the story in the silent era. Ghost stories were early favorites among filmmakers.

4. Sleepy Hollow's Early Afterlives

The First Feature-Length Film

The year 1922 was a landmark for the burgeoning horror film genre. Not only did F.W. Murnau's ill-fated *Nosferatu* appear that year, but so did Benjamin Christensen's *Häxan*—part documentary, part horror fiction about witches. *Nosferatu* violated copyright laws for Bram Stoker's *Dracula* and was nearly lost to history when the copies were ordered destroyed. *Häxan* ran into difficulties with censors in many countries, including the United States. The same year saw the first known feature-length film of Sleepy Hollow. Edward D. Venturini's *The Headless Horseman* not only demonstrated the feature-length viability of the short tale, it took the first tentative steps toward horror. The special effects of the Horseman alone must've been a draw to directors who enjoyed a challenge.

The Headless Horseman, while not a featured character in these early films, would ultimately be essential to transforming the story into a myth, as we saw in Chapter 2. Instead, early film makers focused on Ichabod Crane, making him the protagonist. It would take the Horseman to make it mythic, but Edward Venturini seems an unlikely myth-maker. He's credited with directing nine films, mostly forgotten. But *The Headless Horseman* was his first, and he understood the concept of star power.

The film's writer, Carl Stearns Clancy, was best known for being the first person to circumnavigate the world—or at least the dry parts—on a motorcycle. His writing credits included his accounts of his journeys, which helped finance the venture. He was also a film producer, and he also holds that credit for *Headless Horseman*. But what of the story? Is it simply Knickerbocker translated to celluloid? Although even a silent film would require extra material to transform to the full-length film format, Venturini stayed fairly close to Irving for the action. Added material, however, focuses on religion.

Before you get the wrong idea, I refer to films by their directors' names. This convention masks the fact that movies are collaborative projects with many influences. I want to emphasize up front that I follow the convention merely as shorthand. Directors' names are loaded names.

Venturini's star was Will Rogers, famous for never meeting a man he didn't like. Already known for his Vaudeville work and film roles, Rogers was well qualified to be an Irvingesque Ichabod Crane. Ironically fitting for America's ghostly labyrinth, he was part Cherokee from both parents; a living reminder of what had been stolen from his ancestors. He'd become a famous humorist, and Irving's story was written in a humorous vein. Consider the description of Ichabod that Irving offers: "He was tall, but exceedingly lank, with narrow shoulders, long arms and legs, hands that dangled a mile out of his sleeves, feet that might have served for shovels and his whole frame most loosely hung together. His head was small, and flat at top, with huge ears, large green glassy eyes, and a long snipe nose, so that it looked like a weathercock perched upon his spindle neck, to tell which way the wind blew."

This verbal parody fits the folkloric tone of Irving's humorous story. Venturini took a "literalist" approach in making Crane almost a caricature. Perhaps not as spindly as some current actors, Rogers nevertheless sports an odd hairstyle and clothes clearly too small, creating a believable outsider Crane. The film is funny, but with a haunting potential.

Overall the movie tries to capture many of the details described by Irving. The story, however, features a couple of new scenes in the 70 minutes it fills. Rogers' Crane is comical but also somewhat unsympathetic, in keeping with Knickerbocker's tone. The question of whether Crane is essentially good or self-serving will constantly come up throughout this maze. Irving seems ambivalent about him but overall, Knickerbocker casts Yankees as problematic. For example, perhaps in an effort to be true to the time, the film presents Crane violently beating a student with a switch.

Will Rogers as Ichabod Crane, from Edward Venturini's *Headless Horseman*, lobby card.

He's also somewhat vain. He's a bookworm but his efforts in the community are entirely selfish.

This cinematic version suggests there is a real ghost of a Headless Horseman, rumored to be a Hessian soldier, but the "ghost" that chases Ichabod off is also revealed to be Brom Bones. Shown early only in a brief cutaway shot, the actual Horseman plays no role in the action. The only character that the story really develops is that of Crane.

The opening card of the film reads "On a late summer's day, about the year 1790, the little Dutch village of Sleepy Hollow was agog with excitement—for the new school-master was due to arrive on the weekly mail stage from 'Nieu Yorke.'" There's something new here (apart from the strange spelling "Nieu," likely borrowed from Irving's *History of New York*). This film portrays the start of the story as Ichabod's arrival. Nearly every future rendition will follow this somewhat obvious introductory device. In Knickerbocker's tale, yes, Crane is an outsider, but he's already established in Sleepy Hollow. It doesn't begin with his move to the community. What spurs the action is his eventual meeting of Katrina Van Tassel, according to Irving. Notice also in Venturini's introduction the stagecoach is coming from New York—although Crane's a Yankee he's been to the big city (as we'll see in Burton) and he comes to the small town from there. The school committee awaits him.

The first individual character introduced is actually Katrina (Lois Meredith), who is the neighborhood belle (again, an object). She's followed by Brom Bones (Ben Hendricks, Jr.), her favored suitor. Ichabod arrives aboard the coach, reading *History of New England Witchcraft* by Cotton Mather, 1653, and complaining about the coachman's driving. Once the coach arrives, Crane's met by the school committee, which plays an active role in the movie. Katrina is, as will be typical for films based on Irving, an under-developed character, but she's there at his arrival for Crane to see and fall in love with.

After the establishing scene, setting up the love triangle, the Headless Horseman—transparent and with a skeleton hand—is shown by way of foreshadowing. The scene is spooky, but it's the only view we'll have of the actual ghost. The Horseman will become a major character over time, but for this first feature film, he's a few seconds of a mere shadowy presence. Myths take time to build.

While the film is generally faithful to Irving, some of the padding shows through, especially in the form of two extended scenes. The first is, significantly, the church service. The myth of Sleepy Hollow has a strong religion element. After the psalm-singing lesson, where Brom begins to express open resentment to Ichabod, we see the community in church. The scene is handled with considerable humor—a boring preacher with a long sermon and the discordant psalm singing led by Ichabod—that makes this otherwise tortuous religious meeting a little cinematic fun.

Clancy and Venturini clearly did their research well. For example, an intertitle for the sermon reads "and fiftiethly, Brethren." Historical records show, after Irving's time—and remember, Irving was never a member of the Old Dutch Church—that one preacher really did read 50 verses of a hymn based on Psalm 120. Even the presentation of the congregation falling asleep and the minister calling out "Fire!" is historically based. The Rev. Thomas Gibson Smith did this once, following up the response to "Where?" with the line picked up by Clancy, "In Hell—for such sleepy Christians as you are!"* This actually happened, although it's not in Irving's cut of the story. Knickerbocker doesn't describe the church service at all. Everyone knows what church is like.

Remember, Christianity was, and still is, the fabric from which America was snipped. Not founded as a Christian nation, nevertheless the early politicians couldn't imagine another religion taking over from it. Not personally religious, they were mostly mainly practical Deists. As children of the Enlightenment they may have thought religion would fade over time, but it has remained crucial for national identity. Just watch any political election in America and beg to differ. Christianity has an important role in laying out labyrinths. The first major addition to Irving is thus in church. But back to the movie.

Between Sunday services Ichabod entertains or teaches the children by reading gravestones to them. When some of the boys tell him they've found the Headless Horseman's grave, he informs them that it's haunted and they should keep away. This unconventional religion—Christianity tends to avoid ghosts, as we've seen—accepts the reality of the spiritual world and allows for another conjured episode that stretches the tale to feature length. In Knickerbocker's telling, Ichabod does read gravestones for the children, but he doesn't claim the churchyard itself is haunted. The scene also reintroduces the threat of the Horseman as foreshadowing. Irving started "The Legend" by using the Horseman as the chief example of the supernatural beliefs of the Dutch. Headless here is introduced to viewers just after Ichabod arrives, but not to Crane himself.

In the second major innovation, the movie presents Dame Martling using Crane's belief in ghosts and witches to set a trap for him. Dame Martling is an introduced character, not in Irving. Her ruse allows Crane to be accused of occult crimes. It involves Bones talking a boy into drinking something. Dame Martling, upon finding the "bewitched" boy, accuses Crane of witchcraft. His knowledge of the occult is used as evidence

---

* Allen and Griffith, *The Old Dutch Church of Sleepy Hollow*, 98–99.

against him and the villagers attempt to tar and feather him and ride him out of town on a rail. The tone here is darker than Knickerbocker, and besides, everyone likes Ichabod except Brom Bones, especially the women, according to "The Legend." This scene nevertheless manages to be disturbing, edging toward horror, from an unexpected angle. Witches also move us in that direction.

The American witch hunts, most notably at Salem, are clearly another labyrinthian component of America's nightmare. By 1692—nearly a century before Irving's birth—witch trials were a thing of the past in Europe. Frightened American Puritans with their own local authority blamed individuals—mostly women—of the community for bewitching children. Historians have shown that there were multiple causes that led to this miscarriage of justice, one of America's true hauntings. Nevertheless it lives on in American horror. Indeed, much of the horror literature produced in America points back to Salem, at least as early as Jonathan Scott's "The Sorceress, or Salem Delivered" from 1817. Nathaniel Hawthorne's "Young Goodman Brown," foregrounding Salem, was published 15 years after "Sleepy Hollow." The tradition lives on. This additional scene of threatened tarring and feathering for witchcraft is a reminder of our days of slaying innocents based on fear of the supernatural. At least the supernatural beyond the control of church. It also addresses the very real terror of lynching. America's nightmare doesn't fall evenly among races or genders in our national experience.

In the film, the mob mentality in Sleepy Hollow is arrested by the school committee. Those who are presumably educated try to bring reason to the vigilante crowd but only succeed when the boy pretending to be bewitched confesses. Even though Dame Martling wanted to trap Ichabod, Brom takes the heat for fraud. The drink he gave the boy made him act bewitched. It's only a prank, Brom suggests, that went too far. Perhaps also true of Salem.

These extra incidents added within this early cinematic treatment show a sensitivity to the importance of religious belief at the time. In the 1920s, of course, most Americans still openly identified as Christian. Recovering from the trauma of the First World War where there were no atheists in foxholes, to be respectable was to be religious. Even so, in earlier days religion had more public expression. It becomes more dangerous when it's sublimated. In the film Crane is willing to let all this pass, convinced, as he is, of his superiority. This Crane isn't exactly a hero, but he's not one to seek revenge.

From this point on, the film follows Irving's plot in general form. A note comes to Crane, inviting him to a frolic at the Van Tassel estate. Reading this as a sign of his favor, Crane envisions himself as heir and future husband of Katrina. At the frolic he eats and dances. When the men repair to the porch to smoke and talk, they turn to tales of the Headless Horseman. Crane, already a firm believer in such things, is frightened by the accounts of men meeting the ghost and being chased by it. Bones sees his opportunity here and adds his own tale. Ichabod remains behind and alone at last with Katrina, asks her to marry him. Her rejection is already his rejection from Sleepy Hollow, but as he makes his fateful ride home he encounters the Headless Horseman—Brom Bones, actually—who drives him off with a pumpkin. All of this follows Irving faithfully.

Wrapping Up Venturini

The Headless Horseman is a landmark in the maze. Venturini had demonstrated that a feature-length film could propel the story to a wide viewership. As films grew more popular and Irving's work aged into a classic, more and more people would be introduced to the story first through visual media. Already we see inklings of how horror might develop, and how religion might play a hand in it.

Irving was a religious skeptic but the Old Dutch Church was a prominent feature of Sleepy Hollow then, as now. An accomplished writer like Irving knew to engage with the culture. He wrote the Old Dutch Church into the story because being openly not religious was (and frequently still is) a quick march to ostracism.

Irving knew that making it to the Old Dutch Church was to reach safety, even as decades later Abraham van Helsing knew enough to keep a crucifix handy in case of vampire. To be realistic, Irving had to add religious details like Ichabod teaching psalmody and the church representing safety. Many reformed Protestant traditions allowed only hymns that were Psalm settings. In Venturini, that scene is drawn out and Katrina, ever the flirt, even helps Ichabod choose the Psalms for Sunday.

But more than that, religion begins to introduce horror elements in this early movie. It's the fear of things outside of church control—witches and ghosts—that truly scare. The movie has a somewhat prominent minister although the parson is merely mentioned in passing in Irving's tale. Fear and religion work in concert and over time we'll see them come together to make the tale a horror standard. All of these are elements of myth making. A good part of that will involve presenting the ghost as real. Following Irving, Halloween is not even mentioned.

What of Venturini's Headless Horseman? It really is Brom Bones that chases Ichabod from the Hollow, but an earlier scene uses special effects to show Headless as a skeleton summoning his horse. As noted, special effects were part of the legend's draw from the outset. They grow more elaborate, of course, as time goes on. No doubt this was spooky stuff before *Dracula* showed up on the silver screen in 1931. It's easy to forget that in the twenties and thirties even Disney cartoons showing silly dancing skeletons were considered gruesome. The Headless Horseman nevertheless has to become real for the story to become a myth. Religion, with its ghosts, will make that possible.

This early film was primarily played for laughs, but, as we'll see throughout this labyrinth, fear is sometimes—often, even—enhanced by humor. Given how brief the story is, and kid-friendly, early on it also suggested itself as appropriate material for cartoons. Indeed, perhaps the most famous early afterlife is animated. The myth began before Disney; we still have to step ahead a dozen years before the next well-known version appears. Notice that as we move into the cartoon world that the church will fade. Nobody wanted to be accused of mocking religion.

5

Sleepy Hollow Animated

He's exposed, out in the open air. Ghosts shriek from the woods around him. Frogs croak his name. Reeds whistle and cattails thump like hoof-beats. Then come actual hoof-beats. A gigantic rider armed with a cutlass gives chase. Inches away from Ichabod, his evil laugh reveals his intent. The Headless Horseman will kill Crane if he can. The sword barely misses and Ichabod whips Gunpowder toward the church bridge—to safety. He hopes.

Animation, as a means for making films, has a history as early as the industry itself.* The idea wasn't Walt Disney's, although he was its greatest promoter and he worked with the greatest innovators. Cartoons had become big business in Hollywood with the major studios opening divisions to handle animation. A number of players would come to dominate the market, with Disney eventually taking the lead, especially for feature films. Disney, like Venturini, didn't do all this alone.

The first known animated version of "Sleepy Hollow" appeared a dozen years after Venturini and the other lost live-action films discussed. Once it was released it became part of the growing mythology of the Hudson Valley. And it was the first of many cartoons to come. But it wasn't a Disney production. That would come several years later.

The First Cartoon

Before Disney's direct involvement, an early animated short, titled *The Headless Horseman*, was released in 1934. It was directed by Ub Iwerks, Shamus Culhane, and Al Eugster (the latter two uncredited). Given the comic tone in Washington Irving's story, animation naturally suggested itself for a visual medium. Cartoons were still short at this period and the

---

* Histories of early cartooning may be found in Iwerks and Kenworthy, *The Hand Behind the Mouse*, and Hanna and Ito, *A Cast of Friends*.

story is brief. Intensive movie special effects were to come later, but a headless character presented no difficulties for a cartoon, and certainly not for a man as talented as Ub Iwerks.

Born as Ubbe Ert Iwwerks (he worked under the shortened name Ub Iwerks), this early friend of Walt Disney was a first-generation American film animator. Although his name isn't widely known today, he collaborated with fellow cartoonist Walt Disney when they were both young and untested. The most famous of their collaborative efforts was an illustrated character—perhaps you've heard of him—called Micky Mouse. For several years Iwerks worked for Disney as the latter started building his empire. Iwerks was a great innovator and inventor. His creativity enhanced what Walt Disney was developing.

Iwerks had shown his early horror chops with the first of Disney's Silly Symphonies series, *Skeleton Dance* (1929), alluded to a couple of times above. This harmless cartoon of skeletons dancing in a cemetery was, according to some critics, too macabre for audiences of the time. This was two years before the release of Universal's *Dracula* and *Frankenstein*, so popular horror fare was still in the future. As with most things in which he was involved, Iwerks was ahead of his time.

Although Iwerks got his start with Disney—rather like Tim Burton—he left to find his own path. He parted ways with Disney for about a decade, during which Iwerks produced cartoons at Iwerks Studio, beginning in 1930. It was in this context that he produced *The Headless Horseman* as part of his Comicolor Cartoon series. This was the first film shot with the multiplane camera built by Iwerks himself. Multiplane cameras, as the name implies, shoot multiple levels simultaneously. This creates the illusion that objects at different distances from the camera are moving at different speeds relative to each other. It adds depth to an animation.

Following Irving and anticipating Disney, there's no spoken dialogue in Iwerks' short. The show begins with a literal love triangle, introducing Katrina, Brom, and Ichabod. The rivalry of the men is made clear by the daggers Ichabod stares at Brom. Ichabod is then next shown at school, secretly reading about the Headless Horseman while the students study. An invitation to a "brawl" at the Van Tassels' arrives and "Icky" grooms himself up for the occasion. The "brawl" is really just the ball ("frolic") from Irving. Brom races past Ichabod on the way to the Van Tassels' farm, but Katrina favors Ichabod and he dances up a storm. Up until Burton, dancing scenes will be favored in most adaptations.

When the old men tell stories about the Headless Horseman, Brom gets the idea to scare Ichabod off. Katrina, really doting on Brom, refuses Ichabod's proposal—something Disney won't show. The Headless Horseman follows Ichabod through a graveyard and throws a pumpkin at his head. After Ichabod runs off, the Horseman reveals himself as Brom. At Brom and Katrina's wedding, however, the Headless Horseman walks in, frightening everyone off. He then reveals himself as Ichabod, snickering at the gullible locals.

A few things stand out here. This appears to be the earliest animated version of Sleepy Hollow. The cartoon isn't set at Halloween—Disney will add that. There's no jack-o'-lantern, although one may have been present in the Étienne Arnaud short 22 years earlier. Somehow the cartoon manages to bring in the racist stereotypes of the Black messenger and musicians, even with its eight-and-a-half-minute run time. The racist tendencies of the period are well recognized and justly lamented. Disney will leave the Black characters out—it's just easier. So will Burton.

There's no ambiguity in Iwerks that the Horseman is Brom—and in a cute twist ending, Ichabod. As with most cartoons, there's also plenty of subtlety here. When Brom leaves the party shunned by Katrina, she's shown imagining an idealized version of him in her head. And yet, when it's all over, brains win out over brawn—Icky has the last laugh. Since this was before television, cartoons competed for theatrical space. The theatrical cartoon industry began in the 1910s, before either Disney or Iwerks got their start.

Iwerks rejoined Disney in 1940. After he returned to the Disney studios, the famous and familiar Disney Sleepy Hollow cartoon appeared a few years later. In the early days of animation (and even in recent times) various studios would "borrow" ideas from their competitors and repackage them. Iwerks' cartoon became source material for Disney's *The Adventures of Ichabod*. Cartoon versions would continue to appear ever after.

Anticipating Disney

While Iwerks was away, Disney was building a reputation as *the* cartoon studio.* When referring to the famous animated movie, directed by Clyde Geronimi, Jack Kinney (and James Algar, if adding Mr. Toad), I'll simply refer to it as "Disney's." His name is better recognized than the directors in this case. So influential would this rendition become that it will be referred to elsewhere in the maze as "the cartoon." Everyone knows which one.

Disney's version borrowed some ideas directly from Iwerks, however. One of the most obvious specific borrowings between the two cartoons is a scene where Ichabod uses chalk dust to powder himself before attending

---

* For a readable history of Disney, check out Goldberg's *The Disney Story*.

the Van Tassel party; Disney lifted that straight from Iwerks. Another borrowing was the name "Icky" used for Crane. In both cartoons Ichabod is shown getting in front of his horse during the final chase. In common with Edward Venturini, an extended dance scene dominates the Van Tassel party. In both cartoons it shows off animation skills—every part of Ichabod moves. There's some justice in this emphasis on dancing since Irving liked to parody dances from his earliest writing days in Manhattan.

"The Legend of Sleepy Hollow" was, however, beginning to share an unfortunate trait with much other early literature in that it was becoming known as a children's story. Children's stories can be mythic. It's not difficult to see why Sleepy Hollow was kid-friendly. No sex or violence mark it as adult, and there's no real heavy moral to the tale that requires thinking through. Kids like scary stories and although Ichabod's inner life is glimpsed, nothing is too deep. Katrina and Brom are character parts. Nothing profound here. Once branded as children's literature, any story will have a difficult time peeling that label off. It will take a long time after this before the story can become an actual horror tale. Interestingly when Disney's copyright on characters expires, they often appear in horror films. This happened with both Winnie the Pooh and Mickey Mouse. But back to Sleepy Hollow.

While it may seem odd to speak of "reality" in a cartoon, the Horseman is not yet real in Iwerks' version. He wasn't real in Venturini either. To become a myth the threat of the Galloping Hessian must be supernatural (religious). Given the reception of *Skeleton Dance* a few years earlier, it may have been a bit too early to take that particular step, even in cartoon form.

Although today overshadowed by the Disney empire, Iwerks was recognized in his own time—he received three Academy Award nominations as well as being posthumously named a Disney Legend. But ask people today who came up with Mickey Mouse and you already know the answer. I have to wonder, given the timing, if America's most famous animated ghost story wasn't really the idea of Ub Iwerks. His cartoon was in many ways the template for Disney's. At under nine minutes, it would require some work to become half a feature length. Since this was the pre-television era, Iwerks' cartoon was shown in theaters in October of 1934. The tug of Halloween was starting to be felt about the same time. The labyrinth, like that of the Overlook Hotel, is quite capable of luring in the young.

Disney Takes Over

Disney's first animated feature, *Snow White and the Seven Dwarves* revolutionized cartooning when it was released in 1937. Over the next decade, Disney would dominate feature-length cartoons. With Iwerks back in house, there was no threat of competition there. Disney didn't always do its own distribution yet, and it cranked out 13 more feature films before reaching the one we're primarily interested in seeing. Notice that after 1942 the feature films were anthologies—not a single story line. This trend continues into Disney's adaptation of Irving. Even this involves a labyrinth.

Intended as a feature itself, Disney's adaptation of Kenneth Grahame's *The Wind in the Willows* was halted by the Second World War. In 1946 Sleepy Hollow was planned as one of a series of folktales—an idea Shelley Duvall would take up in the eighties (see Chapter 7). Instead, Disney decided to add the material from *The Wind in the Willows* to Irving's very different tale.*

It would be simplistic to suppose decisions about which stories are to be included in anthologies was a straightforward process. Nevertheless, a question that will arise from time to time is why Disney didn't pair Sleepy Hollow with Rip Van Winkle. In the earliest cinematic treatment of Irving, the two were combined. Perhaps afraid of being accused of being "too scary," Disney paired Sleepy Hollow with an unexpected partner in its 15th feature film.

The Adventures of Ichabod and Mr. Toad (1949) followed Iwerks' *The Headless Horseman* by 15 years. Distributed by RKO, the film credits Ub Iwerks as in charge of Special Processes—essentially special effects. In the minimal credits of the day he's not mentioned as being involved in story although the Disney version clearly takes several cues from Iwerks' earlier rendition.

Despite the unusual combination of stories—Grahame's *Wind in the Willows* and Irving's "Sleepy Hollow"—for many children this would be their first introduction to America's mythic ghost story. Audiences were still unsure that cartoons would be able keep up with rapidly developing cinema. Disney wasn't yet a major studio, and it was still using other distribution companies. Nevertheless, the force of Disney's superior animation led to the closing of animation departments in other studios that focused mainly on live action movies. In any case, Toad and Crane's feature was originally titled *Two Fabulous Characters*, and continued Disney's string of anthologies.

The Ichabod segment, later released separately as *The Legend of Sleepy Hollow*, runs for 34 minutes. Using the book-off-the-shelf trope to introduce the story, in keeping with Disney's title, Irving's tale is renamed

---

* For the pairing of Ichabod and Toad see Squire, "The Pleasures and Pains of Text," and Neuman, "Disney's Final Package Film."

"Ichabod Crane, or The Legend of Sleepy Hollow." It is presented as a stand-alone book, the rest of the sketches in the *Sketch Book* forgotten. The title indicates Ichabod is the protagonist.*

As for the storyline, it really is a faithful retelling of Irving's plot, exaggerated Disney style. Three musical numbers are added, each based on a character: "Ichabod Crane," "Katrina," and "The Headless Horseman." Poor Brom has no song, but he will reappear in another Disney classic, as we'll see. The only dialogue in this film is crooned by Bing Crosby so there's not a lot in the way of character development. Much of the narrative involves pratfalls and pranks, in keeping with early Disney's half-serious style. Many brief episodes are omitted: Brom doesn't stuff up the chimney, and Ichabod doesn't read gravestones to kids. Still, it is a major step in creating a myth.

This is the first film to set the action of Sleepy Hollow explicitly on Halloween and it introduces several other elements that will soon also become canonical for the myth of Sleepy Hollow. Irving made the quilting frolic an autumnal event, but the use of the pumpkin suggested Halloween to the Disney crew. Perhaps someone had seen Arnaud's version with its pumpkin lantern? Not only does Crosby announce that this all happened on Halloween, the pumpkin hurled at Crane is shown as a flaming jack-o'-lantern, by now a standard American Halloween tradition. That idea has had staying power and has become an essential part of the Sleepy Hollow myth. Even modern novelists have trouble shaking it. A plain old pumpkin is never thrown any more, although for Knickerbocker, the pumpkin was a symbol for dreaded Yankees, essentially a "Yankee go home!" statement.

Halloween became popular in America only well after Irving's day, as we'll see in the next chapter. With a Revolutionary War to fight and a new country to organize, there were more pressing matters on hand at the time, slavery and women's suffrage among them. Halloween celebrations in the new world only began to spread in the mid–1800s as more Celtic immigrants began to settle in the heavily Protestant northern states. Protestants tended to be intolerant of anything Catholic. Halloween's breakthrough as a commercial holiday came only in the twentieth century, and Disney's film is part of that growing Halloween mythology that will join with Irving. If "The Legend of Sleepy Hollow" hadn't been associated with Halloween before, from now on its myth ever would be.

Like Will Rogers, Disney's Ichabod doesn't have an audible line of spoken dialogue. Not only that, the Ichabod Crane to which many children

---

*Some of the details of *The Adventures of Ichabod and Mr. Toad* benefited from Maltin's standard reference, *The Disney Films*.

would first be introduced was Disney's heroic cartoon version. It would be safe to say that Venturini's film hadn't been a major hit. (The term "blockbuster" wouldn't even appear until the forties.) Few Sleepy Hollow tales filmed earlier had even survived. This puts Disney in a privileged position for defining this American myth. Since children are early drawn to cartoons, their promotion hands America's heritage to Disney, not for the last time. And although continuing to treat the story primarily as fun, Disney also made it gateway horror; and firmly established Ichabod Crane as the protagonist. The labyrinth expands.

A number of Disney innovations create an authentically spooky atmosphere. As Ichabod first enters Sleepy Hollow (and Disney opens the story at his arrival, following Venturini's lead), he passes a windmill. This innocuous flood-control device will become the scene beginning the Headless Horseman's chase in Tim Burton's first horror film. The windmill is prototypically Dutch, but also hints at Don Quixote. In his own mind, Ichabod is defeating giants. Indeed, Irving described him as a "knight errant." He doesn't belong to Sleepy Hollow. The windmill also has horror associations going back to *Frankenstein* in 1931.

The Old Dutch Church, interestingly, isn't mentioned at all in Disney. The bridge—across which the church is shown in the distance—is the safety point. Disney also introduced the bridge as covered. Knickerbocker described it like this: "Over a deep black part of the stream, not far from the church, was formerly thrown a wooden bridge; the road that led to it, and the bridge itself, were thickly shaded by overhanging trees, which cast a gloom about it, even in the daytime; but occasioned a fearful darkness at night." The covered bridge innovation gives an old-timey feel, and offers some opportunities for fright by breaking sight lines. Again, Burton will also use the covered bridge to enhance the horror, as will others. It's now part of the myth.

Disney also adds further to the "official" Irving story, beyond introducing Halloween and the covered bridge, venturing into horror territory. Ichabod's mistaking the grasshoppers and frogs chirping and croaking his name on the fateful ride home are so effective and expected that it's difficult to believe Irving mentions nothing like this. No doubt his frightening ride sets the horror tone for the film. There are jump-startle screams and creepy renditions of the woods. Ichabod has to ride through a cemetery at night. (This part was borrowed from Iwerks.)

In the chase scene Disney also adds the Horseman slashing with his sword. Probably necessary for head collecting, this is nevertheless another innovation that doesn't appear in Irving. If Knickerbocker's Horseman is Brom Bones, such aggressive swordplay could lead to unexpected results on a dark night during a horseback chase. Irving's description of the

Horseman is spare, and he doesn't mention any weapons: "He appeared to be a horseman of large dimensions, and mounted on a black horse of powerful frame." And headless, of course. Disney gave him a piece.

The chase scene also inspired Burton as Ichabod finds himself on the wrong horse and even ends up briefly chasing the Horseman. As Disney's Crane assumes some questionable positions on Gunpowder—the animators must've been aware of the implications—the Horseman does seem to be sincerely attempting to kill the schoolmaster. This certainly adds to the Halloween feel of the telling. Perhaps the most important Disney innovation was making the Horseman of the chase scene an actual ghost.

Most retellings from this point on imply, if not outwardly declare, that the Headless Horseman is a real entity. This applies across media; films, television programs, novels, and even games play on this reality. America is a haunted place. Our past becomes our nightmare as well as our myth. Yes, it's intended for children but that doesn't prevent it from having a particularly dark song ("The Headless Horseman") and scary imagery. Don Raye and Gene de Paul, the songwriters, introduce the horror elements that move the legend in a new direction. It is becoming a myth.

This Geronimi, Kinney, and Algar version is also notable for what it omits. It leaves out Katrina's rejection of Crane the night of the Halloween party—he simply has to ride home alone when the party's over. And it leaves out any mention of the church or psalmody. Even the singing lessons Ichabod gives—where in Knickerbocker's story he meets Katrina—involve secular crooning, not really period-appropriate. Of course, this version is largely a showcase for Bing Crosby and Reformed psalmody wasn't exactly his style.

Prior to Disney there were—often unflatteringly portrayed—African American characters. Irving plays on them for comic effect, although they aren't presented as slaves. That comic effect is picked up both by Venturini and Iwerks, each in their own ways presenting Black servants or musicians. Disney makes the cast all white. In this it's followed by Burton and others. The African American element will only come into its own again with the Fox television series starting in 2013.

The Disney Introduction

Perhaps recognizing the mismatch with Mr. Toad, in 1955 in season two of *Walt Disney's Disneyland Anthology*, episode seven, "The Legend of Sleepy Hollow," was aired separately on television. Walt Disney himself introduces a 14-minute short on the life of Washington Irving. This tale offers some new dead ends in the labyrinth of this myth.

Narrated in the first person, Irving gives a fictionalized account of his life. With journeyman animation, this introduction plays fast and loose with history at points. Following Irving's own recollections in his essay "Sleepy Hollow," this narrative makes his boyhood trip to Tarrytown a summer vacation. Historically, Irving's boyhood visits to Sleepy Hollow were to avoid the yellow fever outbreak in Manhattan. The new introduction also combines his two trips to Europe into one undertaken in 1804, after he wrote *A History of New York* (which was actually published in 1809). Illustrated Irving claims to have taken lodgings at the Red Horse Inn in Stratford-on-Avon where he wrote *The Sketch Book*. He actually wrote his *Sketch Book* in pieces while traveling from place to place and almost certainly wrote "The Legend of Sleepy Hollow" in London.* Interestingly, Walt Disney's introduction notes that "Rip Van Winkle" and "Sleepy Hollow" are Irving's two most famous tales. That recognition never seems to have driven an animated Rip to go with Ichabod.

There are numerous historical errors in this prologue, underscoring Disney's role as the maker of myths. For example, during his time in London Irving claims to have met Thomas More and Lord Byron. More died in 1535, well over two centuries before Irving was born, and Byron left England for the last time in 1816, the year after Irving's arrival in Britain. There's no record of their having met. While in very broad sweeps this Irving autobiography resembles his life a little, the details are wrong. In fact, it's implied he may have heard Sleepy Hollow's ghost stories from an old white man fishing. He claims to have heard it originally from a Black mill worker, but Irving may have invented this as well.†

We can't fault Disney too much, however. Irving did spin his own version of events in his "nonfiction" essay "Sleepy Hollow," published some 20 years after "The Legend of Sleepy Hollow." There Irving recollected, under the pen name Geoffrey Crayon, how the story came to be written. It was an exercise in myth making. Irving understood having to stay in character. In any case, in this essay he gives credit for "the Legend" to a Black mill worker on the banks of the river. Disney made him white.

But Disney wasn't through with Irving yet. Another spin-off development from *The Adventures of Ichabod* appeared in 1991. And it comes from a completely different monster story by Disney.

---

* Denis, *Sleepy Hollow*, 91.
† See Irving's nonfiction essay "Sleepy Hollow," in *The Knickerbocker*, p. 408, as well as "Wolfert's Roost."

Beauty and the Beast

One of the characters in this voiceless animated tale further illustrates the myth-building potential of Knickerbocker's story. Disney's Brom Bones led to a newer character later in the Magic Kingdom's constellation: Gaston.* Considered by some to be Disney's greatest animation, *The Beauty and the Beast* (1991) is also a love triangle. Set in France in roughly about the same time period as "Sleepy Hollow," Belle, first a prisoner, becomes the bride of the beast (leading to some interesting possibilities for other interpretations, and perhaps even inspired by those of Angela Carter). The character of Gaston, however, looks familiar, doesn't he?

Disney's *Beauty and the Beast* is also a subdued monster story, ultimately derived from a more rococo fairy tale written by Gabrielle-Suzanne Barbot de Villeneuve and published in French in 1740 as *La Belle et la Bête*. This original, retold through the years, has no love triangle. The tension comes from Beauty's family since she's not an only child. Jealous sisters are outshined by protective brothers (11 siblings in total, in the original) who try to keep Belle safe from the beast, in whose house her father took refuge during a storm. No Gaston attempts to marry Beauty or "kill the beast" (although the brothers do toy with that latter idea). Although Beast/Prince is no Ichabod Crane, there is more than a passing resemblance between Brom Bones and Gaston. And there's no question that Brom and Gaston are the unsympathetic antagonists in Disney. This is played out more fully in *Beauty and the Beast* because Gaston has spoken lines (and more screen time) as well as motivations that clearly function against Belle's wishes. This is similar to the Brom in Alyssa Palombo's novel, discussed further on. The entire Gaston character and plot seem to have been derived from "The Legend of Sleepy Hollow." The two characters are even drawn in similar ways. Brom Bones' character was simply too good to let go without a word.

Further evidence of this connection comes from an unnamed character among Katrina's wooers in Disney's *Adventures*. Among Brom's Sleepy Hollow Boys, there's a very short man is singled out as seeking Katrina's hand. At one point he is stared down by Brom and quietly steps aside. This anonymous character bears more than a passing resemblance to LeFou, Gaston's constant sidekick in *Beauty*. The seeds for one of Disney's greatest animated triumphs seem to have been sowed in Sleepy Hollow, as befits a labyrinth.

---

* Conradt, "11 Hair-Raising Facts About Disney's The Legend of Sleepy Hollow," and Korkis, "Disney's 'The Legend of Sleepy Hollow.'"

Kids' Stuff

As often happens with Disney adaptations, a cartoon version of a story subconsciously labels the underlying tale as "for children." To make sense of the spirit in which it was written by Irving, however, "Sleepy Hollow" has to be kept in the context of Diedrich Knickerbocker. Satire is a form of humor directed at adults and it doesn't preclude serious topics. By pairing it with the lighthearted "Mr. Toad" (which never gained the fandom of Sleepy Hollow), Disney suggested that the legend is children's fare.

It seems that perhaps Disney bears a special responsibility to the Western canon. Think of it: for many of our common cultural references, the Disney version is often the first that children see. It suggests that this is the way the story *ought* to go. Is there any other way *The Beauty and the Beast* could play out, for example? This despite the fact that the original version, that of Gabrielle-Suzanne Barbot de Villeneuve, has any number of notable differences, including Beauty's (Belle's) five sisters and six brothers, and the beast's having a trunk like an elephant, and scales instead of fur. That version wasn't for kids and it's even a chore for adults to get through today.

Of course de Villeneuve's version was rewritten and slimmed down by Jeanne-Marie Leprince de Beaumont, also in the eighteenth century. This version became the best known, and ended up retold in *The Blue Fairy* book by Andrew Lang in the next century. This story laid its own maze. Then Disney entered it.

Once Disney claims a story, all other versions, including the original, are merely variants. Children see them first. Consider what is perhaps Disney's darkest tale, *The Hunchback of Notre Dame* (1996). It has to be displaced by the versions of Lon Cheney, or, ironically, Victor Hugo, later in life. There's a responsibility in being first. Our childhood is our first impression. Children are also drawn to mythology.

What's the harm, you may ask. Children can "correct" the story once they learn to read. But can they? Or more importantly, do they? As a nation of literalists you might think we'd pay more attention. Even to an adult who's read Irving's tale multiple times, speaking for myself, the visual that comes back by default is generally the Disney version. We need to pass our heritage on, of course, but those who do so commercially bear more cultural weight than the rest of us. Break out your copy of Irving and see if you don't agree.

This is especially the case in the light of a quote from the famed author Clifton Fadiman. Although originally about "Rip Van Winkle," it equally applies to "The Legend of Sleepy Hollow." This comes from the afterword of a bound edition of both works. Fadiman wrote, "I think it's the feeling for the past that makes this simple story cast such a spell. It seems to be about the childhood of our country, which we can never relive, except in fancy."* That's it, isn't it? This is the myth of our lost childhood, both national and individual. It appeals to adults who are now seeking the truths they once knew in this maze. Fadiman calls out the Disney movie for "retain[ing] nothing whatsoever of Irving's charm, sweetness and delight in spinning a slow, lazy yarn." We have no time to be lazy, and barely time to read. Fadiman's remark is, not surprisingly, in an edition meant for children. And yet it speaks to adults, if we'll listen.

Disney won't leave ghosts out of future movies but Halloween isn't a theme for which it's widely known, despite monsters in blockbusters like *Beauty and the Beast.* Pixar's *Coco* (2017) is based on *Dia del las Muertas,* and *Tim Burton's The Nightmare Before Christmas* (1993) blends Halloween with the titular holiday. Both are Disney productions with the theme of ghosts and death. *Soul* (2020) is yet another example. Still, silly mouse, Disney movies are for kids.

The long influence of this Disney version—nothing really challenged it for half a century—put the story in children's territory. And on Halloween. It set it out on a mythic path. We now need to consider the holiday most associated with Sleepy Hollow. We've found the origin of how Halloween entered the afterlife of Sleepy Hollow, but how did it too become part of the American myth?

---

* *Rip Van Winkle & The Legend of Sleepy Hollow: With an Afterword by Clifton Fadiman,* 80.

6

How Halloween Met Sleepy Hollow

We see things through his eyes. We hear kids running from house to house trick-or-treating in the small town of Haddonfield, Illinois. He makes his way to the back door. In the kitchen he picks up a butcher knife. He watches, unseen, as his sister's boyfriend leaves. Slowly he makes his way upstairs to his sister's room. We hear him breathing as he slaps on a clown mask. His sister is brushing her hair after just having had sex with her boyfriend. He raises the knife. As she cries, "Michael!" he stabs her repeatedly, leaving her dead on the floor.

The scary holiday season of the autumn is such a prominent fixture in America that it's difficult to believe it's not even as old as Washington Irving. "The Legend of Sleepy Hollow" has become a Halloween story—that's a large part of its myth. The two go together. Still, Halloween had not yet become an American tradition when Irving penned "Sleepy Hollow" and no mention is made of it anywhere in his tale. The pumpkin used as the Horseman's head confirms it's the right season, but Irving had a history of using pumpkins in his writing, mainly to symbolize Connecticut Yankees. He could have predicted neither the advent of Halloween on these shores nor how his story would become standard Halloween fare. Disney's version would eventually add the jack-o'-lantern, as we've seen, but this was only after large numbers of Celtic peoples had immigrated. Celtic immigrants had to navigate the maze. And then get lost in it.

This labyrinth of holidays comes with a disclaimer: holiday celebrations can be quite regional, with complex histories.* In this era of internet homogenization, it may be difficult to believe that prior to the twentieth-century different holidays, including Halloween, were

---

* Several of the observations in this chapter owe their origins to Bannatyne's books *Halloween* and *Halloween Nation*, as well as Skal's *Death Makes a Holiday*, Morton's *Trick-or-Treat*, and Roger's *Halloween*.

celebrated quite differently in different states. What follows is a description that necessarily jumps around this particular labyrinth to offer a wider view both of the holiday and of Sleepy Hollow.

Irving also had a hand in another holiday aspect of Halloween: Christmas. As we'll see below, the two holidays have a long association. Irving, largely from his Christmas stories in the *Sketch Book*, inspired Charles Dickens to write *A Christmas Carol*. Read on to enter this spooky and strange part of the maze.

Halloween in Sleepy Hollow

Nights get scarier as they grow longer. Monsters lurk in the stygian darkness. Headless, our Horseman is seeking something that belongs to him, whether his head or Katrina van Tassel. There's love amid the dimness, as directors from Edward Venturini to Tim Burton and beyond have explored. They've wandered through this labyrinth as the hours of darkness increase.

From ancient times people have been aware of how weak our control over our lives really is. We depend on the sun and the weather to cooperate for our crops to thrive. We fear the darkness when our eyes can't compete with those of our predators. As the year descends into longer and longer nights, we secretly fear that eventually night will not end. The dark time of the year belongs to the spirits. Halloween has developed its own mythology and Sleepy Hollow is part of it.

More than just one of our first national ghost tales, "The Legend of Sleepy Hollow" has also become America's Halloween story. Ghosts, harvest, pumpkins. Although the eerie atmosphere comes mostly from tales told for Ichabod and his famous ride, the subtle humor of horror clearly persists. Ichabod Crane is difficult to take seriously in Irving's own words. Brom Bones is a roustabout who loves fun. And there's that love triangle, a situation that sometimes turns deadly in real life but can be funny in fiction. All of this is set in the Halloween season, even if Irving didn't know it. Perhaps this story was key to setting the autumnal season as spooky in the first place?*

With Celtic and other old European roots, Halloween has become an American holiday. A reflection of who we are. Outselling any other occasion but Christmas, capitalism has declared it quite valuable. But there's something more going on here. There's a story that can't be told too many times. It reflects who we are. Narcissus, so the myth suggests, must be kept

---

* Jones, *Washington Irving*, 189.

away from all mirrors. Mirrors have had long associations with ghosts, as many horror films attest.

The Headless Horseman is among the earliest of such American literary specters, but he's by no means the only one. His association with Halloween began innocently enough with Knickerbocker noting that "As Ichabod jogged slowly on his way, his eye, ever open to every symptom of culinary abundance, ranged with delight over the treasures of jolly autumn." By the end of that night, however, the jolly autumn will become a season of fear. For Ichabod the "night grew darker and darker; the stars seemed to sink deeper in the sky, and driving clouds occasionally hid them from his sight. He had never felt so lonely and dismal." A shattered pumpkin was found at the scene of the crime. In the twentieth century, when Halloween had evolved along with "Sleepy Hollow" to occupy October nights, and to claim pumpkins as its own, a mythic union was born.

Halloween Arises

America has contributed an outsized share toward commercial holidays. Our version of Christmas, for example, is recognized around the world with its spending and its Santa Claus (originally a Dutch character). Although Christmas originated in Europe, largely among Catholics and pagans, in America it began to take on other elements and become something else—an idea that other nations adopted. Like Christmas, the second great holiday export of Halloween was originally an import here also. A number of divergent traditions meshed into a distinctly American holiday. Other countries, in turn, have borrowed aspects of American Halloween. So much so that Halloween celebrations can turn deadly as happened in Seoul in 2022.

"The Legend of Sleepy Hollow" may have had a hand in the development of the scary autumn. Washington Irving seems to have inscribed a ghostly nature onto the bountiful and joyous harvest season. Certain it is, the Celtic tradition of Samhain—the main source behind Halloween—predated Irving's tale by centuries. It seems to have been Irving, however, who cast the nightmare shadow over the autumnal season in America with his tale of Ichabod Crane.

Samhain had been celebrated at least since the early Middle Ages among Celts in the British Isles. Even the fact of the British Isles' being the setting—with its own imperialism and racism, locally against the Irish—shows that the nightmare labyrinth isn't uniquely American. Still, the holiday's origins are lost in the storied lack of written sources and the imperialists' lack of interest in those they rule.

We may not have descriptions of their holidays by the Celts themselves, but Samhain was clearly one of the four pivotal fire festivals of their year, along with Imbolc, Beltane, and Lughnasadh. The beginning of winter, Samhain was such a deeply revered celebration that the Catholic Church appears to have moved All Saints Day to November 1 at least partially in order to compete with it. We know little of how the festival was originally celebrated beyond building bonfires. Disguises and divination—telling the future—seem to have been part of it as well.

Historians connect the fragments and try to construct the beliefs behind the day. The Celts appear to have believed that the otherworld—a place where the dead continued on—was separated from our world by a veil of some kind. That veil was especially thin on Samhain, and perhaps also on Beltane (May Day). This meant that the dead might cross over into our world at that time. This can be pretty scary stuff, a maze you don't want to get lost in. It may not be so bad if those souls that come over are good, but Halloween jack-o'-lanterns may have originally served to frighten off the evil spirits that also came.

The word "Hallowe'en" first appears some 40 years before Irving was born. The word itself comes from the Scottish name for All Saints Eve, or All Hallows Even(ing). The Catholic festival of All Saints commemorates those who have lived and died as exemplary Christians. It is followed by the more democratic All Souls Day, when the rest of us get celebrated, after death of course. This major two-day holy day observance revolves around death. Perhaps officially a celebration of the lives of the saints and faithful, it only applies after life, bringing that darker element into focus. Instead of All Hallows E'en displacing Samhain, it appears to have borrowed from it and the holidays began to blend.

American Halloween

Since the eve of All Hallows is October 31, the observance spanned three days and at least two religious traditions. Technically speaking Halloween is Christian in origin, but like many Christian practices it makes use of other traditions. Those other traditions were considered pagan. And like most religious holidays, it had a difficult time getting a foothold in Protestant America. Especially in Puritan New England. It really hadn't arrived by the time Irving was writing "Sleepy Hollow."

Many Puritans felt that any religious holiday—even, or especially, Christmas—was far too Popish for Christian recognition. Early New Englanders didn't like Catholics and they didn't celebrate Christmas. New York tended more toward Reformed forms of Calvinism, which also avoided anything that smacked of Catholicism. Nobody really observed Halloween much in America until large numbers of Celtic people came to the New World in the nineteenth century. It took many years for Halloween to become mainstream, and when it did it was largely a secular holiday, despite its religious origins.

Harvest time, particularly the end of the in-gathering, was generally a joyful occasion. What "The Legend of Sleepy Hollow" suggested is that maybe the monsters were out at that season as well. Irving's story may not mention Halloween at all, but as the holiday grew more popular it made sense to put them together. As the initial successful American writer, Irving was the first to tie a monster to harvest season. A large part of the reason has to do with the humble pumpkin.

Pumpkins

Pumpkins are indigenous to the New World. Celtic jack-o'-lanterns tended to be carved from turnips. Hollowing out a large turnip must've been a somewhat laborious task, so the pumpkin would've immediately suggested itself as ready-made for the job, once it was discovered. Scooping out the seeds leaves a hollow fruit just right for carving. They're naturally larger—the largest grown fruit or vegetable in the world—and easily found as head-size. Knickerbocker found pumpkins humorous and wrote about them in his *History of New York* as well, but not associated with Halloween. "Pumpkin lanterns" were associated with Guy Fawkes Night in early New England.

The jack-o'-lantern tradition came to the United States when large numbers of Irish immigrants arrived. Even the name has eerie associations. "Jack-o'-lantern" was another name for will-o'-wisps. Will-o'-wisps are naturally occurring but still unexplained lights that flicker above peat bogs and other swampy areas—in other words, swamp gas. Why it glows we still don't know. Will-o'-wisps can occasionally be seen at night floating over these dismal areas and that led to tales to explain them that often involved ghosts or fairies. They're also known as "ghost lights" or *ignis fatuus*. The jack-o'-lantern may have been intended to imitate these spooky nighttime lights. And frighten off evil. Even before that, the term "jack-o'-lantern" was in use to describe a night watchman, a "guy with a light." Irving used it that way in his pre-book-length writings.* This is a pumpkin maze.

---

* Irving himself uses the phrase to refer, satirically, to male society dancers, naming them as "these jack-o'-lanthorn heroes." *Salmagundi* 1, 77, pointed out in Burstein, *The Original Knickerbocker*, p. 53. The phrase here clearly means watchman.

Large pumpkins can be scary in their own right. The largest weighing in at over a ton, the pumpkin possesses a kind of innate majesty that the turnip lacks. It's impossible to determine when the first carved pumpkin was made in North America, or who made the connection of pumpkins with Halloween.* The first recorded use of "jack-o'-lantern" for a carved pumpkin was in 1834, over a decade after "The Legend of Sleepy Hollow" published. Carved pumpkins seem to have predated their use at Halloween. Associated with harvest, a celebratory time, they also have Thanksgiving connections. In Irving's day, Thanksgiving would've not resembled the food-centered holiday we know today. Also keep in mind that he was living in Europe when he wrote this story.

Although the modern Halloween would've been completely alien to Irving, and the modern Thanksgiving equally puzzling, the pumpkin grew into something of an icon. It would also become associated with Christmas as pumpkin pie was a seasonal treat then as well. All of these are fruitful paths through this labyrinth. In the United States, however, the carved pumpkin of harvest and the jack-o'-lantern of Halloween coalesced. This is so much the case that the pumpkin remains perhaps the main symbol of Halloween. It features in Halloween horror movies.

Some of these elements seem to have been in the air around the time Irving published his story. Since he had been living in Britain for about five years at this point, it's difficult to say whether he'd caught wind of this very young American tradition before he left. The hurled pumpkin in his story, however, later tied the tale to the holiday that would burst into popularity some decades further on in America. Of course, that it was a pumpkin thrown at Crane is only implied by the discovery of a shattered one near his hat the following day. It was a dark night when the chase took place and the Horseman threw his head at the teacher, rather than trying to lop the pedagogue's off. According to Irving, anyway. As the labyrinth winds its way through America, it almost always leads back to Halloween.

Meanwhile Halloween grew as a cultural force that remained unanalyzed for years. There are multiple reasons for this lack of attention. In the serious world of adulthood, Halloween was considered a children's holiday, rather like Disney made "Sleepy Hollow" a children's story. Derived from folk tradition rather than church decree—although with considerable fuel from All Saints Day—no church was declaring how the day should be celebrated. Many churches, in fact, discouraged (and still discourage) Halloween as "satanic." Historians have to comb many disparate sources to make any kind of coherent account. The same applies to Christmas, the winter Halloween.

---

* For a history of jack-o'-lanterns on Halloween, see Bannatyne's *Halloween Nation*.

"Christmas—the Other Halloween"

Unbelievably from today's perspective, Christmas also had a difficult time getting established in the United States. Two of the key elements in bringing the holiday to American attention go back to Washington Irving. In his *History of New York* he makes repeated reference to the Dutch patron saint, Nicholas. That's the first element. He mentions that Saint Nicholas brought Dutch children presents in December.* The second element, however, was more influential.

As Irving was writing *The Sketch Book of Geoffrey Crayon, Gent.*, he was sending it for publication in America in small volumes. Volume five was dedicated to how the English gentry celebrated the holiday of Christmas. This account, in turn, caught the attention of a British fan of Irving named Charles Dickens. And as one book would proclaim in its title, Dickens was "the man who invented Christmas."† That's only part of the story. Irving had set the stage. And he followed it up with action. He co-founded the Saint Nicholas Society in 1836 to collect gifts for the poor.‡

As pumpkin pie earlier suggested, the holiday for telling creepy stories was, historically, Christmas. This makes sense—it's darker (darkest) at Christmastime in the northern hemisphere and thoughts naturally gravitate towards ghosts in the dark. Even today horror fans know there are more Christmas horror movies than Halloween offerings. Sleepy Hollow helped shift the scary time to autumn.

Holidays with their origins in folk celebrations often have a great deal in common. Without church authorities declaring the doctrinally correct behavior (apart from the usual suspects), Halloween and Christmas were periods of celebration, presumably dedicated to specific gods. They both often included building fires, eating special foods, and general merry-making. Halloween and Christmas share many features. In fact, in some ways they're difficult to tell apart. What did you expect in a labyrinth?

The Halloween-Christmas connection long predates *The Nightmare Before Christmas* and Jack Skellington. As already noted, Christmas was the original ghost-story holiday. This practice predated Charles Dickens, but *A Christmas Carol* is, after all, a ghost story. The immense popularity of that book helped spread the celebration of the holiday. Even the modern Christmas song "The Most Wonderful Time of the Year" (written by Edward Pola and George Wyle and published in 1963) includes the line "there'll be scary ghost stories." It was Christmas tradition.

---

* *A History of New York*, book seven, chapter nine.
† "The man who invented Christmas" is taken from the book by that title by Les Standiford, who makes frequent reference to Dickens' taking cues from Irving.
‡ Foster, *Author Unknown*, p. 245.

That tradition has deep roots. Dickens' justly famous novella isn't really scary (rather like Irving's "Sleepy Hollow"), although the ghost of Christmas yet to come is definitely unnerving. It is, however, part of an old tradition tying Halloween to Christmas. Dickens was a great admirer of Irving, and Irving's "Christmas Dinner" in the *Sketch Book* includes an old parson spinning scary tales on Christmas day. (*A Christmas Carol* was published more than two decades later, in 1843.) So Irving also had a role in "inventing" Christmas and his experience of it involved telling frightening stories.

Even Shakespeare, as cited by Crayon in his essay "Christmas," knew the connection with ghosts. In *Hamlet* (act 1, scene 1) Marcellus, discussing the ghost with his companion Horatio, says:

> It faded on the crowing of the cock.
> Some say that ever 'gainst that season comes
> Wherein our Savior's birth is celebrated,
> This bird of dawning singeth all night long;
> And then, they say, no spirit dare stir abroad,
> The nights are wholesome; then no planets strike,
> No fairy takes, nor witch hath power to charm,
> So hallowed and so gracious is that time.

Notice that Christmas, in Shakespeare's time, also had the power to fend off witches. Scary things abound in the winter season.

M.R. James, who overlapped Dickens' final years (even as Irving overlapped Dickens' earlier ones), is the Dean of ghost stories. Montague Rhodes James was provost of King's College, Cambridge. A Medievalist by trade, he told ghost stories as part of his Christmas Eve tradition. He is famous for his five collections of such stories, beginning with *Ghost Stories of an Antiquary* (1904). He's often credited with reinventing the ghost story genre. (Clearly the connection, to anticipate the next chapter, with Sears James and the old men telling ghostly tales in Peter Straub's *Ghost Story* is intentional. Straub's narrative is set, however, in October.) Christmas and Halloween are close kin beyond their shared association with ghost stories.

The two holidays are also tied together by soul cakes and the tradition of begging. Halloween begging led to trick-or-treating. Begging also survives in the Christmas tradition of caroling for a donation, sometimes food. The soul cake takes its origin story from two practices. One was the rich giving cakes to the poor to commemorate the dead, thus the name. This was naturally associated with All Saints' Day and All Souls' Day, and therefore Halloween. It may also be the origin of trick-or-treating, although others would suggest different paths through that particular maze. The second origin story for soul cakes is that the name was derived from "Wassail Cakes."

Wassailing was an English Christmas tradition that gave birth to caroling. Groups of singers would go from house to house among the affluent, singing for wassail (hot mulled cider) and cakes. Meanwhile souling, which was a similar practice, was done at both All Saints and Christmastide. These are both English, as opposed to Celtic, traditions. Nobody contemporary with these practices thought to write their origins down, so we don't know how they got started, but we can see Halloween and Christmas are clearly connected through them.

The tradition of carving jack-o'-lanterns is generally traced, as noted above, to the Irish tradition of lighting hollowed-out turnips with a candle. If we follow the Celts to Brittany in northern France, carved lanterns made from beets are part of Christmas Eve celebrations.

Pumpkin pie—as noted above—is yet another connection, although more American. Pumpkins are ripe by Halloween and although pumpkin pie is today generally associated with Thanksgiving—additional connective tissue between Christmas and Halloween—it also appears in another Christmas carol, "Sleigh Ride." Although not explicitly a Christmas song, sleigh bells are now associated with Christmas rather than Thanksgiving. Composed by Leroy Anderson, the tune was published in 1948 but the lyrics by Mitchell Parish were added in 1950. First recorded with Parish's lyrics by the Andrews Sisters, pop performances have made it into a standard Christmas piece. It does mention pumpkin pie, tying it back through Thanksgiving to Halloween. Up until the twentieth century, jack-o'-lanterns were sometimes used as Thanksgiving decorations.

In the popular imagination, among the poorer classes at least, Halloween and Christmas already had a long connection. In some locations mistletoe was used for a kissing prompt at Halloween, for example, which had a long tradition of matchmaking. It's now a Christmas tradition. Many holidays at the darker season of the year had similar features. Fire, for one, was practical for both light and heat when those necessities were lacking in nature. Feasting, particularly on foods previously not available (you couldn't run to the grocery store and pick up some Libby's pumpkin if the mood hit in summer) was a holiday practice. Animals slaughtered for winter food and grain newly harvested were at hand (hopefully) in abundance. In Christianity it was often the fine points of theology that made a difference between holidays.

This connection has its own continuing afterlife. Just a few examples will suffice: Ray Bradbury's novel *Something Wicked This Way Comes* is set in October. While it builds up the spooky childhood aspects of the season, the carnival settles into town. Charles Halloway, noticing the changes, hears a Christmas song "incongruous for October" yet somehow appropriate.* Or consider that Robert Louis Stevenson wanted to finish his gothic novella *Dr. Jekyll and Mr. Hyde* in time for Christmas purchasing. In more traditional settings, we also find several Christmas monsters in various European cultures. Perhaps the best known is the Dutch Krampus, who has even had horror films made of him. He's not alone, however, as the Icelandic, troll-like Gryla—one of several Christmas witch-like figures, the Welsh ghost horse Mari Lwyd, and Greek Kallikantzaroi demonstrate. Even Dr. Seuss' Grinch has become a standard Christmas monster.

A 2013 blog, *Scary Little Christmas*, was subtitled "Christmas—the Other Halloween," giving this section its title.† Horror movies set on holidays congregate around Christmas with Halloween coming a distant second. This all may relate to the British custom of seeing the Christmas season as a scary time of year. Or perhaps it shows we're only beginning to explore this maze. Either way, Washington Irving had a hand in both Christmas and Halloween as they came to be celebrated in America.

Evolution of Halloween

Halloween has taken in not only Sleepy Hollow and Christmas, but a number of other autumnal observances. Mischief Night was another custom from the British Isles, originally associated with May Day. As its title suggests, Mischief Night was when children (mainly) were permitted to get away with socially unacceptable behavior. In America it slipped around the calendar toward Halloween.

In England, until fairly recently, Guy Fawkes Day celebrations, on November 5, took precedence over Halloween. Characterized by bonfires and effigy burning, it also played into the ever-expanding Halloween associations. Of course, Guy Fawkes had to do with its namesake's ill-fated attempt to blow up Parliament, and not All Saints Day (Fawkes was, notably, Catholic). In Puritan New England, Guy Fawkes Day continued to be celebrated nearly until the twentieth century. In fact, Guy Fawkes celebrations were fairly common in the U.S. colonies that had large English populations. Mischief Night eventually migrated from spring to autumn, settling around either Guy Fawkes or Halloween. It still exists in pockets around Britain and North America. It made its way to the United States in the 1930s and '40s.

Pranks threatened, unless paid in candy, may have evolved into

---

* Bradbury, *Something Wicked This Way Comes*, chapter 5.
† A Scary Little Christmas blog is found at https://scarylittlechristmas.wordpress.com/, accessed 9 April 2023 (Easter, no less).

trick-or-treating. Earlier origins may have been in the "souling" mentioned above—remember, this is a maze. Halloween experienced a slow evolution, and it's still evolving. Now many adults look forward to it and celebrate it just as much as children do. As a commercial holiday it's second only to its longtime associate, Christmas. Both are seasons haunted by ghosts.

Around the turn of the millennium, Anglo America began to notice the separate, but related Hispanic celebration of *Día de los Muertos*, the Day of the Dead.* (Cue *Coco*.) Rather like Samhain, the Day of the Dead is a religious ceremony blending Catholicism and folk religion. It generally occurs November 1 and 2 (All Saints and All Souls for European Christians) but can stretch a few days on either side of this.

The basic idea is that home altars or tables (*ofrendas*) are set out with food offerings for deceased family members. Candles, flower petals, and photos of the recently deceased, are also placed among the goods. Offerings are also placed on the graves of the family dead. The tradition of sugar skulls, often colorfully decorated, has made a connection with the late development of candy for Halloween. Decorating and visiting family graves is important. The origins of the holiday are debated, with some suggesting indigenous traditions and others claiming Spanish ancestry. It may very well be a combination of both. Holidays are like that. In the United States the crossover with Halloween and Day of the Dead has led to a mixing of the symbols of the holidays. Mazes can be confusing and holidays are also examples of active myth making. Just ask the average American about the first Thanksgiving and you'll hear a myth in action.

All of this underscores America as a melting pot with its many ghosts. Halloween as it's known today is a conglomeration of Celtic otherworld beliefs, a Catholic festival, the death of a treasonous English subject, kids playing pranks, Christmas, and an Hispanic remembrance of ancestors. To this we've added America's ghost story, "The Legend of Sleepy Hollow." Ever since the late 1940s, it has generally been treated as a Halloween tale. This part of America's nightmare labyrinth also offers some hope. We're always at our best when we blend, rather than fearing and hating those who differ. Myths can heal. If only every day could be like Halloween.

Halloween on Film

Disney's film may have introduced Halloween to Sleepy Hollow, but another formative cinematic influence on the holiday is John Carpenter's

---

* Brandes, *Skulls to the Living, Bread to the Dead*. Brandes also contains information on All Saints and All Souls, in his introduction.

Halloween (1978). If you didn't recognize it, the opening paragraph of this chapter recounts the first few minutes of that movie. It remains, still, the most influential cinematic Halloween. Horror films focused on holidays (mostly Christmas) had been around for some time. *Halloween*, however, portrayed Laurie Strode babysitting and showing Tommy Doyle *The Thing from Another World* (which Carpenter would himself shortly reboot) on television. Watching horror movies on Halloween has developed into part of the ever-growing tradition for many. There's even an October challenge to watch a horror movie every night. So if your co-workers are jumpy this time of year, maybe you can understand why.

For children, of course, Ichabod Crane met his fate in Disney's version, on Halloween night. This connection would become so strong that most people simply assume "Sleepy Hollow" is a Halloween story. It has certainly become one since stories also evolve. It's America's first Halloween tale.

In America Sleepy Hollow and Halloween grew up together. The idea of having media dedicated to this spooky holiday doesn't seem to have occurred before Disney, just after the world was busy tearing itself apart during World War II. Someone at Disney seems to have had the idea of making the connection between Irving and Halloween explicit by setting Ichabod's chase on that day, and arming the Horseman with a jack-o'-lantern. It would be another half-century before a true horror movie based on the story was released. In the meantime, Americans gathered around the television—that great myth-maker—and there they also found Sleepy Hollow when autumn rolled around.

7

Xennial Developments

Trudging through the snow carrying a bag with all his possessions, the man suddenly hears something scary. Dogs baying. Two large hounds are suddenly chasing him through the woods. He begins to run but the dogs are faster. Gaining on him. He leaps, catching a low tree branch. He pulls himself out of reach of the angry canines, baring their teeth. A horse-drawn sledge slides up, driven by the burly owner of the dogs. The stranger asks the driver to call them off. Instead, the driver reaches up and breaks the branch, dropping Ichabod Crane down to his pursuers. They are, it turns out, playful, not angry hounds. Brom Bones, the dogs' owner, warns Crane that he does what he wants in Sleepy Hollow, especially to Connecticut Yankees.

Perhaps it's because Disney had such an early, definitive word about it, or maybe it's because of its incipient humor. Or changing tastes and mores in adult fiction in the twentieth century. Whatever the reason, "The Legend of Sleepy Hollow" is often treated as a children's story. And this is a very sticky label. It wasn't written as children's literature, of course, as we've seen. Washington Irving's descriptions of Ichabod Crane and Brom Bones are cartoonish, in keeping with Diedrich Knickerbocker's trademark style, but it's an adult story. In other words, it's kid friendly, even if not intended for children. Children's literature at the time was nothing like it is today. As we would put it in current terms, *The Sketch Book of Geoffrey Crayon, Gent.* was marketed to adults.

Whether this had anything to do with it or not, explicit remakings of "The Legend" seemed to take a hiatus until the 1970s. There were still references to it, of course. Mario Bava's *Black Sabbath* (1963) film poster featured a headless horse rider bearing his head in his hand, although no such scene occurs in the movie. There is a beheading victim, but the closest we get to a headless horseman is that one of the characters passes the corpse while on horseback. The poster, however, made its own nod to Sleepy Hollow, counting on the recognition.

Sleepy Hollow also continued to be referenced in specific episodes of established television series: *Scooby-Doo, Dark Toons, Shirley Temple's Storybook, Hold Tight!, Most Haunted, Diggers, Dark Days, Dead by Dawn, Wishbone* and more have Sleepy Hollow episodes—the story is irresistible to those targeting the young and curious. Many children's short movie versions also exist. Irving's characters suggest themselves for caricature and relief from adult-sized troubles. Overall, however, everyone seemed to think Disney pretty much said all that had to be said about it theatrically.

Since the legend was treated as "kids' stuff" it wasn't always taken seriously by adults anymore. Keep in mind that the category of "teenager," let alone "tween," wasn't recognized in Irving's own day. Certainly not teenagers with spending money. Books were adult business. And apart from the two pieces in the *Sketch Book* by Knickerbocker ("Rip Van Winkle" and "Sleepy Hollow"), the rest of the book is pretty much of interest only to adults. Still, there's childhood magic here. Remember Clifton Fadiman's sentiment from Chapter 5: these stories seem to be about the childhood of our nation. The childhood of the country taken literally, but also of our childhoods *in* this country. It's an American maze that has been adapted for children many times, becoming mythic along the way. This went hand-in-glove with the popularization of America's baby-sitting myth-maker—television.*

Sleepy Hollow in 1970s Television

The things we attend school to learn—reading and math—don't come naturally to people. That doesn't mean they're not important, just that they're difficult. Television appeals to our visual nature and our innate love of stories. Watching does come naturally. Like the computer, television had been in development for many decades before the device became widespread. In the fifties American homes started to accommodate television. About the same time, social historians were starting to treat childhood and teenage years as their own distinctive phases of becoming an adult. Weekend morning cartoon blocks ran in the sixties, offering adults the opportunity to sleep in a bit while the kids watched the tube.

Adults could claim the television for the evening news and later, but as TV schedules grew more aligned with viewer demographics, the after-school hours before dinner became prime time for advertising aimed at younger people. And therefore programming aimed at children. This

---

* Joe Nazare's essay, "Eerie Rider," details some of the television episodes not covered here.

was pretty much solidly in place by the end of the sixties. And "Sleepy Hollow" proved itself ideal for televised adaptation. This development also meant that horror elements in the story were subdued. Although it was building into a myth, this was more kids' stuff.

Disney may still have a privileged position in American consciousness of the tale, although adults may not have really forgotten Irving's original. There's something uniquely bankable about a story that can be made to fit children's interests as well as becoming the nepenthe for adult nostalgia. Those old Looney Tunes cartoonists understood that well enough, as much as writers for *SpongeBob SquarePants* do. After all, it's adults who are being paid to make these things, as well as to bankroll children's watching habits. We live in a time when not only teens, but tweens and younger, often have disposable income. Anything can be merched, even forgotten hamlets in the lazy Hudson Valley. Sleepy Hollow became a favorite children's television tale.

The received wisdom that to catch kids' attention you had to do so with after school programming became a boon for a short story like "Sleepy Hollow." As Disney discovered, Irving's plot isn't really long enough for a feature-length cartoon. Here we'll explore two examples of the afternoon special variety, but to find, watch, and parse all such adaptations would be the task of a lifetime. Who doesn't like the brain versus brawn trope? This story televised even as nerds were moving to positions of power. And nerdy Ichabod had become the hero of this myth.

Disney's claim on the story was considered in Chapter 5, but it certainly wasn't the last attempt at telling the story via cartoon. In 1970 Zoran Janjic directed an animated television movie, *Tales of Washington Irving*. Janjic was an Australian animation pioneer who headed Hanna-Barbera Productions in that country.* Hanna-Barbera was an American animation studio that had its start in 1957 and has since become part of Warner Brothers. They produced many very successful children's programs. They would also play a part in the myth of Sleepy Hollow.

Janjic's Hanna-Barbera connection accounts for the "Scooby-Doo" quality of this particular movie. Already at this early stage in the myth "Rip Van Winkle" was paired with "The Legend of Sleepy Hollow"—something Disney might've been well advised to have done. Janjic treated the two stories discretely, starting with Rip. Both are presented as spooky and this cartoon originally aired on the first of November, Halloween season. All together this movie runs an hour, putting Sleepy Hollow at about 30 minutes, similar to Disney.

Presenting Ichabod (George Furth) as completely noble, if nervous

---

* Hanna and Ito, *A Cast of Friends*.

and a bit silly, the Sleepy Hollow segment of the film follows Irving pretty closely. It tries to build up the scary setting better than Disney, portraying Ichabod as already present in the area and talking incessantly of ghosts. He's the one who brings up and tells locals about the Headless Horseman. Katrina (voice uncredited) is kindly and yet smart, but not an only child. If the writers were aware that this meant she wasn't likely the only heir to the estate, they don't let on.

Since it has plenty of dialogue, Katrina's expanded role is more easily developed. We'll see her become a stronger character as time goes on, like a ghost becoming physical again. The story emphasizes the mixed cues Crane receives and has Katrina point out something that will become common in later versions—although Crane is charming as a schoolmaster, Katrina notes that he's not equipped to be a rich farmer. Katrina is smart here, and aware that running a successful farm requires a skill set that Ichabod just doesn't have.

This Crane bursts into hymn singing when he thinks the schoolhouse is bewitched, and on his ride home after the Van Tassel party. In a strange turn of this maze, his singing lessons are songs by Henry Purcell, including the somewhat libertine "Nymphs and Shepherds." While not explicit here, sex will eventually enter the labyrinth of this tale. This is one of the rare versions that has Brom (voiced by Lennie Weinrib), following Irving, stopping up the chimney to end the singing lessons—as well as using his truly annoying dog to help interrupt. He apparently knows what such songs imply. Adults take notice. What would shepherds do with nymphs, do you suppose?

Ichabod also makes up songs about Katrina after school—Knickerbocker states that he tried to write poetry about her. Brom Bones is meaner here than in many other versions and Katrina doesn't reciprocate his affection. At the Van Tassel party it's Ichabod who starts the ghost stories and tells the tale of Old Brouwer. The chase scene is somewhat subdued, despite the spookiness. As Ichabod heads for the bridge that fateful night, the Headless Horseman hurls a jack-o'-lantern at him and the final scene mentions briefly that Brom wed Katrina, but then it cuts to an eerie shot of the abandoned schoolhouse and emphasizes something other versions tend to overlook.

Irving himself says the school fell to ruin after a new one was built elsewhere, and that the old one was said to be haunted by Ichabod Crane. This is a decidedly scary way to end the narrative that few have followed. The Headless Horseman is implied to be real in this telling of the tale. The Old Dutch Church, however, is left completely out of it.

This atmospheric Australian-American collaboration was released just after Halloween. It seems never to have been produced for home viewing after the VHS revolution. More's the pity since, despite the famous Hanna-Barbera limited animation, it offers a more substantial retelling of the tale steering toward horror. The jack-o'-lantern seems here to stay. It digs deep into the story and plants itself there, perhaps as an improvement to the original. The myth of Halloween influenced Sleepy Hollow just as the myth of Sleepy Hollow has influenced Halloween. So the seventies began with a new cartoon, but it couldn't displace Disney.

Just two years later, in 1972, an animated short narrated by John Carradine and directed by Sam Weiss, was released. This 13-minute *The Legend of Sleepy Hollow* pretty much follows Irving's lead as well. A few extra lines are added and much is left out. There is no church scene, for example, and although Ichabod teaches Katrina a psalm in her singing lessons, there is no Old Dutch Church in which they present it. The church is shown visually, even prominently, in a shot or two as background, but it plays no role in the story. Not as sumptuously animated as the Disney feature—or even the Janjic version—it nevertheless requires little time to watch and conveyed the basic story line. It helped set the spooky mood and kept the tale going.

Following the fateful dance—again Ichabod's animated dancing is emphasized—at the Van Tassels' house, Ichabod sings his psalm when he first meets the Horseman. The hurled head, as is now expected, is a jack-o'-lantern. Is the Headless Horseman Brom Bones? That's left unclear. Brom is drawn somewhat malevolently here, as in Janjic's rendition. The narrator notes that Brom was outclassed at every turn by Crane. Bones also laughs a lot, showing that he's not entirely evil, right? This may be a dead end in the maze. Released in August, it was a bit early for Halloween and isn't noticeably referenced by later renditions.

Overall, it's difficult to assess the impact of shorts. They aren't major theatrical releases and they aren't always aired widely on television. The fact that you can find many of them on YouTube for free suggests their owners are no longer making profits from them. Such postings, however, offer them in a place where people who've perhaps never heard of them can make up for that deficiency in the internet age. Tracing their historical impact isn't straightforward, unless they're widely discussed or referenced in other versions. The same is true of individual television episodes as parts of various standing series. These appear in addition to the many movie review shows that broadcast at least parts of one or another retelling of Sleepy Hollow filmed by someone else. Many sit-coms or dramas have also devoted an episode, usually around Halloween, to a version of the story. They are all, nevertheless, helping to build an American myth.

Before we leave 1972, we're obligated to consider John Kirkland's truly awful *Curse of the Headless Horseman*. This 75-minute low-budget

7. Xennial Developments 99

production only touches on the myth of Sleepy Hollow in a tangential way, a false turn leading to another dead end, if you will. It's live action, but that makes it no better. There's a payoff, in this maze, however. Read on. It begins with Mark Callahan, an internist, who has inherited his uncle's ranch. It has survived by being a crappy tourist attraction and Mark has to turn a profit in six months or lose the property, according to his uncle's will.

He invites his way-out friends to help him and the group of kids try to revive the place. Solomon, the old caretaker, tells them a headless horseman haunts the ranch because of a shootout that took place in old western times. How the shootout led to headlessness isn't explained. Then the psychedelic kids start getting attacked. It's all a ruse, however, since Mark knows there's gold on the land and has started killing his friends to bring publicity; otherwise he loses the mineral rights. Believe me, it's worse than it sounds.

What about that payoff? For one thing, this television movie shows how mythic Irving was becoming. For example, when Solomon tells the kids the tale of the headless horseman, Mark assures the gang it's all just a story. "Like Washington Irving," he says. Also, when a wealthy French countess (Ultra Violet, sporting a Superman lunchbox—I kid you not) tours the ranch wanting to buy it, she asks about Will Rogers. Will Rogers, of course, starred in Edward Venturini's 1922 *Headless Horseman*. This is a surprising bit of self-awareness in the film. Not set in the Hudson Valley, this may be the first movie to place the Headless Horseman in another state. It won't be the last. Another payoff is an unexpected connection with a director we'll shortly see again.

And whose name do we find on this groovy groaner? Look at the credits for cinematography. Henning Schellerup. Schellerup held a number of credits and roles in the film industry over the years. He was, for example, in the camera and electrical department for *A Nightmare on Elm Street* (1984), the film that includes Johnny Depp's first major film role. We'll see Depp in 1999 as the star of Tim Burton's version, of course. It's a maze. Schellerup, however, will turn up again in 1980 as the director of a television version of "The Legend." Clearly Sleepy Hollow is deeply entangled in the entertainment industry. But before watching more television, a word about philately and the written word.

Stamp and Novel Club

Irving's star had been holding steady in the seventies, but it hadn't risen beyond Disney's now classic treatment. His visage had appeared on a postage stamp from 1940. The first postage stamps date from 1840, a century earlier—still during Irving's lifetime—and stamp collecting likely began shortly thereafter. Irving, along with James Fenimore Cooper, was one of the first two of the Famous Americans stamp series, both in the category of authors. Those with the earliest birthdates, such as Irving, appeared on one-cent stamps.* Even before the Disney film, Irving had been one of a select few "famous Americans" chosen, based on recommendations of regular citizens. In an effort to boost stamp collecting, the United States Post Office would occasionally produce special issue stamps that appeal to philatelists.

Stamp collecting is one of the world's most popular hobbies.† Even in this digital era, in 2013 the *Wall Street Journal* estimated the number of stamp collectors in the world at 60 million. In 1974 the Post Office issued a commemorative ten-cent stamp based on "The Legend of Sleepy Hollow." Commemorative stamps had been produced since the 1890s. They normally appeared on a significant date or anniversary to mark an important event, person, object, or place. Issued on October 10 in Tarrytown, this stamp commemorated American folklore. The blue and orange dime stamp showed Ichabod mid-chase, the Horseman practically near enough to hear his horse's breath. A spooky, leafless tree reaches across the amber full moon. The stamp eerily evoked America's ghost story, engraved and printed and stuck to letters that crossed the country that autumn. This nation was a haunted one with stamps traveling every inch of the maze. Note it was issued in October. The seventies went out with several versions of the legend suggesting that more than just stamps would be navigating the national labyrinth.

That same year the episode "Chopper" on the popular ABC series *Kolchak: The Night Stalker*, featured a headless motorcycle rider with a sword. Making no explicit reference to Sleepy Hollow, the story's worth mentioning because it introduces the return of the head to the headless as a means of stopping an angry rider. Kolchak (Darren McGavin) throwing the head back to him is a solution Tim Burton will also use a few years down the road.

The year 1979 proved to be when Sleepy Hollow reentered public consciousness both in novel and television format. Some of the modern literary retellings are read into other stories by Knickerbocker fans, and are barely recognizable without their guidance. That's so much the case that it

---

* See https://www.mysticstamp.com/Products/United-States/859/USA/ (accessed 26 April 2023).

† See the *Wall Street Journal* interactive here: https://web.archive.org/web/20141028222154/https://online.wsj.com/news/interactive/stampgraphic?ref=SB10001424127887324009304579047070874399370 (accessed 26 April 2023).

requires some detective work to see that they're based on Irving at all. For example, *Ghost Story*.

Peter Straub's *Ghost Story* (1979) is a modern horror classic. Overall the story isn't based on Irving, but one of its vignettes is widely regarded to be. The jauntily named "Chowder Society" is a group of older men who meet together and end up telling stories within the story—almost Poesque. Some readers suggest that the first ghost story, that of Sears James, is based on Sleepy Hollow.* There are indeed some commonalities, although the teller's name suggests Henry James' *The Turn of the Screw* instead, as do many elements of the story. Of course, the old men telling ghost stories is itself reminiscent of "The Legend."

Sears James recounts being a young schoolteacher in a one-room schoolhouse in upstate New York, thus planting the Sleepy Hollow imagery. He's boarded with local families and is not paid well, just like Ichabod. There's no Headless Horseman, but there is the ghost of a pedophile, Gregory Bate. Bate had sexually abused his younger sister, and especially his younger brother. Then Gregory died in a school repair accident. James sees the dead Gregory without realizing he's a ghost and a couple of scenes look like they could have been vacationing from Henry James' masterpiece. If this is based on Irving it's in the latter-day Ichabod Crane character, and although the story has a ghost, it lacks Katrina Van Tassel and Brom Bones (unless that's Bate) and the only love triangle is between siblings.

There's enough here to suggest Sleepy Hollow to some readers. It's a tribute to Irving that starting off with a schoolmaster in upstate New York brings his tale immediately to mind. Of course, within Straub's novel the pedophile theme has connections with other stories in his narrative, so this may be more the borrowing of a setting than an actual conscious retelling of "The Legend." It does contribute to the myth, but perhaps it's another dead end in the labyrinth. The Legend continued toward myth on television.

Television into the Eighties

In October 1979 CBS aired *Once Upon a Midnight Scary*, hosted by Vincent Price. This was the first of the "CBS Library" series, aimed at children. Presenting live-action versions of children's books, the point of CBS Library was to get kids to read. The series ran for eight episodes, until it

---

*The suggestion about Peter Straub's *Ghost Story* came from Nazare, "Literature of Sleepy Hollow."

ended in 1983. Sleepy Hollow featured in the initial, Halloween-themed chapter.

Directed by Neil Cox, *Once Upon a Midnight Scary* features adaptations of three ghost stories: *The Ghost Belonged to Me*, a young adult novel by Richard Peck, "The Legend of Sleepy Hollow," and John Bellairs' juvenile novel, *The House with a Clock in Its Walls*. The last of these receives the longest run time. The Sleepy Hollow segment is the only one based on a single short story. Notice that Sleepy Hollow is again being presented as kids' stuff by the company it keeps. This despite the fact that the title of the special is based on Edgar Allan Poe's opening line of "The Raven."

Poe had been exploited quite frequently in the 1960s by Roger Corman. American International Pictures released ten films that are now called the "Corman-Poe Cycle." Many starred, of course, Vincent Price. While not intended for children, by the next decade these films were being aired alongside Saturday-afternoon monster movies, meaning that kids already associated Price with horror. *Once Upon a Midnight Scary* built on that connection.

The three stories presented are necessarily truncated, of course. "Sleepy Hollow" is again presented as a book, alongside two full children's novels, keeping alive the illusion that Washington Irving had published Sleepy Hollow as a stand-alone work. Irving was also being classified with Poe. Although the two corresponded with one another, their approach to writing scary stories differed quite a bit. Knickerbocker was claiming the autumn. *Once Upon a Midnight Scary* leans toward horror in the Halloween season, and you really couldn't leave Sleepy Hollow out of Halloween, could you?

Since all the stories are kept quite brief, this "Legend" segment picks up toward the end of the tale, just before the famous chase scene. The Headless Horseman is a "soldier" whose head was shot off. Ichabod Crane, played by Rene Auberjonois, is courting Katrina Van Tassel (Pamela Brown) at a dance when Brom Bones (Guy Boyd) intervenes. He offers to see Katrina home—the dance isn't at her father's house (although later Crane says he's going home from the Van Tassels')—due to the recent sightings of the Headless Horseman. Crane is presented as skeptical here, setting the stage for future renditions which will present him as having to be convinced that there are ghosts, as in Burton. This fits the xennial spirit. On his ride home, filled with rather annoying patter to his horse, Crane meets the Horseman and the famous chase ensues. The only reference to the Old Dutch Church is "the church bridge" that Ichabod wishes to reach. That bridge, however, does have a cross on it. After he crosses the bridge, Ichabod taunts the Horseman, who throws his actual head at Crane.

The next morning a smashed pumpkin—but no, a jack-o'-lantern—is found on the bridge. Whether the ghost is real or not is left up to the viewer, and the suggestion is to read "the book" and find out. If you read Irving, of course, you still have to decide for yourself. Price plays up the scariness aspect in his narration, but it's all in good fun. At the end it's revealed that his role as host has been a very much shorted version of Bram Stoker's *Dracula*.

There's not much new here beyond the skeptical Crane, but that's not the point. Entering the scary season, the show was pointing the way to child-friendly scary stories. It was contributing to the myth. Bram Stoker's *Dracula* may fall somewhat beyond young children's reach, but for what we now call tweens, it was accessible. Vincent Price was a horror icon for children by this time. Truly scary horror was brewing for adults during the seventies, with *The Amityville Horror* also being released in 1979. Interestingly enough, three episodes of the eight CBS Library series stories featured monsters of one kind or another.

Keep in mind that it was also during the xennial period that Scholastic began to publish books of scary stories for children, as we saw in Chapter 2. There was also a maturing of adult horror films at this same period starting with *Rosemary's Baby* and *Night of the Living Dead* in 1968. Irving's legend participated in the spirit of the times, it seems, and the story itself moved closer to actual horror, becoming what America needed it to be at the time—spooky children's fare.

Sleepy Hollow is evolving and each aired iteration has the potential to influence those that follow. Clearly, by the late seventies it has firmly become a Halloween tale and Halloween is becoming part of the myth. *Once upon a Midnight Scary* was released, after all, in late October. Also, beginning with Disney we see "The Legend of Sleepy Hollow" presented as a book. Even then it was in the public domain, but a story of only about 12,000 words can only very loosely be made to fill an entire book for adults. Publishers of young readers' materials often got around this by binding it together with "Rip Van Winkle" and/or illustrating it. Many editions of these two stories together, or "Sleepy Hollow" with other stories, appeared about this time.

A truly original animated take on Irving's characters also appeared in 1979 in the form of the Canadian television special *The New Misadventures of Ichabod Crane*, directed by Vic Atkinson. With a half-hour run time, it rivals Disney's and Janjic's versions in length. Despite all the musical and sound cues for comedy, it actually has some of the scariest visuals for an early animated production of the story. After a spooky poem, it begins with the Headless Horseman robbing a stagecoach. A musical number then introduces Ichabod Crane (voiced by Kreskin) as a local hero. Nerdy, yes, and timorous, he's elected to take on the Horseman because he knows all about witchcraft and the weird. He reluctantly agrees to his charge, accompanied by Rip Van Winkle (Larry D. Mann, who, as a joke, keeps falling asleep), the horse Washington (after Irving), and bloodhound Wolf. The latter two are voiced by Pat Buttram and George Lindsey, paired as Napoleon and Lafayette in Disney's 1970 *Aristocats*. (Buttram and Lindsey were frequent Disney voice talents but the *Aristocats* connection is especially obvious here.)

As the audience, we're clued in that the Headless Horseman is actually a spell cast by Velma Van Dam, a local witch who lives outside town. The four heroes pass through some scary woods until they find the wrecked carriage that Velma robbed. Seeing her house out on its rocky pinnacle, they investigate only to be driven off by the Headless Horseman. Rip, however, falls asleep and is captured. He learns about the Headless Horseman spell before being turned into an opossum by the witch.

Meanwhile Ichabod can't abandon his friend and guide, so the remaining three come up with a plan to pose as a traveling salesman selling witchcraft items. Through madcap spells and chases the four manage to escape, but Velma turns some scarecrows into living monsters to chase them. Ichabod, who stole her spell-book to change Rip back, accidentally turns himself into the Headless Horseman and cuts down the scarecrows. The friends realize they needn't fear Velma anymore because they now control the Horseman.

This is all for amusement, of course, and the "new misadventures" presume the Headless Horseman is still real, even if the result of a witch's spell and not an actual ghost. This monstrous Horseman can cause physical harm without being a ruse of Brom Bones.

In fact, Brom Bones and Katrina Van Tassel don't appear at all. There's no love story here. The Horseman is shown in Disney style, holding a flaming jack-o'-lantern. Even the less polished sketching of Wolf resembles Napoleon from *The Aristocats*. The faux French accent on the Ichabod Crane song resembles the *Aristocats* theme song. This cartoon is taking its cues from Disney. Although the victim is a scarecrow, this short also shows a beheading with the scarecrows ending up like the Straw Man after a visit of the Wicked Witch of the West's flying, blue-faced chimpanzees. That's important because up to this point, beheading has only ever been implied in both the original and retellings. Brom beheading a scarecrow in Disney's version has only an inanimate victim. From now on, heads of the living may roll. This is moving toward horror, even though a cartoon.

Two final points about this production: there's no church and it isn't set at Halloween. Most re-imagined versions since Disney have taken this to be, in essence, a Halloween tale. Other children's adaptations appeared from time to time over the next few decades. Most set the story around

Halloween. There is a jack-o'-lantern here, however. And this is the first version showing humans controlling the Horseman's actions—a part of the myth that will also grow.

Perhaps because it's a Canadian translation, the centrality of the church isn't assumed. Also, the narrative has broken loose from Irving's plot. The lead character is here, as is the Horseman, but the rest of the story is new. Although witches will feature in the future, not too much is added to the myth from here. It's another fun dead end in the maze.

Before stepping through the portal to the eighties, let's pause to consider that the growing state of children's horror might help to understand the myth. "Monster boomers" were those baby boomers who grew up when horror and sci-fi movies invitingly aired on Saturday afternoons before cable. *Scooby-Doo* was on Saturday mornings, and *Dark Shadows* played after school. *The Twilight Zone* was in evening reruns, early enough to watch. Networks discovered kids could handle some of the more innocent horror on offer at the time. This eased the way for a ghost story to become an American myth. Theatrical horror had grown up just as the seventies began, but kids could get a friendly fix after school and on the weekends. Also at this time Alice Cooper was extremely popular with young rebels. "School's Out" and, for those slightly older, "I'm Eighteen" became anthems. Midway through the decade, Cooper launched his solo career with *Welcome to My Nightmare*. He would go on using horror themes in rock that appealed to the young. Horror was becoming an inescapable part of the labyrinth. But still, family-friendly fare was on offer on television, bringing Henning Schellerup back into the picture. Such was the state of things moving into the eighties.

Second Feature-Length Film

As the eighties began a full-length television movie appeared, moving Irving's legend in a different direction. Myths evolve and even as expectations such as Halloween and religion took hold in some quarters, they loosened their grip elsewhere. A labyrinth is the best way to understand this evolution.

A feature-length film of "The Legend" by itself had not appeared since 1922. Remember, Disney's version had to be paired with Kenneth Grahame's *The Wind in the Willows* to reach a standard running time. Zoran Janjic's television movie had been more naturally paired with "Rip." Short stories had been made movie length before, of course. Roger Corman was famous for doing this with Edgar Allan Poe's short stories throughout the sixties, as we saw. To get these results Poe had to be padded considerably.

Corman seemed to have no underlying mythic message to build—just staying alive in Hollywood. Sleepy Hollow was different.

In 1980 the television movie *The Legend of Sleepy Hollow* aired.* Directed by Henning Schellerup—whom we met in *Curse of the Headless Horseman*—it stars a young Jeff Goldblum as Ichabod Crane. This adaptation was surprisingly important to the myth. Although Tim Burton doesn't recall seeing it,† it influenced the twentieth-century's myth-making culmination. Although a skeptical Crane had appeared before, this one's rationalism carried over into Johnny Depp's rendition. Goldblum's Crane tries to convince the locals there's no such thing as ghosts, but he comes to believe. Schellerup also demonstrated that a feature-length movie was possible with enough development.

Remember, Washington Irving had no heirs and his stories were completely in the public domain. There was no-one to object to altering things

Jeff Goldblum as Ichabod Crane, from Henning Schellerup's *Legend of Sleepy Hollow* (© 1980 Jensen Farley Pictures and Schick Sunn Classics, All Rights Reserved).

---

* The information on Schellerup's movie, and those prior to it, derived from watching them (repeatedly), as well as using their pages on IMDb.
† On Schellerup and Burton, see Salisbury, *Burton on Burton*, 165–67.

completely. The names hadn't changed, but apart from Brom Bones, just about everything about them has. Ichabod's still a teacher and Katrina's still a prize, but there's a lot more scheming and plotting happening in Sleepy Hollow in this adaptation. Eyes forward, we'll see this again in Burton. To become a myth the story must fit the needs of the time.

As we've seen, Halloween has a connection with the festive season at the end of the year. For some reason perhaps related to this, Schellerup's legend is set in winter, not around Halloween. Although Schellerup's story is set later in the year his Headless Horseman still carries a lit jack-o'-lantern, now fully expected, if out of season. Harvest imagery is otherwise lost beneath the snow. Burton doesn't use the jack-o'-lantern convention with his horseman, apart from Brom Bones' stunt. That movie is set on Halloween, however. In 1980 Schellerup tried to move away from the by then traditional Halloween atmosphere.

Ichabod Crane enters Sleepy Hollow one winter day as a complete skeptic regarding ghosts. After being chased by Brom's dogs, as we saw in the chapter opening, he's met by Fritz Vanderhoof, played by the irrepressible John Sylvester White. Vanderhoof is an important added character who has an agenda to get Crane to marry his daughter Thelma (Laura Campbell), a young widow. Brom Bones, played by Dick Butkus, resents Ichabod's interest in Katrina Van Tassel (Meg Foster), but because of Thelma, the story becomes a love quadrangle rather than the usual triangle. Ichabod ends up with Katrina, staying in Sleepy Hollow, while Brom is blackmailed into marrying Thelma. The payoff for this complexity is minimal but it shows how the myth evolves along different paths. Myths tend to construct variants into the labyrinths they build.

This Ichabod Crane is likable and sympathetic, as well as logical. At the schoolhouse the children inform Crane that his new home—for he sleeps at the school—is built on an Indian burial ground. That detail marks the tale as a period horror piece. Beginning with *The Amityville Horror* the previous year, genre films latched onto the Indian burial ground trope. Despite its overuse, this too is part of America's long nightmare. Our collective guilt over our treatment of American Indians, despite not having improved their current situation, has come back time and again in horror. So much so that *Room 237*, directed by Rodney Ascher—a 2012 documentary about *The Shining*—includes a segment suggesting the whole movie was about the indigenous American genocide.

Some of the current best written horror comes from the pen of Stephen Graham Jones, a Blackfoot author. There's another whole book to be written on horror and American Indians. It's another labyrinth. Supernatural fear pervades Schellerup's Hollow, although the movie doesn't make too much of it. Fritz Vanderhoof dresses as an Indian to frighten Crane at one point, somewhat insensitively by today's standards, but the theme is dropped after that. Knickerbocker left the indigenous Americans out of it almost completely.

Vanderhoof is, in fact, a main character in this adaptation, capturing more screen time than Bones. Vanderhoof's role in the community is never really explained, but he does function somewhat like a Greek chorus, or Edward Venturini's school committee, informing Ichabod that previous school teachers have been driven away, or even killed by Bones. This idea will recur in future tellings as well. The most recent schoolmaster before Crane, Winthrop Palmer, was drowned because the Headless Horseman—later revealed to have been Bones—drove him into the river. Apparently to dissuade Baltus Van Tassel from allowing his daughter to be courted by Crane, Vanderhoof orchestrates "hauntings," so he can claim the teacher has gone strange when he reacts to "ghosts," just like the past schoolmasters have. In this way he can arrange for Crane to marry Thelma, who's in love with Bones. Meanwhile, Katrina has fallen in love with Ichabod, after a rocky start. Emphasizing marriage and comic scheming, the horror aspect is clearly subdued in Schellerup's film.

This level of backstory appears to be either padding to fit this short story into a two-hour television slot or an attempt at improving upon Irving's storytelling by adding complexity. Or it may be simply getting lost in the maze. The mythic influence of Knickerbocker shouldn't be underestimated. Additional episodes were required to get the story to fit Venturini's 70 minutes with the first feature-length attempt, and Disney couldn't make it stand alone, as we've already seen. Since the actual running time for Schellerup's version is nearly twice that of Venturini, it requires even more material than the silent version. Some of it seems to be just for the fun of getting lost.

The obligatory choir rehearsal scene is included but Crane and company are never shown going to the church. Indeed, the Old Dutch Church has become lost in this section of the maze. America had been secularizing throughout the xennial period, despite the looming Religious Right.

Much of the comedy here comes from Bones and his sycophantic sidekick Frederic Dutcher, rather than Crane. Although portrayed in family friendly manner, Brom is seriously dangerous in this adaptation, and not above murder. He hates schoolteachers, not just Crane. Bones and Dutcher make plans to take care of Ichabod for good, but the former pedagogue Palmer reappears, finally convincing Crane to believe in ghosts. Palmer reveals himself to Crane as somewhat insane, but nevertheless out for revenge on Bones for killing him, and also, surprisingly, revenge on the Headless Horseman as well. Although he makes fire magically appear, and Crane's furniture moves by itself in his presence, Palmer is himself later revealed to be the actual previous schoolmaster, not drowned as everyone thought. He's "gone strange" and his role seems to be to convince the viewer that he is the Headless Horseman. Misdirection in the maze.

The Van Tassels throw an annual winter ball. Katrina and Thelma conspire to manipulate the men to their liking. Palmer appears to Crane at the party, setting him off on a clumsy streak that ends with Bones throwing Crane through the window. Baltus Van Tassel dismisses Ichabod, but Katrina vows her love. There are no ghost stories told, and Ichabod is in high spirits as he leaves the party, assured that Katrina really does love him. On the ride home, Bones, dressed as the Headless Horseman, tries to drive Crane off. Instead, the real Headless Horseman—who Crane thinks is Palmer—chases Bones. Then in a reversal that upends the character of the original story even further, Ichabod chases the Horseman. The ending reveals that Palmer couldn't have been the Horseman, but Crane ends up with Katrina anyway and decides not to make an issue of the very real ghost he's encountered.

When Bones falls from his horse, the Vanderhoofs learn he's been "the Horseman" in the past and agree not to inform on him if he marries Thelma. Although the film has three Horsemen, including the implied Palmer, the climax of the previous versions—the Halloween chase of Ichabod ending up with an attack—never takes place. Echoes of Schellerup's previous Headless Horseman work bleed through. It seems we've perhaps been walking in a circle in this maze.

Some elements of the Schellerup story made it into the Burton version, including the music cue for a scary figure in the woods and the skeptical Crane. As noted, this is one of the two versions that somehow influenced Burton (the other one being the Disney rendition) before filming his adaptation. Each telling grows the myth.

Vanderhoof and his attempt to get his daughter married to Crane adds more filler to the story that may serve as comic relief, but the plot raises questions about forced marriages. Ichabod's skepticism adds a fresh element that will be treated again in future versions directed by more skillful hands. Ichabod ends up with Katrina, plot turn that Burton's version will use at the expense of Brom Bones.

The supernatural pervades Schellerup's story, despite the missing church. The owl in the school room is said to be the ghost of Chief Running Buffalo. America's nightmare is lurking in the rafters. Palmer's able to perform supernatural feats. The actual Headless Horseman chases Brom. Another dead end in the labyrinth? Nevertheless, the ghost remains real in this largely secularized version. The Headless Horseman lurks to ride another night.

It's unclear what the winter setting accomplishes—the movie aired on

Halloween. The Horseman still carries a jack-o'-lantern (and sword). Following Irving's tale, it doesn't mention Halloween, which would be accurate for the period. Setting the climax in winter, however, suggests a move to put ghost stories back closer to their Christmas-time setting. The starkness of a snow-covered landscape is atmospheric. Black-clad Ichabod shot against this white backdrop suggests a gothic undertone. It's difficult to say this film was completely effective, but it has an outsized portion of the maze dedicated to it. Clearly influential on Burton, it demonstrates how myths take on lives of their own.

It would be almost two decades more before another feature film was released. But when it was, it had company. Not exactly triplets, three Sleepy Hollow films appeared in 1999.

8

Moving Toward the Millennium

He's beyond cruel. He stalks the battlefield after winning, in case he's missed anyone. He spies a dying soldier leaning on a cannon wheel. The wounded man begs for mercy. The Hessian laughs and instructs the man to tell the Devil to keep the fires hot for him. He runs the man through with his sword. He doesn't notice that the stricken soldier still has enough life to light the cannon, if only he can reach it.

A change was in the air following Henning Schellerup's *Legend of Sleepy Hollow*. Moving toward the millennium three new feature-length movies of Sleepy Hollow would appear. One of them included the scene above, giving the Headless Horseman a new prominence. Tim Burton's 1999 film would give the Horseman more of a backstory. So much backstory that he became mythic. By the time we reach Fox's *Sleepy Hollow* in 2013, he's just as important a character as Ichabod Crane. (For two seasons.) This new outlook on the Horseman accompanied a new view of Crane as well. No longer silly, Ichabod would become heroic in his own right. Almost mythic. A man with sex appeal. In this labyrinth Sleepy Hollow was becoming a myth.

Two of the three Sleepy Hollow films of 1999 were television movies.* Both of them were released not long before Burton's adaptation. After Burton there would be a slow explosion of new interest in Sleepy Hollow. Novels would begin appearing. Feature-length renditions—there were only two in the previous century—would become standard. "The Legend" had been around for nearly two centuries, but clearly it was becoming something more. And the next rank up from legend is myth.

Before we reach 1999, however, two more paths through the maze

---

* Most of the information conveyed in this chapter came from repeated viewings of the Duvall, Gang, and Williams adaptations of Sleepy Hollow. They haven't been written about much.

would take wanderers in new directions through Sleepy Hollow. The first took its shape from the former horror icon, Shelley Duvall.

Duvall's Legend

Disney's original plan for Sleepy Hollow had been a series of legends. This series never materialized, but the idea was a compelling one. It led to another creative rendition. The next serious retelling effort came in 1985 as part of Shelley Duvall's *Tall Tales and Legends* series that initially ran on Showtime. A total of nine tales and legends were included in the series. Her first entry? Sleepy Hollow, of course.

Ed Begley, Jr., starred as Ichabod Crane. Like Jeff Goldblum, Begley's tall, lanky physique fits Knickerbocker's description of Crane. His Katrina Van Tassel is Beverly D'Angelo. Both Begley and D'Angelo were known for their comedic roles, although Begley had been in horror films such as *Cat People* and *The Entity* (both 1982) and some may have remembered D'Angelo from *The Sentinel* (1977). Duvall's *The Legend of Sleepy Hollow* features several clever asides and a few insider nods to horror. Duvall herself was already known for *The Shining*, just four years earlier. The maze takes in not only these other horror films, but family connections as well. Ed Begley's father had narrated Sleepy Hollow in 1968 for Caedmon Records—later Caedmon Audio—so this was a kind of family interest.

This mix of comedy and horror presents the story in the spirit of Irving's original. Directed by Edd Griles, it was advertised as "A retell of Washington Irving's 1820 Halloween novel."* Let's pause here for a moment. Recall that Irving wrote a short story—too brief to be produced as a book itself. It's now become a novel in the advertising copy. And not just any novel, but a Halloween novel! Can there be any doubt that whether trying to be faithful to Irving, or even when set in winter, Sleepy Hollow is part of America's growing Halloween myth? It fits the needs of its society, even as traditional religion was declining. America embraces its autumnal scary season with all its ghosts and nightmares. We've come to expect this to be a Halloween legend—throwing Schellerup's version into even more abrupt chiaroscuro—and so it is.

Duvall begins with an introduction in which she recommends curling up with a scary book. This adaptation is narrated by Doffue Van Tassel (Charles Durning), brother of Baltus. The name "Doffue" seems to have

---

* From the log line on IMDb, https://www.imdb.com/title/tt0717645/?ref_=ttep_ep1, accessed 13 June 2024.

8. Moving Toward the Millennium

Ed Begley, Jr., as Ichabod Crane, from Edd Griles' *Legend of Sleepy Hollow* (©1985 Platypus Productions, Inc., and Gaylord Productions, Inc., All Rights Reserved).

been borrowed from the tavern keeper in Edward Venturini's silent adaptation, which, in turn, borrowed it from an unrelated character in Knickerbocker's original telling. A traveling salesman, Doffue enjoys scaring people and Ichabod, thrashing through the woods in fear, ends up at his camp one night. This Crane is extremely nyctophobic—he's afraid of the dark. Doffue uses his fear to sell him a potion by telling him the story of a headless highwayman who rides at Halloween. From the beginning this is treated as a Halloween tale. In this case, Headless is a highwayman, not a Hessian mercenary. And he's not central to the story.

Despite his fears, Crane determines to take the schoolmaster job after meeting Doffue's niece, Katrina. During the day Crane is nervous but unafraid. For the most part. This Crane never really commits to staying in Sleepy Hollow. He says the next morning he'll leave by Halloween. Doffue takes him to the Van Tassels, and along the way he meets Brom Bones (Tim Thomerson). And Katrina's little brother. Like both Zoran Janjic and Henning Schellerup, this version underplays Katrina's heiress role since she has a sibling. Brom visits Katrina and is there when Ichabod arrives. She's pretty clearly using Crane to make Brom jealous, and Brom's anger rises. Katrina tells Ichabod that he has a famous singing voice and the women can't wait to hear him sing in church. But she really seduces him with cookies. Cookies, by the way, were originally Dutch treats and the word itself derives from Dutch.

Rooming with locals, Crane prepares for bed by praying and laying out garlic, a cross, and other symbols of good luck. The next day Doffue tells us that Crane sees the Devil in everything. He balked at the horse name Daredevil, and expresses fear of Hell. He tells the children they're possessed. When he spies a spider on Katrina's brother, he assumes it's the Devil and sends it back to Hell. By the way, this scene, in which he's picnicking with a student, fits Knickerbocker's telling as well. Irving said he was a companion to older students after school. But notice how religion has been added—a cross, numerous references to Hell and the Devil. This is a secular-religious Crane. It is possible to be secular and religious all at the same time in this labyrinth.

Choir practice here is as secular and suggestive as it was in Janjic's production. The women host choir practice at their homes instead of church. Ichabod leads them in "Drink to Me only with Thine Eyes," a song with lyrics from a poem by Ben Jonson. The imagery, like "Nymphs and Shepherds," tends toward the erotic. No hymn-singing Crane here.

Meanwhile, at the tavern, the local men express their dislike of the cowardly Crane. Bones hides in the cemetery and scares Ichabod with a headstone with the teacher's name on it. The next morning, Crane finds the schoolroom in disarray and decides to leave Sleepy Hollow. Katrina visits and asks him to stay for the fair. He finally agrees but Katrina rides to the fair with Bones. The fair features a horserace that demonstrates Brom's riding skills. This will be revisited in an adaptation by Pierre Gang, mere weeks before Burton's movie. Remember, Palmer had "drowned" after a horse-driven chase in Schellerup's story. In the context of Duvall's episode, it serves to demonstrate that Daredevil, Brom's horse, is the fastest in Sleepy Hollow. A broad hint, of course, to those who've been wandering in this maze for a while. During the fair, Katrina urges Crane to stay for the Halloween party. Duvall's Ichabod loves the ladies, however, he's far more interested in staying alive than being in love, it seems.

Brom rages against Crane. He encounters Katrina's little brother who has a jack-o'-lantern. He says Crane made it for him. Brom gives him a ride and places the pumpkin on his saddle pommel, note. Ichabod never goes out at Halloween, but Katrina has persuaded him to attend. The party convinces Crane to stay in Sleepy Hollow—the food, Katrina, and wealth sway him, just as in Irving. Also, Duvall gives us a Black fiddler and a Crane who can dance.

Brom tells the story of how the Headless Horseman came to be. A highwayman—essentially a pirate on land, robbing travelers—was caught by ten men with swords. In the melee his head was chopped off. Now the highwayman rides on Halloween looking for a new head, carrying his moldering one in front of him. Crane stays on to propose, but Katrina won't let him. The spooky ride home is emphasized and he's chased away by Bones, carrying a flaming jack-o'-lantern. Rather than throwing it at Crane, however, he tosses it in a pond after the teacher rides off.

Doffue tells us nobody knows what became of Crane, and that things would've worked well for Brom had he not met the real Headless Horseman the night after Halloween. The ghost is real here, but never really shown.

While the church is mentioned it's also never portrayed, and it plays no part in getting to safety in the expected chase scene. Crane doesn't mention Cotton Mather in this version, but the idea of the Devil is played up. Ichabod carries a cross (and garlic) to ward off evil. Crane assumes the black cat of one of his choristers is the Devil in another form. Mentions of the Devil and the use of a cross strangely imbue the tale with a religious urgency without the Old Dutch Church. And religion summons horror. By 1985 everyone knew that crosses (and garlic) kept vampires away. They knew the Devil was real because both *Rosemary* and the *Exorcist* told them so. It is possible to be secular and religious all at the same time in Sleepy Hollow. There's even a "Vampire Butte" near Sleepy Hollow in this version.

Interestingly, the first popular literary vampire actually appeared about the same time as "The Legend of Sleepy Hollow." Written by John Polidori, friend and physician of Lord Byron, "The Vampyre" appeared in 1819, attributed to Byron. If Irving had read it he didn't mention vampires at all in his story, which was published the following year.

Burton's film also bears some striking resemblances to Duvall's. The emphasis on Hell, absent before Duvall, is taken up by Burton. Ichabod's antics mounting Gunpowder also seem foreshadowed here—even calling him "horsey." This, along with some of Johnny Depp's mannerisms suggest that either he or Andrew Kevin Walker, the writer, had seen this adaptation. Both feature a large spider with apparently occult significance.

Begley's Crane is underdeveloped, and we don't really get a sense of his motives. His fear keeps him threatening to leave Sleepy Hollow. He's not really drawn too much by love or money. Some just wander about in the maze all day. It's all told with Irving's smile. This humorous retelling demonstrates that the myth always has an element of fun. Of course, the Horseman is really real in the end. All of this is fit into 50 minutes. Sleepy Hollow was making a comeback, and Irving's star was ascending.

The End of the Eighties

Other developments were taking place in Sleepy Hollow as the decade drew to a close. T.C. Boyle's sprawling, award-winning novel *World's End* was published in 1987. Not a retelling of the Legend, it's nevertheless part of the myth in that it uses both the fictional van Brunt and Crane families as characters. No Ichabod or Brom lurk here, but rather a story of land taken from American Indians and held tightly by white supremacists across the generations. While there's no Headless Horseman there are ghosts and a footless real person. It's worth mentioning here because it demonstrates that Irving's characters have taken on afterlives in some unexpected places. Even as the xennial period progressed, it made its way into literary fiction. This will accelerate in the new millennium.

The next year, Rabbit Ears produced an animated short of "The Legend of Sleepy Hollow" in 1988. Featuring the minimally animated paintings of director Robert McNutt, the 20-minute video is narrated by Glenn Close. Noteworthy because of the awards it won, the story stays close to Irving. Rabbit Ears produced a set of Story Book Classics from 1984 through 1990. Known for their high production values, the series was aimed at children. If you meet Ariadne before you enter the maze, perhaps as a child, you may find your way out.

Although the Rabbit Ears story stays pretty true to Irving, it does continue to use the jack-o'-lantern that the myth now demands for the tale. Interestingly enough, Katrina is first introduced with a green ribbon around her neck. This appears both at her first introduction as well as during her wedding. Remember the ribbon from Chapter 2. It's like a clue dropped on the path of the maze. Also, Brom is shown leaping over a barrel on Daredevil in the background the night of the party and it seems he has no head. Some fans acclaim this as the best adaptation to film.*

The seventies and eighties were notable for their growing secularization, even as religiously motivated forces were eyeing all three branches of the U.S. government, and the broadcasting power of mass media. There were hints that Sleepy Hollow could be considered mythic, that it wasn't just for children. Darker elements aren't too pronounced just yet, but these would be picked up by the end of the next decade, even as horror began to appeal to the mainstream.

After all this activity, there was a gap of just over a decade before a dozing Sleepy Hollow would come roaring back. Although the legend had been growing into a myth, a sea change awaited at the end of the nineties. Tim Burton wasn't the only one to be thinking of Sleepy Hollow as the

---

* According to user reviews on IMDb.

story continued to appear in both amateur and professionally produced versions. Nevertheless, Burton's film would prove to be the new mythic standard. After the change of the millennium, no future telling could afford not to tip its hat, or its head, in that direction. Two other films, however, also haunted Halloween that year.

Like It's 1999

In the year 1999, "The Legend of Sleepy Hollow" became a full-blown myth. The momentum had been building for years—ever since the story left Washington Irving's pen, in fact. Even in the nineteenth century, writers were suggesting that there was something strangely compelling about this tale. Irving wrote a couple of reminiscences of its background. It was clear that it might grow into something larger than a legend. The year 1999 stands out because of Tim Burton's *Sleepy Hollow*, but also because two other Sleepy Hollow films also appeared that year. All were released within weeks of each other. Each told the tale quite differently.

In most cultural landscapes there are defining beacons—markers in the maze. These beacons set directions for further exploration. For example, fans of demonic possession movies look to *The Exorcist* as the godfather and trend-setter. For "Sleepy Hollow," Disney's early animated version clearly formed the expectations of how the story goes for generations of children. No serious theatrical attempts were made for half a century after that. Then Burton's 1999 *Sleepy Hollow* set the story off on a new trajectory. Not only was the movie itself a hit, it directly inspired the Fox television series by the same name and set off a spate of novel-length books—sometimes series of novels—based on various characters, locations, or ideas that find their ultimate origins in Washington Irving's tale. This rich and flourishing afterlife is remarkable and shows no loss of energy with the passing years. It has become its own mythology. Religion played a key role in this development. It's also Sleepy Hollow's grand entrance into horror proper. Burton's film, however, wasn't first out of the gate at the turning of the millennium. Two others made it through the portal first.

The Gang Telling

Released a few weeks before Burton's film in 1999, a television movie directed by Pierre Gang became the third feature-length adaptation of Irving's story. Titled *The Legend of Sleepy Hollow*, the film was almost totally eclipsed by Burton and Depp's rendition. At an hour and 45 minutes, Gang's story also included departures beyond the storyline suggested by Irving, although it stays fairly close. Starring Brent Carver as an unsympathetic Ichabod Crane, its most noteworthy feature is its overall faithfulness to Irving's plot. Remember, Crane isn't Knickerbocker's hero. Indeed, the character Knickerbocker (the pseudonym often used by Washington Irving and credited with "The Legend" in *The Sketch Book of Geoffrey Crayon, Gent.*) comes to a tavern one stormy night to collect stories as the movie opens. The men gathered there remember Revolutionary times and tell the story of the capture of Major André and recount the tenure of Ichabod Crane. They set Ichabod's tale in 1791.

Crane, arrogant and condescending, arrives in Sleepy Hollow from Hartford, Connecticut, to take the job of schoolmaster. Blacksmith Brom Bones (Paul Lemelin) is the first inhabitant he meets. This is perhaps the most sympathetic Bones in the body—hardworking and really in love with Katrina. It isn't until Sunday, when Crane sings the loudest in church, that

Brent Carver as Ichabod Crane, from Pierre Gang's *Legend of Sleepy Hollow* (©1999 Muse Entertainment Enterprises, All Rights Reserved).

Katrina Van Tassel (Rachelle Lefevre) is first seen. After church Crane wheedles his way to offering chorister lessons. His ulterior motive is to have access to Katrina. Most notable in this adaptation is that Katrina is an intellectual and not a flirt. She doesn't encourage Brom Bones but thinks for herself. This more developed Katrina will feature particularly in novels of the new millennium. Baltus, her father, sees through Crane from the start. Bones is the protagonist in this telling while the focus remains on Ichabod.

Carver's Crane considers himself an expert on Cotton Mather's work on witchcraft. He claims to have lectured at Harvard College's School of Divinity. Mrs. Van Tassel tells him the tale of the Headless Horseman initially. According to her, the Horseman was a Hessian mercenary turncoat. He was actually helping the patriots against the British when his head was shot off. He rode into battle nevertheless. Katrina, who is not superstitious, doesn't believe. She teasingly tells Ichabod how a local man, after disappearing on Sleepy Hollow road, was found with his head in the ground at the Horseman's grave, his neck stretched as if he'd been hanged. That night Crane mistakes Brom Bones' gang for the Horseman and companions. When afraid he sings hymns. Katrina is cautiously impressed by him.

A horserace is thrown in, as in Shelley Duvall's rendition, perhaps to introduce Daredevil, Bones' horse. Katrina is, however, interested in learning and traveling, and she finds Ichabod interesting. Until her father sets him up. Asking leading questions while Katrina is listening out of sight, Baltus has Crane admit that Katrina's dreams are foolish and that he would remain local and could indeed manage the farm. She then realizes Ichabod wants her for her wealth. The Van Tassels throw a harvest merrymaking. Historically correct, no mention is made of Halloween. Brom convinces Katrina that he loves her while Ichabod otherwise monopolizes her attention for his own gain. At storytelling time, Brom narrates his encounter with the Horseman, saying he had to get across the log bridge, beyond the church, and past the Horseman's grave to be safe. Ichabod stays after the party to propose and is rejected by Katrina, who, of course, heard his earlier admission.

Riding Gunpowder home that night, Ichabod encounters Brom, dressed as the Horseman, carrying a pumpkin. When Brom is knocked off his horse, the actual Horseman appears. Gang is taking cues from Henning Schellerup here. There is no chase, however, but the ghost throws a pumpkin to the ground near Crane—again following Duvall—encouraging him to run off. Back in the tavern, the old men tell Knickerbocker that Brom and Katrina married and Crane was never seen again.

Gang's movie is more Katrina's story of learning life lessons when small town life offered women few opportunities. The dilemma of being faithful to a period when women tended to be relegated—now less willingly—to the home, versus giving them agency, is real enough. Schellerup had the women scheming, but their plans are for attaining husbands. Gang's Katrina has a mind of her own and wishes to set goals for her own life. Burton's Katrina will also have more agency but she ultimately ends up following Ichabod's lead. Women tend to get lost in this labyrinth. Like Disney, all of Gang's characters are white, leaving African Americans out of Irving's problematic servant roles.

For a television film, Gang's version takes care with many historical details. Intended for family viewing, it keeps any horror very much muted. The chase with Brom Bones, before he's revealed, is the scariest part. In general Ichabod is treated as a comic character whose self-importance is clearly seen by most, and Brom's sincerity has the viewers rooting for him. It's also one of the very few post–Disney films not to use any jack-o'-lanterns. Not setting the story as a Halloween tale, however, has almost become Sleepy Hollow heresy in this myth.

Although the ghost is real, there's little supernatural horror here. The church doesn't offer salvation from the Horseman, and Crane treats it as a place to make business deals for his own betterment. Religious elements, while subtle, are nevertheless interwoven through the story. Even if a mere brag, Gang's Crane declares himself a former seminary professor. In his schoolroom he lectures on "pious learning," without actually having the children read from the Bible. The church isn't prominent but Crane's Psalm singing is emphasized. At the party Crane is about to "swear by all that's holy." Katrina confronts him with his lies and stops him, declaring that falsely swearing by all that's holy leads to damnation. This is ambient religion.

Although no mention is made of Halloween, the movie was released on October 23. By 1999 Sleepy Hollow had become America's Halloween story. Even if it doesn't portray Halloween, it *is* Halloween.

Computer Animated Sleepy Hollow

Another noteworthy effort, the first computer-animated rendition of the legend, is the 1999 television movie *Night of the Headless Horseman*, directed by Shane Williams. The opening scene for this chapter is from this adaptation.

This movie aired on October 28, 1999—just five days after Gang's movie—and shortly before Burton's *Sleepy Hollow* was released. Clocking in at just over 48 minutes, it begins with scary music as the Headless Horseman—unambiguously real—follows and beheads an unnamed traveler.

8. Moving Toward the Millennium 121

The scene shifts to Sleepy Hollow Inn on October 13, 1830, where the narrator is telling the story to Washington Irving—rather like Gang's opening. The narrator, using many phrases verbatim from Irving's tale, starts the story when the schoolmaster, several years earlier, met Katrina Van Tassel. The scene shifts to Hans Van Ripper taking Ichabod Crane on a tour of Sleepy Hollow and pointing out the scary locations, including where Major André was hanged and the hut of a local witch. The narrator makes it clear that Ichabod had his eye out for a girl that could bring him wealth.

Brom Bones is then shown awkwardly wooing a racily dressed Katrina, who chides him for refusing to make solid wedding plans. Ichabod, with a windmill in the background, interrupts, boldly praising Katrina, whom he is meeting for the first time. This Crane is confident and this Brom is also a blacksmith. Offering private singing lessons to Katrina, Ichabod angles a dinner invitation rather than being sent to his "cottage"—his room at the back of the schoolhouse (echoes of Schellerup). He begins Katrina's lesson with "Amazing Grace" before rushing off to dinner with a corpulent Baltus Van Tassel. Throughout the film "Amazing Grace" is Crane's preferred "psalm." The squire warns him against being out too late because it's the season that the Headless Horseman rides. The spirits stir as Halloween grows near. Gang omitted Halloween, Williams brought it back.

Brom, meanwhile, broods over his problem. Hans Van Ripper tells Ichabod about the cruel Hessian mercenary who loved killing. And perhaps for the first time, unusual before the Fox television series, the Horseman is given spoken dialogue—he dispatches his victims to Hell in a flashback, the one that opens this chapter. The wounded soldier lights the cannon, taking off the Horseman's head. Buried as an "unknown soldier" in the churchyard, he can't bear that his tombstone has no name and he desires a head. He rides with a flaming jack-o'-lantern, looking for a new noggin.

Katrina confronts Brom about his ogling other women and refusing to plan an actual wedding. Brom, in turn, targets Crane while he's teaching, telling the boys to blame the Headless Horseman. After school Brom initiates a threatening conversation with Crane, only to be interrupted by Baltus who invites Crane to dinner again. Baltus nevertheless warns Katrina that this is a dangerous game to play, pitting rivals against one another.

The Old Dutch Church shows up as Ichabod leads the singing lessons there, only to be smoked out by Brom, who then disguises himself as the Horseman in the sooty mist. Katrina saves Ichabod and kisses him in the graveyard. Brom, admitting he's an oaf, nevertheless loves Katrina and makes a deal with the spirits to take care of Ichabod. In a nightmare,

Crane wanders lost in the graveyard and is engaged by a disembodied head wedged in a tombstone. It wants Ichabod to take him along even as zombies rise, asking him for their missing body parts. In the middle of that nightmare, Brom's henchman awakens Crane to invite him to the Van Tassel quilting frolic on All Hallows Eve.

The scene cuts to Halloween night, 1820. Williams has a Black fiddler portrayed, respectfully, and there is the—now expected—extended dance scene. At storytelling time, Brom's race with the Horseman is shown, accompanied by horror film music. Ichabod's proposal to Katrina is interrupted, and his ride home is beset by ghosts even before the Horseman starts the chase and hurls a flaming jack-o'-lantern at him. The narrator then states that Brom wed Katrina, and Brom "laughed sadly" when the story of Ichabod's disappearance was told. The couple had 30 years together. But two years after Katrina died Brom's debt to the Headless Horseman came due. The narrator then reveals himself to be the new Horseman—Brom had been required to take the original's place. He hands Brom's rotting head to Irving and goes out in search of another.

This animated feature certainly offers horror treatment, just as Burton will shortly. This gives it pride of place, if only by a matter of weeks. Sleepy Hollow had never been a true horror movie before. As a love story this version is quite poignant. Brom is willing to sell his soul, literally, for Katrina. Crane has clearly only self-interest in mind regarding her. He's no protagonist. Katrina knows what she wants. These characters are flawed and likable. The visuals are dated, but Williams uses the horror aspects effectively.

This adaptation also had star power: Mark Hamill voiced Van Ripper and Luke Perry did Brom Bones. Bill Fagerbakke, probably best known as Patrick Star in SpongeBob's world, voiced Brom's sidekick Dolphus. Tia Carrere was Katrina and William H. Macy did Crane. The narrator was Clancy Brown, who, among many other credits, voiced Mr. Krabs, again in SpongeBob's universe. He will also reappear in the mythology in Fox's *Sleepy Hollow* as sheriff August Corbin. This is a labyrinth indeed. Where else would SpongeBob meet the Headless Horseman?

One of the more creative retellings of the legend, with a twist ending, Williams' effort might have caught on had it not been eclipsed by Tim Burton just days later. Had it been on the big screen, perhaps. Clearly inspired by video game graphics of the time, it seems to have been largely forgotten except among gamers. The American labyrinth is one that never ends. We keep coming back to the story that first haunted us in the style of the time.

Before we leave Williams, we need to consider that the Horseman has definitely moved front and center. He's a real ghost and he haunted Sleepy Hollow until Brom made a deal with him to win not a bowl of punch, but

8. Moving Toward the Millennium 123

Katrina. Once Brom takes over his position, he's required to find a replacement, apparently ten years after he got the job. He's shown with a human head and he has spoken dialogue. After 1999 the Horseman will become much more prominent in Sleepy Hollow. In all the versions we've seen he's had a relatively small role. All that has changed now.

We're at an important juncture in the maze. Sleepy Hollow has been tried out as a horror movie. The Headless Horseman has developed beyond a ghost after a head. His association with Hell will make him demonic. All of this becomes part of the mythology. Once it becomes a horror movie, there'll be no turning back.

These 1999 renditions of the story slipped quietly into the background when Tim Burton's movie became the most popular retelling since Disney (see next chapter). Johnny Depp made for an arresting Ichabod Crane in the fourth feature-length film of the legend. More than that, however, it firmly established the story in the horror genre. *The Exorcist* of Sleepy Hollow movies, Burton's vision set the tone for future explorations into this "sequestered glen ... long ... known by the name of SLEEPY HOLLOW."*

---

* The quote is from Irving, "The Legend of Sleepy Hollow."

9

Tim Burton's *Sleepy Hollow*

A church fence post bursts through the stained-glass window and impales Baltus Van Tassel in front of the entire town. Standing in the pulpit of the Old Dutch Church, he is yanked backwards out through the window and dragged along the ground. His head breaks through the fence. Still alive, he watches in horror as the Headless Horseman slowly rides up after this grisly extraction. His head is summarily lopped off. And taken.

This ghastly scene isn't quite the climax of Tim Burton's *Sleepy Hollow*, but it illustrates a point. But before delving deeper, we need to give credit where it's due. I use "Burton" as a stand-in for the ideas in this game-changing and myth-making movie, as in keeping with cinematic convention, as noted above. It's easier than stringing together a bunch of names every time a movie is mentioned. In this case the story itself actually has its own backstory.

It began with Washington Irving, of course, but then came Kevin Yagher, a special effects artist. You may know him from such nightmares as Freddy Krueger (and yes, Johnny Depp's first movie role in this maze was in *Nightmare on Elm Street*) and *Child's Play*. Yagher had the idea of making Washington Irving's "Sleepy Hollow" into a proper horror film. This had not yet been done. He met screenwriter Andrew Kevin Walker and the two reinvented Ichabod Crane as a detective. They found a producer and got as far as catching Paramount's attention. A Paramount executive suggested that Tim Burton direct the movie. It would be his first straightforward horror film. As with any movie, many people were involved—even Francis Ford Coppola, in this instance. They were all drawn to Sleepy Hollow.*

---

* This information was drawn from Salisbury, *Burton on Burton*.

Tim Burton's Sleepy Hollow

The center of our labyrinth—the treatment that made the legend truly myth—was Tim Burton's *Sleepy Hollow*. An entire book could be written about this movie alone, but in order to get a sense of the mythic whole, it must be treated here with some restraint.

Many versions of "The Legend" have emerged over time, but nobody had taken the—in retrospect obvious—approach of treating it as a horror film before the turn of the millennium. Remember, short stories leave many blanks in their narratives. What do we really know of Katrina Van Tassel, for example? Or why is a schoolteacher like Crane so credulous? Burton exploited these blanks in his retelling, creating some new orthodoxies along the way. There's enough raw material that Irving could've made a novel of this tale, but he didn't have a novelist's outlook. The quick jolt of a brief, ambiguous story that leaves plenty of space for imagination was more his style. Not surprisingly, many writers and directors have picked up his narrative and moved it in different directions, as we've seen. Avoiding, until 1999, actual horror. And Burton used religion to do it.

This film was a watershed in the mythology of "the Legend." From this point on, others looking to cash in on Irving's tale have tended take the horror approach. Some had toyed with the idea earlier, but this version was the first so widely seen as to leave a lasting impression in the growing mythology. Burton noted in interviews* that he was really only familiar with the Disney version and perhaps the Henning Schellerup television rendition, and being more indebted to the former. This, then, was a real departure. And a new path through the maze.

The story starts out familiarly enough—a Headless Horseman is on the rampage, lopping off heads in Sleepy Hollow. He's an angry ghost, essentially a demon. And it all revolves around a plot. The first-time viewer might become lost in the storyline, so here's what you need to know:

Lady Mary Van Tassel† (Miranda Richardson) is out for revenge (her first name is never used in the film). Her family was displaced from their cottage on Van Garrett land in Sleepy Hollow when she was just a young girl. Along with her sister, she survived as a child in the haunted western woods where she first encountered the Hessian soldier. Pledging herself to the Devil for vengeance on Van Garrett, she has been controlling the Headless Horseman since becoming Mrs. Van Tassel. She gained the

---

* Salisbury, *Burton on Burton* is the source for any interviews with Burton that may be mentioned.

† The name "Mary" for Lady Van Tassel appears to have emerged in Fandom, along with the idea that she uses "Preston" as her family name to disguise "Archer." These developments further demonstrate the power of myth.

assistance of four respected townsmen—the minister, the notary, the magistrate, and the doctor. With their silence and complicity, she directed the horseman to kill all of those who either stood in the way of her inheritance, or who knew of the plot.

'Tis no magic. All of this is revealed in Lady Van Tassel's monologuing as she summons the Horseman for his final task. But there's a lot more going on than this simple summary reveals. Herein lies the tale. To get a better sense of this, we need more of the story than Lady Van Tassel tells.

The movie reveals, before the opening sequence, that Peter Van Garrett has been involved in some serious business that turned deadly. It's nearly Halloween as his son drives him on a nighttime coach ride, presumably to deliver his new will. A horseman, barely glimpsed, beheads son and then father. *Sleepy Hollow* opens with murder in the witching season.

The New Ichabod Crane

Unlike previous movie versions, Burton's Ichabod Crane is not a schoolmaster at all. Although set in the same era as Irving, Johnny Depp's 1799 Crane is an educated detective. The date, by the way, was two centuries before the release date of the film, rather than the usual 1790 or '91. Rather like Edgar Allan Poe's C. Auguste Dupin, Crane uses reason in a world where many others appeal to supernatural explanations. Not only that, but something else from Irving is missing. The comic aspect of Crane's enormous appetite—something Knickerbocker used in his early works of America as a land of plenty—is simply left out. Indeed, from this point on, Crane's eating will pretty much fall out of the myth. Also omitted are Crane's penchant for singing and love of dancing. In short, although some comic elements remain, this Ichabod is no cartoon. He's the protagonist. In this maze he's evolved beyond Irving's vision. And he must confront religion.

Burton's Crane is from New York, but the foreign country of the City. Already, in this narrative, New York is a large city with large city crimes. Living there successfully requires sophistication and education. As a constable, Crane attempts to apply science—which in the film closely resembles magic—to solve crimes. His ardor for this new learning earns him a journey to Sleepy Hollow to solve three murders. We'll learn, once our feet are on the ground, that a young widow named Emily Winship has also lost her head.

To avoid prison himself, Crane takes a carriage on a two day's journey north while the opening credits roll. Although educated, Crane has much to learn when he is the outsider. Knowing a place includes making sense of

Johnny Depp as Constable Ichabod Crane, from Tim Burton's *Sleepy Hollow*. Extras in the background courtroom scene are unnamed (©1999 Paramount Pictures and Mandalay Pictures, All Rights Reserved).

what happens around the clock in that location. And in Sleepy Hollow the horseman rides at night.

The People of Sleepy Hollow

Sleepy Hollow is a gothic place filmed with muted colors. Window shutters are closed when a stranger walks by—people are afraid. Ichabod Crane arrives at the Van Tassel mansion in the midst of a Halloween party. Katrina (Christina Ricci), blindfolded, catches him in the circling game of The Pickety Witch. This game has at least a triple meaning in the film. We'll be coming back to it further along. For now let's consider that it's Ichabod's introduction to Katrina as Brom Bones (Casper Van Dien) looks jealously on. This is the classic love triangle of Irving's tale but Brom falls into the background and ends up dead.

Pickety Witch is a version of an early parlor game called Blind Man's Buff (known as Blind Man's Bluff in the United States). This game was quite popular in the Victorian Era, into which Sleepy Hollow falls. (The original story was published in the previous, Georgian, period.)* One of

---

* Information on the games the pickety witch and blind man's buff/bluff was found on this BBC webpage: https://www.bbc.co.uk/dna/mb6music/A634187, accessed 21 December 2023.

its meanings utilized in Burton is as the first hint that Katrina might be a witch. She says as much.

By 1799—the year Burton's story is set—witch trials were long a thing of the past. Frightened American Puritans had blamed individuals—mostly women—of the community for bewitching children a century earlier. This most famously, or infamously, took place in Salem, Massachusetts, in 1692. Shortly afterwards, witch trials fell from favor. Historians have shown that there were multiple causes that led to this miscarriage of justice in the first place, one of America's true hauntings. Nevertheless it lives on in American horror. Burton makes ample use of the witch theme, so we'll keep an eye out for them.

Baltus Van Tassel, Katrina's father, now makes his first appearance. Ushering Crane into his study, a most telling interview takes place. The main characters—all eventual victims—are introduced: Doctor Lancaster, the town physician, Samuel Philipse (named for Tarrytown's actual founder, Frederick Philipse), the magistrate, the Reverend Steenwyck (Jeffrey Jones), the parson, and the town notary, Hardenbrook. There are a number of factors to note, like an amateur deductor. One is that they are all, except Baltus, in on Lady Van Tassel's conspiracy. They may not know how she controls the Horseman, but they know she does. A second deduction is that the Reverend Steenwyck is the leader of this second tier of plotters. The Lady later explains to Katrina that Steenwyck is committed by lust, but Philipse and Hardenbrook are controlled by fear, and Lancaster by blackmail. The doctor has been fornicating with the Van Tassels' servant girl.

Religion in Sleepy Hollow

The story treats the parson with special attention. Making the minister part of the conspiracy underscores how deeply religion is implicated in Burton's telling. In fact, in the conspiracy Steenwyck is the most committed, sticking with it until his death, and he is the last to die. He is, arguably, the chief conspirator under Lady Van Tassel. He's also not the only minister in the film, as we'll see. In this introductory scene, already singled out by Crane's doubling back on him, Steenwyck tells Ichabod that the answers he needs are in the Bible. This is an important moment, remember it! This Bible will be key to solving the mystery. Although the reverend is contrasting it to science, the Bible contains the vital clue of the family trees that will solve the murders.

This opening interview also presents the backstory to the Headless Horseman. A Hessian mercenary in the Revolutionary War, he fights not

9. Tim Burton's Sleepy Hollow

Jeffrey Jones as Rev. Steenwyck, one minister in Tim Burton's *Sleepy Hollow* (©1999 Paramount Pictures and Mandalay Pictures, All Rights Reserved).

for money but for love of killing. Especially chopping heads. One winter's day in the western woods he's caught by American soldiers and beheaded with his own sword. Little Lady Van Tassel, née Archer, watches all this and she sells her soul to Satan if he will raise the horseman to avenge her. Of course, Baltus doesn't know that—he believes the horseman was a "seed of evil." In reality, his second wife is a witch who knows how to control a demon. It's becoming clear just how entangled religion is in Burton's *Sleepy Hollow* labyrinth.

Between this scene and Lady Van Tassel's confession to Katrina viewers can make sense of the conspiracy against Baltus, intended to funnel his wealth to his second wife. This unnamed Archer woman sets up one of Burton's most intriguing additions to Sleepy Hollow lore—there be witches here. Witches are a form of occult religion in this universe.

The town elders insist that the culprit is a ghost. Not only that, but he takes his victims' heads "back to Hell." This monster is perhaps more than a ghost, and a new trope has been born—the Horseman resides in Hell. Interestingly, Williams' version also emphasizes the connection with Hell, but without making it the Horseman's domicile. Crane, insisting there are no ghosts, will investigate scientifically. The next morning Jonathan Masbath's decapitated body is found. Masbath was on guard duty at the time and his young son will become Ichabod's ward.

Notice that when Crane arrives at the scene of the beheading, Steenwyck is standing above the others in a tableau of a worship scene. Crane's investigative techniques do not impress the locals. In fact, they will be very similar to what the witch of the western woods (yet another witch!) does to summon spirits. Both add ingredients that cause smoke to rise. When Crane notes that Masbath's wound was instantly cauterized, Magistrate Philipse declares it "The Devil's fire." Once again this affirms the infernal nature of the Horseman. The scene shifts to Masbath's funeral where the reverend is again presiding. He takes the lead in keeping the conspiracy going. Philipse attempts to help Crane, but Steenwyck spies him talking to the constable and gives him an accusing stare. Philipse suggests Crane investigate the corpses.

The widow Winship, the original third victim, is now introduced. Crane discovers she had been pregnant when she was beheaded. The body count is up to five. That night, Brom throws a flaming jack-o'-lantern at Crane, prompting the first of three important flashbacks. Indeed, these flashbacks explain Crane's motivations and provide clues, via the Bible we've already seen, as to what's happening. By the way, Brom's prank leads to the immediate resolution in the original story, but here we're only just getting started.

Witches

Crane flashes back to his childhood. His mother was a "child of nature"—interpreted by his father as a witch. When young Crane goes out to his mother, she's blindfolded and playing Pickety Witch, just as Katrina was when he first met her. But his father, Lord Crane, does not approve of his wife's behavior. Wakeful after this dream, Ichabod finds Katrina reading and learns that she, like his mother, practices charms and spells. We've already seen how Pickety Witch implied Katrina is a witch, but when Crane discovers her reading in the wee hours he also discovers her spell books. "They were my mother's," she explains. Both she and her stepmother, Lady Van Tassel, admit their mothers were witches. So does Ichabod. Beth Killian, the town's midwife, will also be coded as a witch. Burton's movie sets witches up against a crooked Christianity led by a sinister minister. This witch theme introduces an occult form of religion that is ultimately shown to be more virtuous than the Christianity practiced by Lord Crane and the Reverend Steenwyck. Katrina insists that Crane keep one of the spell books.

The town elders, sans Baltus, are arguing. Magistrate Philipse, fleeing Sleepy Hollow, also participates in occult religion. He explains to Crane that his talisman—an ankh—protects him from the Horseman. The ankh is an ancient Egyptian symbol of life, but it doesn't help against the demon Horseman. Philipse's decapitation finally convinces Crane that there is a real ghost since he witnesses it himself. The trauma of the attack also leads to the second flashback dream of his own pagan mother and strict Christian father. Lord Crane wears black preaching bands and has his own private chapel, we're shown. (Preaching bands developed in the mid-seventeenth century, and the clerical, or "Roman" collar about a century later.) In the movie script Lord Crane is called "a grim Parson."* In other words, he's envisioned as a minister. The preaching bands suggest as much. He throws down a Bible—apparently the same one the Reverend Steenwyck used—to accuse his wife of witchcraft. This is the Bible's second representation in *Sleepy Hollow*. It's becoming clear just how entangled religion is in Burton's vision. The flashback once more sets Christianity against witchcraft and the occult, misguidedly so.

Overcoming his terror, Crane then heads to the western woods with young Masbath where he encounters an openly bona fide witch. The clash of religions is implied, but the constable doesn't judge her belief system. "Each to his own," he says. Witchcraft, in the form of Wicca and other earth-based religions, is actually a modern form of religious expression. Certainly, pre–Christian folk practices—children of nature represented by Ichabod's mother, and Beth Killian as an herbalist—existed from antiquity. Witchcraft wasn't an organized religion until the middle of the twentieth century, however. In the movie it's folk belief rather than church teaching that conquers the forces of evil.

Peter Guinness as Lord Crane, another minister in Tim Burton's *Sleepy Hollow* (©1999 Paramount Pictures and Mandalay Pictures, All Rights Reserved).

---

* Accessible from www.scriptslug.com.

The witch directs them to the tree of the dead which is a "gateway between two worlds," one of which is obviously the "Hell" from which the Horseman emerges. Unlike Irving's story, this Horseman is buried in the western woods, not at the Old Dutch Church. It's here that Crane discovers that the Horseman's skull is missing, from which he deduces that whoever has the head is controlling the killing. (*Kolchak* anticipated this.) Again in this maze the clash of religions participates in the conflict. This occult theme runs throughout the film, bringing religion in from a different angle. Religion will also be taken up by others who retell the myth from this point on. Witchcraft, which Irving only mentioned in connection with Ichabod's timorousness, will forever become part of Sleepy Hollow mythology after this film.

The Bible

The Horseman's after victims six through eight—the Killians. Brom attacks the Horseman and Crane is wounded trying to help him. Brom becomes victim nine. Crane's feverish injury leads to the third flashback that ends in a significant dialogue with Katrina, who's nursing him back to health. The disturbing flashback equates his father with the Headless Horseman and young Ichabod finds his mother tortured to death in an iron maiden. Ichabod has avoided the Horseman's reality because to admit it forces him to confront his minister father. Religion.

At this point Crane reveals to Katrina that his father murdered his mother. She was "murdered to save her soul, by a Bible-black tyrant behind a mask of righteousness." He indicates he lost his faith at age seven and since then has only believed in reason, "cause and consequence." Crane's refusal to admit the supernatural has held him back from solving the murders.

Using Steenwyck's Bible, Crane discovers the close connection between the Van Garretts and the Van Tassels in its family tree. This is the third scene with the Bible, and indeed, it's crucial to solving the crime. Complicating things, Ichabod has begun to fall in love with Katrina. She had assisted him in investigating, along with young Masbath. Once she realizes that Crane suspects her father, however, she destroys the evidence. Her father, Baltus, in addition to being prosperous, inherited the Van Garrett estate. The Bible demonstrates just how interconnected their family trees are. Of course, the Bible misleads because Baltus isn't directing the Horseman. Logically, there's no need to—he already owns the estate.

When a spider crawls under Crane's bed, young Masbath discovers a witch's sigil that he identifies as the "evil eye." This misreading of somebody else's religion nearly has fatal consequences. Ichabod and Masbath both believe the chalk sign indicates a witch is placing a hex on the constable. Ironically, the book Katrina gave Crane would've indicated otherwise. He suspects Baltus is leading the conspiracy, but doesn't know who the hexing witch might be. Nobody, however, suspects Baltus' second wife, Lady Mary Van Tassel, is both witch and author of the conspiracy.

Shedding further light on the hypocrisy of mainstream religion, Lady Van Tassel lures Crane out to witness the Reverend Steenwyck having sex with her. She's able to set up her own faked death that way, but the scene also anticipates her revelation as a witch. Steenwyck, for his part, is fully committed to keeping the conspiracy intact because of his lust. He knows who controls the Horseman. The others all know parts of the story.

The Church

A meeting is called in the church, and it is Crane who is being challenged. The Horseman, however, attacks but is unable to enter hallowed ground. During the confusion Dr. Lancaster, one of the remaining conspirators, implores Steenwyck that it's time they confess. Before he can, however, Steenwyck bludgeons him to death with a large cross, leading Baltus to shoot the cleric. Too late, Baltus realizes that there is a conspiracy, just as the Horseman kills him as the description at the head of the chapter narrates. The one conspirator intimate with Lady Van Tassel, the one willing to kill to keep it secret to the end, is the Reverend Steenwyck. After the melee Crane notices that Katrina had drawn another "evil eye" on the church floor and assumes she is the one behind the murders. Twelve people have now been killed.

At this point it's important to note that the Old Dutch Church has become the scene of violence and death. Irving had intimated that it was a place of safety, and it mostly is. The Horseman has figured out how to subvert the fact that he can't enter, but the real protection in this maze comes from Katrina's magic and the real threat is the magic of her stepmother. Indeed, Lady Van Tassel conjures the Horseman to kill Katrina, the last person standing between her and the combined Van Garrett and Van Tassel estates. Katrina's magic doesn't prevent her father from being pulled through the window, symbolically shattering the cross on his way to the waiting Horseman.

How It Ends

In the final confrontation, Katrina's spell book—which saves both her life and Ichabod's—is a kind of secular salvation. Crane uses it to determine Katrina's innocence, and thus returns to save her. The book itself stops Lady Van Tassel's bullet, saving Ichabod's life. In both instances it is reason, not the magic contained in the book, that affects salvation. At the same time, the magic is very real.

Lady Van Tassel has been using the Horseman to behead those who stand in the way of her inheritance of the combined families' wealth. She holds Katrina for the Horseman. Katrina is saved, however, when Ichabod returns the Horseman's head (again, like Kolchak). The Horseman (Christopher Walken/Rob Inch/Ray Park), perhaps recognizing her from the betrayal in the woods that led to his own decapitation many years before, takes Lady Van Tassel back to Hell with him. Crane, Katrina, and young Masbath, move back to New York City just as the new millennium ticks over.

So much is packed into *Sleepy Hollow* that it's difficult to know where to begin. This millennial movie, which introduced a new generation to Irving's tale, was also a watershed in the explicit use of religious elements lacking in the original legend. From now on religion could, and often would, be explicit—and even central—to the story. The most successful rendition since Disney, Burton has become a touchstone for any future re-workings of "The Legend." It plays an establishing role in the myth of Sleepy Hollow. The Fox television series and novel-length tellings of the tale make that abundantly clear. As is often the case, when a story is shown to be lucrative, others will try to cash in on it. But what made this Burton-Depp collaboration so successful? It helped Americans believe in Sleepy Hollow.

Believing in Sleepy Hollow

"The Legend of Sleepy Hollow" has been around a long time. Starting with Disney and continuing through the xennial period, three related aspects had grown into the myth: religion, Halloween, and scariness. In *Once Upon a Midnight Scary*, Vincent Price calls it a tale of terror. In the seventies children's scary books began to appear. Halloween had been growing from a fun night for the kids into a major scary-spending holiday, complete with horror films. The movie *Halloween* both underscored and encouraged this idea. Burton brought these three things together into a single mythic package. If "The Legend of Sleepy Hollow" had been legendary, now it was a myth.

Star power no doubt contributed to the success of Burton's film. Johnny Depp's acting career started in the horror genre but really took off when he began collaborating with Tim Burton. *Edward Scissorhands* appeared in 1990 and brought both Depp and Burton into the public eye.

Not a scream king by any stretch, he did horror roles from time to time, such as Roman Polanski's *The Ninth Gate*, also released in 1999. He would go on to superstardom as Captain Jack Sparrow in Disney's *Pirates of the Caribbean* franchise, but would continue to collaborate with Burton from time to time. His growing fame and ability to carry off this role framed him as the new icon of Ichabod Crane.

The creepy atmosphere and capable writing certainly are huge factors in the movie's influence. But what really sets it apart, in my opinion, is its engagement with religion, much of it occult. Also essential here is that Halloween is central to the film. As a cultural holiday, Halloween had its own evolution, as we've seen, and in many ways it parallels that of Sleepy Hollow. By 1999 Halloween had grown into a scary occasion and retrojecting that into Sleepy Hollow wed the two in a way that makes Disney's use of it seem merely casual. The first beheading takes place before a carved pumpkin scarecrow. Crane arrives on Halloween, attending a party to lighten spirits during "these dark times." Americans had begun watching scary movies around Halloween by this point, and the combination of rolling heads, religion, and October's holiday made this treatment a solid horror success.

The addition of religion and Halloween are part of what makes this such a classic rendition of Irving's legend. But there's something more, too. Burton's was the first big-screen adaptation of Sleepy Hollow since Disney, and *The Adventures of Ichabod* was only half of a film back then. Several decades had passed since a major studio stood behind the idea. During these decades, particularly starting with the seventies, smaller adaptations emerged. With its graphic beheadings, Burton's version brought something new to the story. This is the first live-action motion picture, on the big or small screen, where human characters actually lose their heads. We see Peter van Garrett's blood on a jack-o'-lantern as the film opens, and Jonathan Masbath's head rolling along with a frozen scream, as if to start a game of Viking football. Then Magistrate Philipse has his head end up between Crane's thighs. Mr. Killian, his wife, Beth, and son Thomas are all beheaded (the last offscreen). Baltus Van Tassel is speared and decapitated. No retellings before had this level of violence or this high a body count. The R rating indicated it wasn't for kids. This was a nightmare for adults. It was horror for the first time.

Timing Is Everything

By the end of the millennium, in a way that will seem naive to millennials and later generations, there was palpable fear in 1999 that the anticipated Y2K crisis would lead to the complete collapse of society. Some religious groups, mistakenly believing it had been two-thousand years since Jesus had been born, saw this round-number year as a potential apocalypse. Seriously.

Those of us who work in media know that a happy coincidence of circumstances, including social moods and news cycles, can lead to unexpected success for a book, song, or movie. Timing can be everything. Y2K was one of the growing pains of increasingly widespread use of computer technology. Personal computers were common, although smartphones were still in their early days. Nevertheless, worldwide systems such as banking, and local ones like utilities, relied on computers that could not, it was said, differentiate between 2000 and 1900 because early programing had utilized a two-digit, rather than a four-digit, year. (Were they too looking for the world to end with the millennium?) What would happen if systems built on software supposing that '99 was followed by '00 reset to earlier dates—1900 rather than 2000, for example—leading to fatal logical errors?

No less intense, and scary, was the religious fervor. Christians of a certain stripe have been predicting the end of the world for hundreds of years. There was some speculation around the year 1000, but with the growth of Fundamentalist groups at the dawn of the twentieth century (the "Third Awakening," remember), many major events, or speculative calculations, led to the expectations of "the Second Coming." World War I spawned such ideas, as did World War II. The cultural shifts beginning in the 1960s led to a very real fear that the end was near. The best-selling nonfiction book of the entire 1970s was Hal Lindsey's *The Late Great Planet Earth*. The premise was that world events were aligning with biblical "prophecy" presaging the literal end of the world. Fundamentalist groups had been working for decades, in often subtle ways, to spread the idea. The world was going to end and it could be any day now since world events, as demonstrated by Lindsey, met all of God's preset conditions.

These ideas hold considerable power. Social change is frightening. Horror movies, starting in 1968, began to address religious fears directly. *Rosemary's Baby* could be read as biblically literal, although not intended that way. *The Exorcist* scared the hell out of audiences in 1973. Following just three years later, *The Omen* reprised fear of Satan's son, in keeping with Lindsey's scheme (which is explained, without credit, in the film itself). These ideas had been around since an obscure sect, the Plymouth Brethren, under the leadership of one John Nelson Darby, began promoting a "roadmap" of end times in the nineteenth century. This roadmap was also a labyrinth. All of this was well underway before the twentieth century began. Diverse parts of the Bible were "systematized" into an artificial scenario that sounded convincing to many—we were in the final days. Until the sixties, church membership ran high and even mainstream churches wondered if there might not be something in this outlier idea.

This particular adaptation of "The Legend of Sleepy Hollow" is the high-water mark of Irving's original tale (so far). The legend has become a myth. Myths are more deeply planted and have a further reach than legends do. For a story to attain this status it must grow for some time and the following chapters will chart that continuing growth. The rapidity of its expansion following Burton indicates that something happened with this film. A tall-tale that had been around for nearly two centuries gained a currency that pointed to its relevance for contemporary viewers. There are many more obscure versions of Sleepy Hollow, and since new films are in the works, it's time to give the Horseman his due.

The New Horseman

In Burton the Horseman's beheading was intentional because he enjoyed chopping heads in battle. His love of taking heads had nothing to do with losing his own; he wasn't looking for a replacement—that was Disney. This Headless Horseman has recently arisen, however, again looking for heads. The important innovation here is that being beheaded, the Hessian's head is not actually missing but is buried with him. Only when it's taken does the Horseman ride.

Making the Horseman an actual monster was, and will be from now on, necessary. That also started with Disney. Xennial treatments continued moving in that direction anyway. In no small part, the design of—and convincing green-screen lack of a head for—the Headless Horseman represented the horror of Burton's story. This Galloping Hessian is credible. Unlike generally accepted conventions, he kills women and children. Not an actor with false shoulders throwing off bodily proportions, he is a believable ghost of a man cruel in life and remaining so after death. Not Brom Bones in disguise, we know from the opening scene on that this ghost is real and that he means business. And he does mean *business—* America's labyrinth is financially charged. The Horseman is an unwitting tool for financial gain on the part of the newly minted Lady Van Tassel. Money without regard for the lives it discards. America's labyrinth leads us to nightmares and ghosts.

Perhaps this level of evolution from Irving is another key to the movie's success. Indeed, the traditional end should've been Brom's chasing down of Crane, but most of the story occurs after that. Looking for the "why" of Sleepy Hollow's mythic status is perhaps the thread to follow out of this labyrinth, but clearly the key is that the Headless Horseman is unambiguously real. And real dangerous. An actual monster. Instead of racing Brom for a bowl of punch he cuts him in half. There's no ambiguity to that. The gothic atmosphere builds higher than Irving, slotting the story where it best seems to fit. And the supernatural threat, so much a part of gothic literature, defies rationality and bodily appears.

Nevertheless, Burton freely borrowed from Disney, despite his alterations of Knickerbocker's base story. Apart from the Halloween setting, Ichabod's creepy ride home when the frogs seem to croak out his name—arguably the most tension-building moment in the cartoon—also appears. The bridge which he must cross is a covered bridge, as Disney innovated. And Disney introduced an actual ghost Horseman who seeks to chop heads. He's real, and in Burton's telling he's demonic.

Burton not only shows the Horseman's beheading, it also places him in Hell. A religious concept in its own right, along with the Old Dutch Church massacre and witches and the Bible, this movie foregrounds religion and horror. This demonic Horseman and the idea that he resides in Hell will reemerge, just like the Hessian from his grave, further along in the labyrinth. Religion and horror are a winning combination. All of this departs from Irving's "Sleepy Hollow" and makes a demon out of a mere ghost. The story has a lot going for it, and it ushered in "The Legend" as proper horror. And in that, it has had many followers. Irving created the monster, but Burton brought him to life.

10

Burton's Aftermath

Diana's severed head rolls down the hill with nobody to see it. She'd fought with Shannon earlier and stomped off into the Sleepy Hollow woods alone. That was the teenager's final mistake. In the woods Diana encounters a monster with a sword and a pumpkin for a head. He's been killing young people around here. Diana screams as he swings his sword. Shannon will be the final girl but three other friends and her teacher have to fall victim to Pumpkin Man first. He's waiting for them, and he kills without regret.

Tim Burton's movie unlocked the true potential for Irving's legend to become a myth. It changed the way "The Legend of Sleepy Hollow" is understood. Yes, generations still rely on Disney to tell the tale to the young, and those uninterested in horror may never watch *Sleepy Hollow*. Nevertheless, to follow how the story reappears in the American consciousness—it is America's ghost story—it's clear that Burton's version started something. From now on there would be reinterpretations with Ichabod Crane taking new roles and the Headless Horseman, now inevitably real, receiving a backstory and sometimes even becoming a hero. Brom Bones will often slip out of the story, but Katrina is generally there, and often empowered. And it would have to be a horror story.

If the myth of Sleepy Hollow was a maze before Burton, after the film it began laying out an enlarged and even more complex labyrinth. Much of this could be traced to *Sleepy Hollow* and its use of religion to make the story real. The most obvious way to secure this hold on the legend, however, was to make a novelization of the film available.

Novelizations

Fans of Sleepy Hollow in the new millennium are at no loss for literary retellings as well as cinematic ones. One obvious example of this is

Peter Lerangis' novelization of the Tim Burton movie. Published in 1999—the same year as the film—the novel is quite similar to the movie, as you'd expect. Movie scripts are, by nature, brief. The story does add a few episodes which are helpful in explaining some flashback scenes in the film. The characterization of Ichabod Crane is a bit edgier than in the movie, but overall the narrative is obviously the same.

It must be both difficult and easy writing the novelization of a movie. The confines of the story are already fixed, and yet there's freedom to explore motivations and states of mind. *Sleepy Hollow* is a film based on a story already, but Washington Irving's tale isn't a novel and the movie was a collaboration between Irving's original, re-envisioned by Kevin Yagher, Andrew Kevin Walker, and Tim Burton after over a century of afterlives. As a novelizer, however, you need to try to make sense of some scenes where a film only implies what's going on. If a viewer's seen the movie many times, any deviations might come across as "that's not the way it goes." We still tend to think myths go only one way. The movie is canonical. Still, the novel's competently done. Novelizations are, of course, yet another path through the maze, sometimes running parallel with their screenplay partners.

In the "book or movie" debate many of us tend to think a book should be read first. Sometimes it should go the other way around. Novelizations are, of course, intended to increase the profits for a film. They follow the movie. You've got the box office take, and if there are advertising tie-ins or other merch, you can add to the haul. A novelization can also reap benefits. In this case, the movie has a somewhat complex plot with revenge and double-crossing, and so a novel helps to make all of that clear. However, when the novelist asks you to accept what a character is thinking you may have already come up with your own ideas on that point.

This novelization was intended to go along with the movie since true fans can never get enough. The recasting of all the characters into unfamiliar roles in the novel follows the movie, of course. Brom, for example, is a minor part, whereas Katrina is a witch and Ichabod a constable from New York City. The new mythology. All of that having been said, there really aren't any surprises in Lerangis' telling, if you've seen the movie.

As originally released, the novelization also includes Washington Irving's tale (the novel part of the book is short). The juxtaposition is pretty stark. The reader moves from an action horror story with a cast of quirky characters to a descriptive, almost soporific narrative that really develops only three characters in ways closer to caricatures than serious attempts at realistic description. And it's funny. Irving had his own way of telling things. The original story was published less than 50 years after American independence and has memories closer to the time. It tells us something of what it was like in those early days. And this new novel both retells and redacts a movie which itself is a retelling. The maze grows even more complex.

Beyond the novelization of Burton's film there are a number of original novels that use either the characters or the situation to keep "The Legend" alive. And evolving. Many of these seem to have been spurred on by the success of television's spiritual successor to Burton, Fox's *Sleepy Hollow*. In recasting Ichabod Crane as outside teaching, and a sex symbol, Burton broke open Pandora's box. Even *Sleepy Hollow High* keeps the schoolteacher aspect intact, as we'll see next. From 1922 up until 1999 Crane was essentially always the schoolmaster and generally the protagonist. New avenues now lay open for getting readers to the Hollow, not all of them kind to Crane. And some of them land you back in high school, while appealing to a slasher aesthetic.

High School Horror

Burton's distinctive cinematic taste had been on display since his short *Vincent* (1982), but his first full-blown horror effort, still with his distinctive humor, was *Sleepy Hollow*. As noted above, this wasn't his idea but he developed it in such a way that there would be no going back only to Disney. Burton, of course, had his start at Disney before branching off into his own style and interests—just like Ub Iwerks. This labyrinth turns back in on itself in many places. This movie became the touchpoint for any future treatments, spinning off its own mythology. In fact, its success likely led an independent project filmed much earlier to seek a public airing. *Sleepy Hollow High* (2000) was shot in 1995 but only released after Burton's film, making it chronologically earlier but available only later.* And this film also brings back the young. Remember, Sleepy Hollow is part of America's youth.

The opening scenario for this chapter is drawn from *Sleepy Hollow High*. It's one of those movies often classified as "so bad it's good." This isn't a retelling of Irving at all. The film itself, being earlier than Burton, shows no direct influence of course, but it does take the story into horror territory—specifically in the slasher region. And that region lies in Sleepy Hollow.

---

*Information about *Sleepy Hollow High* comes mostly from watching it and the extras available on the DVD and IMDb. The same is true of *The Hollow* and *Ichabod!* Little commentary has been generated on these more modern renditions. This bit of trivia comes from IMDb (https://m.imdb.com/title/tt0232657/trivia/?item=tr1487478, accessed 15 June 2024).

The high school crowd is a prime horror film audience. They are clearly the intended viewers of the direct-to-video movie *Sleepy Hollow High*. At about 90 minutes, it's only the fifth feature-length Sleepy Hollow movie. It's also horror. But don't you hate movies where the action all turns out to have been a dream?

Kevin Summerfield's very low budget effort features some adult themes such as sex and violence, smoking and drug use (the latter off screen, and no actual nudity appears). Although set in Sleepy Hollow the monster is "Pumpkin Man" (not to be confused with *Pumpkinhead*). He's never explained, but he has a pumpkin for a head and he likes to kill teens. The violence erupts in the form of Pumpkin Man's attacks, but no hacking of heads is shown in any kind of close-up as in Burton. Perhaps the fact that heads are chopped at all meant waiting on Burton—remember, the first released live-action version to include people actually losing their heads—to clear the path. Or it could be the special effects budget to do this convincingly simply wasn't there.

During the opening credits of *Sleepy Hollow High*, we're shown a man clipping newspaper articles of missing persons, but we're not shown who he is. A woman jogging in some admittedly spooky woods is attacked by

Antonio Benedict as Pumpkin Man in Kevin Summerfield's *Sleepy Hollow High* (©2000 Scorpio Pictures, All Rights Reserved).

10. Burton's Aftermath 143

an assailant who's not clearly shown but who has a pumpkin head. The scene cuts to a student named Justin whose car has broken down at night. He's accosted by Zeke (Z) and Bobbi, two Black students, for ratting out their drug selling in the school parking lot. As they approach Justin's disabled car, Z wears a pumpkin mask, implying he attacked the jogger. As Z is monologuing, he says there are lots of missing person cases in Sleepy Hollow, but there's been a massive cover-up (thus the clippings at the start). He also mentions the Horseman, who, he says, is real. He and Bobbi strip Justin and plan to leave him tied up in the Sleepy Hollow woods the night before Halloween, but they're caught before they can finish their plan.

The next day, five juvenile delinquents: Shannon, Diana, and Jay, along with Z and Bobbi, are given an ultimatum by the high school principal. Do community service, starting that very afternoon, or be expelled. Threatened with no graduation, they reluctantly agree to the community service. They're assigned to work with a teacher, Mr. E. During trash pickup in the remote Sleepy Hollow park, hands break through the ground and grab Shannon, pulling her down. She wakes up in Mythology class screaming. It was all a dream.

Mr. E. gathers the five students after school and gets them to the park. On the way Justin, the student Z and Bobbi attacked, is shown putting a pumpkin mask into his car trunk, implying he's Pumpkin Man. Once at the park, Mr. E. divides the five up into pairs (including himself) to pick up litter. Shannon and Diana have words—Diana had been in a sexual harassment case with Mr. E., but she initiated the relationship—and a pumpkin-headed man decapitates Diana when she's off on her own.

Z and Bobbi are a couple and Bobbi is trying to tell Z she's pregnant, but Z's the gangster type and she's afraid. When she finally does tell him and runs off, Z witnesses Pumpkin Man beheading her. The remaining students and Mr. E. regather but the cars have been sabotaged. Mr. E. offers to run to a garage, just four miles away, as darkness sets in. Pumpkin Man decapitates him and circles back for the other teens. Z and Jay are killed and Shannon, the final girl, pulls the pumpkin off the killer and screams. She wakes up in Mythology class—it was all a dream.

After school, Shannon is walking home with Diana. They note that the principal went home early that day. This implies the dream even includes the meeting with the principal (if the principal's home early, they aren't picking up trash that very afternoon). He's then revealed as the mysterious man cutting newspaper clippings, implying that he murdered the woman at the beginning of the film, outside the dream.

Adults don't fare well in this story. Mr. E., while in the woods, is presented as not only a potential sexual predator, but also a teacher with anger issues who has used excessive force in the past. These two elements, along with the principal's behavior, suggest the school officials are kidnapping and killing people. Of course, the entire Mr. E. story only occurs during a dream, so we have no way of knowing. It's a maze.

The film lacks a Headless Horseman proper. Pumpkin Man is shown on horseback only once, when attacking Mr. E., so maybe he's the Horseman? He prefers to run through the woods with a sword and although he haunts nightmares like Freddy Krueger he isn't a Hessian mercenary, at least not that we know. He isn't dressed like one. The film seems to ask with Poe, "Is all that we see or seem/But a dream within a dream?" The pumpkin is decorated with a face, but it's not lit up because it's worn. The movie seems to be set around Halloween, although the holiday's not mentioned.

Disregarding the dream for a moment, Pumpkin Man is a punisher of bad behaviors. The kids are all delinquents and Mr. E. has issues. Set in Sleepy Hollow, the movie shows kids all considering the Horseman real, but he never really receives an explanation. We don't see what final girl Shannon sees when she pulls off Pumpkin Man's head. Both headless and horseless.

The reported budget for the film was about $16,500 and Kevin Summerfield is credited with writing, co-directing, co-producing, doing special effects, as well as playing Mr. E. The co-director and co-producer is Chris Arth (who's also the editor). One has to wonder if the newspaper clipping byline of Dale E. Wood, Jr., isn't a nod toward Edward D. Wood, the director whose famously bad films are legendary.

Garnering some attention on television shows that feature cheesy movies, despite the budget and the "it's all a dream" ending, *Sleepy Hollow High* isn't all bad for an ultra-low budget independent horror effort. Throughout, from Justin's torture scene and through Shannon's dreams, the legend of Sleepy Hollow is referred to as historical. Clearly intended as a Halloween movie, it plays up the seasonal scares. There are plenty of holes in the plot and improbabilities (to put it politely), but it may help keep interest in Sleepy Hollow alive among the teen crowd. And it may be on its way to becoming a cult classic.

While it seems to be lost in the maze, it also plays a part in America's nightmare. The kids' stuff masks darker issues such as racism and actual violence. There's no avoiding the fact that Z and Bobbi, the only two Black students, are the ones selling drugs after school. They're also having sex. Bobbi carries a knife and Z has a piece in his car. Sex is only implied for the others and they carry no weapons. The first victim is an African American woman jogger (unconnected to the remainder of the plot). Although the villains are implied to be the white teachers, lingering tones of racism persist. At least Summerfield retains some African American characters, something that Irving embedded in his tall tale. The maze turns back once more. *Sleepy Hollow High* was released in 2000, just after the story had changed forever with Burton's addition to the myth. But notice that, like Disney, Burton left Black characters out altogether. And what should we be telling our kids about Sleepy Hollow? One thing is that Black characters can be a good influence. This will become clear in Fox's television series, as we'll see in Chapter 11.

New Millennium Youth

Burton's *Sleepy Hollow* seems to have led to a renewed interest in filming the story. As mentioned above, *Sleepy Hollow High* was only released after the success of Burton's film was evident. Another animated video feature, *The Haunted Pumpkin of Sleepy Hollow*, appeared just three years later in 2002. Running for 47 minutes, it was directed by Vong Zeven. It's aimed even before high school—at middle school level—growing the labyrinth back toward Disney's target viewership.

The story opens with dramatic music as the Headless Horseman chases Ichabod Crane on horseback. The ride takes them through a graveyard before Ichabod sees the church and exclaims he'll be safe there. Of course, once he crosses the bridge the Horseman throws his jack-o'-lantern at Crane, abruptly ending the scene. This winds up being a video within a video—more echoes of Poe—for a school field trip at the new Sleepy Hollow Museum, where the original copy of Irving's book (dated 1819) is kept. A juvenile love triangle appears as Nick Crane and Kate talk about how Nick could be a descendant of Ichabod, only to be interrupted by a burly Tucker—the cartoon's young "Brom Bones." This is the day before Halloween and the next day is a scary pumpkin contest, as the teacher informs us. Nick and Kate are also working on animatronic frights for the class haunted house. As they head out to carve their pumpkins, Tucker chases them down the hall with a jack-o'-lantern head, scaring them into believing him the Headless Horseman (without an actual horse).

Meanwhile a couple of dim-witted thieves steal Irving's manuscript (a strange idea for a museum heist), planning to sell it. They hide the manuscript inside a pumpkin in the woods. Kate and Nick head to the woods to look for a pumpkin to carve—one guess which one they pick. As it storms outside, the pumpkin (which they don't realize has the manuscript inside) becomes a glowing jack-o'-lantern. The ghost of Nathaniel Wiley, killed at the battle of White Plains, emerges from the pumpkin and tells the kids that it's the Horseman's head. He then explains that the Hessian mercenary made a deal with the powers of darkness to make himself undefeatable. Revolutionary elders, Wiley says, knew their own magic and beheaded the Hessian. The Hessian's head turned into a pumpkin and has remained so. Since Halloween Eve is the anniversary of his death, if the Horseman regains his pumpkin head precisely at midnight it will become his actual head and he will be unstoppable once again.

This seems to anticipate Fox's version of the story, borrowing heavily from Burton's magic. Like Burton, the Horseman's beheading was intentional. Also like Burton, the Hessian engaged the powers of darkness and is therefore demonic. None of this had been suggested before Burton's movie added these paths to the labyrinth. On with the story.

The kids and ghost must keep the haunted pumpkin away from the Horseman until after midnight. The criminals follow them, after their booty, while the actual Headless Horseman rides. As the kids run through the woods, the pumpkin animates the trees so they decide to take it indoors, into scary Castle Van Tassel, followed by the crooks. Wiley's ghost boasts of parrying off a musket ball with his sword at White Plains, borrowing the phrase from Irving's original legend. Then the ghosts of Baltus and Lady Van Tassel appear. As the ghosts chase the kids through the castle the Horseman and the manuscript thieves close in. Everyone converges on the castle but the kids and Nathaniel play keep-away with the head until a minute after midnight, defeating the Horseman. Nick, it turns out, is indeed a descendant of Ichabod Crane.

For a cartoon *The Haunted Pumpkin of Sleepy Hollow* lays out a maze comparable to Vic Atkinson's *New Misadventures*, essentially spinning its own story from characters invented by Irving. Drawing a young love element into the story—but not enough to lose juvenile interest—latter-day Crane and Kate battle a demonic Headless Horseman. While it's obviously for fun, there are scary tensions in this kid-friendly adventure. And it's self-aware of being part of Knickerbocker's mythology. And a Halloween story.

Displaying diversity awareness, the teacher, Mrs. Wentworth, is drawn as an African American. A major Black character will appear in the legend's next major television reincarnation on Fox. This cartoon also seems to anticipate Tim Burton's *The Corpse Bride* (2005). The Van Tassels, animated from their portraits, closely resemble Burton's Everglots in *Corpse Bride*. PorchLight Entertainment released this short as a video, so it's difficult to say how influential it was. The resemblance of the Everglots to the Van Tassels is uncanny, but may simply be coincidence. Anything's possible in this maze.

Following on from this, ABC aired a television movie, Kyle Newman's *The Hollow* (2004), which was another early effort to pick up on the horror potential for the story. Although a teen-movie, it attempts to make the original story scary. It also reframes it as occurring in the "present day."

This trend becomes increasingly common, even as *Sleepy Hollow High* and *The Haunted Pumpkin* show. At about 83 minutes, this is the sixth feature-length film of Sleepy Hollow.

Ian Cranston (Kevin Zegers), whose father is the high school football coach, has just moved to Sleepy Hollow. Head cheerleader Karen (a pre–*Big Bang* Kaley Cuoco) is sweet on him but the star of the football team, Brody (Nick Carter), thinks she's his. This new setup of the love triangle is made out to be a replay of old times. Brody is the Brom Bones of this adaptation. Like other versions set in the present day, *The Hollow* treats the Irving version of the story as a factual account of the past. As a myth, everyone in the movie knows the legend. This one also ends with "Ichabod" winning "Katrina," à la Burton and Henning Schellerup.

Claus Van Ripper, the drunk who takes care of the graveyard, opens the film by slashing an axe at Washington Irving's grave. Hans Van Ripper, by the way, was only in charge of Crane's effects in Irving's story and he gains new prominence in modern retellings. He becomes the school superintendent in Pierre Gang's movie, and Ichabod's guide in Shane Williams' animation. He's one of the few other characters named by Washington Irving, so he suggests himself for larger roles in more expanded stories. Claus, in any case, declares the story is all true. Meanwhile, Ian is narrating the legend of Sleepy Hollow to a bunch of kids the night before Halloween. Three of Karen's friends, including Brody, are bored and wander off from the outdoor presentation into the graveyard. Brody splits off and the other two are beheaded. Van Ripper, clearly drunk, warns

Kevin Zegers as Ian Cranston, a descendant of Ichabod Crane in Kyle Newman's *The Hollow* (©2004 The Hollow LLC, All Rights Reserved).

Cranston—whom he calls "Teacher"—that the real Horseman is after him. This Van Ripper is an actual descendant of Irving's Hans Van Ripper, of course. He has a book, kind of like this one, that tells the true story.

Nobody believes sloshed Van Ripper, but on the next night—Halloween—during the annual hayride, the Horseman is back. He's awoken because a Crane has returned. "Cranston" is a disguised form of Crane. Ichabod survived the Horseman's attack, married and had a family in New York City, as Knickerbocker reported. Ian is his last descendant. Bested by Crane making it over the bridge that night long ago, the Horseman wants a Crane head. To complicate things, during the hayride Brody is playing the Horseman. As in the Schellerup version, we have two horsemen simultaneously. Karen is portraying a ghost in the graveyard for the event and Ian is the narrator on the hayride. The love triangle survives the centuries with their confused paths.

When the real Horseman shows up, with a jack-o'-lantern head, he kills a teen couple that are trying to have sex in his shed, bringing the film into the realm of slasher morality. He then kills the sheriff. Now everyone believes Van Ripper. Ian, who is on the high school fencing team, has to take on the Horseman in a sword fight. Brody, Van Ripper, Karen, and Ian team up to stop the ghost. When Van Ripper's instructions fail to halt the Horseman, Ian throws him onto the bridge where he bursts into flames. The final scene of Van Ripper implies the Horseman has arisen yet again.

Clearly not a big-budget theatrical release, this film nevertheless isn't a bad effort. As a teen movie for television, with some of the toned-down effects expected of such a production, its horror isn't always explicitly shown. Borrowing from Burton, Crane and "Bones" pair up to fight a real Horseman. There are clearly elements borrowed from the Disney version as well as the Burton rendition. And, of course, as myth, some expected innovation appears.

From Disney we have both the Halloween setting—in Ian's retelling of "The Legend of Sleepy Hollow" it's explicitly set on the holiday—and the covered bridge. Both of these were picked up by Burton as well, of course. Interestingly enough, when Karen asks Ian if he doesn't have all the details of the story already memorized, he replies that he only watched "the cartoon" as a child. Disney, no doubt, is "the cartoon." Disney's deep in America's labyrinth. Indeed, Disney might just be Daedalus here.

If you roam around this maze long enough, you'll come to the same turns time and again. Not only did Newman take the beheading of a running victim from Burton (both Masbath and Philipse die this way), but also the concept phrased by Van Ripper as "You can't kill what's already dead." In Burton's version, after the exploding windmill starting the climatic chase, young Masbath asks if the Horseman was killed in the explosion. Crane replies, "That's the problem—he was dead to begin with." Also Van Ripper, in Newman's rendition, knows the Horseman has returned because vines filled with blood have grown over Irving's tomb. In Burton's retelling, the tree of the dead has roots full of blood, and vines growing over the Horseman's body are a sign he's about to rise. Note how central the Headless Horseman really is.

The only pumpkin thrown in Newman's version is tossed by Brody— the real Horseman's jack-o'-lantern head stays firmly attached. The Horseman's an actual monster, and one that has been after Crane, always an outsider, from the beginning. He's physical enough for a sword fight. Since America's nightmare involves the stranger, even though this Horseman isn't conventional—the pumpkin *is* his head—he enforces that nightmare. But again, the story's a white one.

The most glaring omission tying *The Hollow* back to the original story is the Old Dutch Church. Given that much of the movie takes place in the graveyard, and the graveyard is right next to the church, this is a curious omission. Granted, the town is never explicitly named "Sleepy Hollow" in the movie, but Washington Irving is buried there. The high school is Knickerbocker High, and their football team is the Horsemen. Also the fact that Cranes have returned to "the Hollow" leaves no doubt as to which Hollow is meant. "The church bridge," however, is simply the bridge and on the other side there's no church. Nobody considers any kind of truly supernatural solution to the ghost—only a sword-fight and getting him onto the bridge. Is America growing shy about its religion?

This film further underscores how the standard Disney version has been canonized. Even characters within the movie know it only from "the cartoon." Still, it's Disney grown up into a myth with horror. Heads are chopped. Teens have sex in a shack. It's part of America's maze. And if you listen closely you may hear some music in that labyrinth.

The Musical

Perhaps one of the most unexpected presentations of the story, post–Burton, was *Ichabod!: The Legend of Sleepy Hollow* (2004). The film of this musical, which has become very difficult to locate, appeared the same year as *The Hollow*. Rick Ramage, the director and writer, had some horror experience before. He'd written the screenplay for *Stigmata* (1999), so he knew about horror writing as well as music. The musical, in keeping with Sleepy Hollow's overall reputation, was for children. At 70 minutes it may technically count as the seventh feature-length film of the myth.

Ichabod Crane (Peter O'Meara) is portrayed from the beginning as arrogant and deceitful. The story itself is quite different from Knickerbocker. The soft rock show tunes, by Cy Frost and Doug Olson, are clearly inspired by Andrew Lloyd Webber. There are only four songs in the movie, with another written but left out from the final cut.

The film opens with a bearded Washington Irving trying to write "The Legend of Sleepy Hollow" and breaking through the fourth wall to tell viewers of his difficulty with finishing the story. As he sings the first song, "Imagine," he becomes Crane stumbling into Tarrytown (Sleepy Hollow here is the Van Tassel estate). Scanning the local broadsheet, Crane decides he'll apply for the advertised teacher role. He's introduced to the local situation by Millie Cooper, an introduced character. He immediately sets designs on the richest girl in town, Katrina Van Tassel (Charisse Stewart). Millie is the one to tell Ichabod about the Headless Horseman.

The play then has a long stretch introducing Brom Bones (Nathan Anderson) and the Sleepy Hollow boys, one of whom is a woman. This takes place at the Knickerbocker Inn where Crane is watching everything, calculating. Brom is about to pummel Ichabod when Katrina arrives and stops the fight. Baltus and Dame Van Tassel, meanwhile, are very impressed with Crane's self-aggrandizing résumé, and decide Katrina will marry him although they know she's in love with Brom. This leads to the main musical number, "Ichabod." Katrina is very accomplished in this version, more so than Ichabod. Crane is more of an opportunist, as Irving presented him.

The fall celebration here is an Oktoberfest—no mention is made of

Peter O'Meara as Ichabod Crane in Rick Ramage's *Ichabod!* (©2004 Write on Film Enterprises, All Rights Reserved).

Halloween, although pumpkins are all around. Katrina accepts Ichabod's proposal to avoid disappointing her parents and explains this to Brom, who gracefully bows out. This Brom is cut from the same cloth as Pierre Gang's Bones five years earlier. The rivalry between Ichabod and Brom is cleverly played out, and in quite a humorous vein.

At the party, which is a masquerade, Baltus overhears Crane bragging to Millie about his success at how he won his fortune, not really being in love. Baltus consults Brom, admitting that he was wrong. Bones points out that Baltus can't break the engagement without losing public esteem, but he comes up with the idea of scaring Ichabod from Sleepy Hollow. This he does with a musical number, "The Legend." The entire town is clued into what's happening and together they all scare Ichabod from the village by song.

Once in the haunted woods Ichabod encounters the presumably real Headless Horseman and pledges to change his ways. Washington Irving, who's been stepping in as narrator from time to time, ends the story here. He explains in a postscript that Brom and Katrina married and that opinions differ on what happened to Ichabod, although the implication is that Irving is Ichabod and that he is telling an autobiographical story and that he married Millie. Washington Irving, in reality, never did marry.

There's quite a bit going on here. The movie draws its main influence from Gang's version, discussed in Chapter 8. Here Brom is a horse trader instead of a blacksmith, however. In both versions Brom is noble and Crane excessively arrogant. Here Crane claims not to believe in ghosts and is an entirely unsympathetic character. Both Schellerup and Burton had skeptical Cranes. Katrina sees through Ichabod, and in fact, tells him "You seduced my mother and my father, sir, but not me." There is no chase scene, no pumpkin hurled. Concerning America's nightmare, there are, as in Burton, no African Americans in the film. The agency of the women, however, is greater than in most renditions. Even one of the Sleepy Hollow boys is a girl.

This particular branch of the labyrinth really hasn't borne any additional fruit. Yet. Mazes have a way of turning back on themselves, so we shouldn't be surprised if more musical films eventually appear on the path.

This is an unusual hybrid. The story was originally a play written for Ramage's children and has been promoted for school productions.* The film was made primarily for young viewers and emphasizes comedy. The point of the play seems to be trusting the reality of imagination. Brom tells Crane that Sleepy Hollow is a mindset. He's quite right about that. As with the after school specials we saw in Chapter 8, the hope is to make children

---

* As noted in the extras on the DVD.

interested in reading what is, in this case, a very different original story. The myth continues to be aimed at the young.

Keeping with our youthful post–Burton Sleepy Hollow renaissance, we have two more departures to consider in this chapter. The first is the eighth feature-length movie, which takes us away from Sleepy Hollow while keeping its monster.

Nightmare on the Road

One last horror flick before moving into the era when Fox's television series came to dominate Irving's myth: Anthony C. Ferrante's *The Headless Horseman*, first aired on the Sci Fi channel (now SyFy) in 2007. Set far from Sleepy Hollow in Missouri, it takes America's nightmare on the road. The labyrinth grows even larger. The chronologically challenged backstory is that of a nineteenth-century serial killer, named Calvin Montgomery. He decapitated children and sent their heads to Hell. A priest then beheaded him with a blessed sword, but every seven years, when the constellation Hydra is visible, Montgomery returns from Hell to claim seven—preferably non-local—heads. This appears to be the first version where the Horseman is given a name. In the present day, seven teenagers in a van get trapped in Wormwood Ridge, where this drama unfolds. This rendition, although a distant departure from the "canonical" myth, clearly borrows from Burton's vision. Not only is the Headless Horseman costume similar to that of Burton's villain, some of the weapons used and the regrowing of the Horseman's head look eerily familiar. The Horseman collects heads in a repository that's a gateway to Hell, as in Burton. Even the scene of Lizzie's beheading—open eyes staring down through a crack in the floorboards—is taken from Beth Killian's demise in Burton's adaptation.

Since this is now a Halloween story, "Headless"—as the fiend is known—often appears with a jack-o'-lantern for a head. The opening Civil War sequence features a bridge that the Horseman can't cross. The Civil War occurred more than 50 years following the origin story—here set in 1806, the year the Horseman first returned. The Horseman is a repeat monster, and he works on a strict schedule.

As the seven young people get lost on their way to a Halloween party, there are clear nods to *The Texas Chainsaw Massacre* (the van trip), and *Deliverance* (cited by name in the movie). We're lost in horror central. The teenagers have fallen into a trap, of course. They are "delivered" by Candy, the teenaged daughter of the local mechanic, Rusk, who shows up with a tow truck shortly after the van "accidentally" experiences a flat tire via bear trap just outside town.

Once the kids meet Candy, she tells them they arrived just in time for the Headless Horseman celebration on All Hallows Eve. Liam, one of the van crew and a literature tutor, asks if it's the Horseman in the Washington Irving story. Here's a tangible connection to all that has gone on before in this maze. Liam then notes Irving's story is set in New England, apparently unaware that Sleepy Hollow is, in fact, in New York (he's not the only one, in the long retelling history, not to know the difference). Candy replies that *this* is the original story, since Irving's is a "whitewashed" version. The people of Wormwood have lived through the real predations of Headless for two centuries and know the true story. The young people are beheaded one by one, until Liam and his student Ava are the only ones left. With Candy's help they destroy the Horseman and the entire town is taken to Hell, literally. Introducing Hell was, of course, a Burton innovation.

Headless Horseman isn't a great movie. Its writing doesn't inspire and it leaves too many gaps in the narrative to carry the viewer along easily. Its most egregious error, however, is killing off the Headless Horseman. Doing so destroys the myth. It makes this into just another horror movie.

Still, it is a creative continuation of the myth. Here the American heartland is openly compared to *Deliverance* territory. Inbreeding is a problem—everyone in Wormwood is literally family—thus it perpetuates an unhealthy stereotype of the rural south. A south with no African Americans, however. They like strangers here, though, since they need seven of them as victims for Headless. Self-aware of Irving's original, Ferrante changes it boldly, continuing the tradition of freeing the story from its literary roots.

Religion plays an important role in this rendition. The original serial killer who offered his victims' heads to the hydra that guards the entrance to Hell now is the Horseman. After the killer was stopped and his own body sent through the gateway, he comes back every seven years to chop heads. Lots of infernal imagery here. The town where all this takes place bears the biblical name of Wormwood (from Revelation 8), and the person who originally stopped the serial killer was the local priest—not part of the family. This area of the labyrinth circles back to its own complicated version of the Old Dutch Church. Revelation will enter the story again with Fox.

There's other heavy and loose religious imagery revolving around the town church. It was burned down around the interloper priest and rebuilt in 1801. Nevertheless the Horseman arose in 1806, presumably seven years after his death. The people didn't appreciate the righteous, outsider priest, but they know if "Headless" doesn't get his seven heads every seventh year then the entire town will go to Hell with him, so apparently they want a church. It's not clear why they rebuilt it unless it was to protect themselves.

There's no current priest. It may not be the Old Dutch Church, but it's pretty firmly part of Wormwood history, and it's linked to the monster's origins.

Not a major studio release, the movie is nevertheless very aware that it's riffing off Knickerbocker. Setting the origin story in 1806 and claiming it was rewritten much later by Irving is a bit strange. Not naming the state or the year, it allows for ambiguity. (Filmed in Romania, as movies wanting a remote look often are, the state is determined by local license plates.) The town was established in 1799 (also from Burton) but Irving's tale took place around 1790. Although there's no Ichabod Crane here, the surviving young people are a teacher (Liam) and a student with whom he's secretly in love. Squinting hard enough, you can still see America's original ghost story in this part of the maze.

One more path through the labyrinth will wind up the first decade of the millennium. And to find it, you need to go back to the books.

Young Adult Novels

The maze appears in paper form also. In 2005 the publishing world, still reeling from the success of J.K. Rowling's Harry Potter novels, came to realize that novels for the young were not dead after all. In fact, they were rising from the dead. That was the year that Stephenie Meyer published *Twilight* and many things happened simultaneously. One is that vampires edged their way back in amid the growing zombie craze. *Twilight* had literary agents telling writing clubs even years later that publishers wanted vampires. Anne Rice's *The Vampire Chronicles* had perhaps laid the groundwork but *Twilight* had publishers talking and readers opening their wallets. This simply couldn't be ignored.

Another result of *Twilight* was that paranormal romances attained new currency. Longish novels for young adult readers were lucrative, and if those that featured vampires sold, wouldn't the same hold for other revenants? Sleepy Hollow had ready-made ghosts and a love triangle to give writers a head start. Meanwhile, Johnny Depp had redefined Ichabod Crane and he was now a sex symbol for the young adult crowd. Captain Jack Sparrow didn't hurt this status, but *Sleepy Hollow* had not been forgotten. Jessica Verday pulled "The Legend" into this swirling sea of hormones. Her *The Hollow* trilogy, published by Simon Pulse, hit the *New York Times* bestseller list. Taking cues from Washington Irving, Tim Burton, and Stephenie Meyer, Verday crafted a series that captured the spirit of the times and added further to the myth.

The three novels, while not retellings of Irving's story, are romantic explorations that incorporate the world Irving spun in "Sleepy Hollow." Abbey Browning, the protagonist, is a rising junior in high school when her best friend Kristen dies mysteriously in Sleepy Hollow. Volume one, *The Hollow*, first published in 2009, narrates Abbey's difficult initial year without her best friend while tying the narrative back to Irving's story at several points. His grave, for example, is a touchstone for the story. Each chapter begins with an epigraph from "The Legend."

Toward the end of *The Hollow* it becomes clear why this is a paranormal romance. Two of the characters turn out to be Katrina Van Tassel and, yes, the Headless Horseman. To get the full effect, however, the other two novels in the series have to be included. By the end of *The Hollow* it appears that the Headless Horseman, who married Katrina, is really benign. The two live on, but aren't visible to many. Abbey is one of the few who can see them.

In *The Haunted*, published in 2010, we learn that Brom Bones was skin and bones and Ichabod Crane was no catch, but both were historical people in the world of this trilogy. Katrina could see the Headless Horseman, a shade, who was clearly in love with her. They managed to make it work. This parallels the story of Abbey whose boyfriend, Caspian, is likewise deceased.

Verday also adds the suggestion that Washington Irving, who could see "shades" (not ghosts proper), learned the legend from the Headless Horseman—Nikolas Degenhart—and Katrina. Meanwhile several shades have appeared in Sleepy Hollow. Since Abbey can see them they seem to be intimating that she too will be dying soon. Sleepy Hollow, it appears, has many ghosts. Verday points out that Irving wrote as much.

The series concluded in 2011 with *The Hidden*. The story grows much more complex here and much of it has to be spelled out by the Revenants—kind of like shades, but slightly different—who are trying to help Abbey complete Caspian so that the young couple can take the Horseman and Katrina's place, and, following the movie *The Hollow*, Caspian is a descendant of Ichabod Crane. Clocking in at well over a thousand pages, there's much more to this paranormal romance than this brief summary indicates. It is the first retelling with a strong female protagonist. She isn't Katrina, but she does stand in for her. We'll see more women taking the tale from here.

The story is set in Knickerbocker's realm and engages the myth throughout. Still, one might ask, how did Burton influence such a story? Timing, for one thing.

Direct descent isn't really obvious but it's difficult to imagine that a major publisher such as Simon & Schuster would've been interested in such a trilogy had not Burton's film rebooted public interest in Sleepy

Hollow. The movie showed people would spend on this. There was more story to be told. If they were handing over cash for vampires, why not for the Headless Horseman as well? There had been further cartoons, television movies, and even a musical. Irving's star was high in the sky.

Next we'll move on to the proliferation of adaptions that took place starting with the Fox *Sleepy Hollow* series that ran from 2013 through 2017—a proliferation that's showing no signs of slowing. Fox's series is the first version to face directly America's nightmare and foreground a strong African American character, who teaches the teacher what it means to be an American in the twenty-first century.

11

Fox and Friends

She can't believe what she sees. Her mentor's body. Headless. Strange, violent crimes are suddenly happening in the not-so-small town of Sleepy Hollow. Gruesome murders. An apparently insane man appears, claiming to have known George Washington personally. She's an African American police lieutenant, and she's eventually won over as she comes to see that this crazy man knows too much about the bizarre happenings abruptly occurring in this quiet town. He is, in fact, a relic from early America. Washington Irving's America. An America that still lives on beneath Sleepy Hollow, and Abigail Mills knows she's deeply entangled.

Sleepy Hollow began to appear in other visual media, as well as novels, after Tim Burton's adaptation. Washington Irving's star was high in the sky and new forms of telling the story began to appear. Graphic novels have been around at least since the 1970s, but such books didn't really break into the literary world until the current millennium. Up until Johnny Depp's portrayal, there weren't graphic novels foregrounding the cartoonish Ichabod Crane, schoolmaster. Or the silent, mysterious Headless Horseman. Part of it may have been that such a tale really only lends itself to one book rather than offering any real serializing potential. Who's interested in judge Crane, happily married? And we never hear of the Headless Horseman again. Fox's *Sleepy Hollow*, however, will suggest routes of serialization, and thus a commercially viable horror graphic novel treatment.

Graphic Novelties

Focusing on the education market, Stone Arch's graphic novels—often conscious of inclusivity—are aimed at younger readers. Several literary classics are represented in their catalogue. *Washington Irving's The Legend of Sleepy Hollow* was actually written and inked in 2008, but copyrighted by Stone Arch Books after the success of Mison's Crane. It falls between Burton and Fox but Crane, in some panels, resembles Jeff Goldblum. Blake A. Hoena and Tod Smith respectively wrote and drew it. This is a straightforward retelling of Irving, but with a few shifts.

As is fitting for a post–Burton retelling, it's clearly horror-based. Brom is first introduced as a blacksmith—we seem to be following Pierre Gang here—preparing to prank Crane's schoolroom. That night one of the Dutch wives tells Ichabod Crane the story of Raven Rock which sets up a spooky walk back to the Van Rippers' farm, where he stays (also from Gang). On his way he encounters the Headless Horseman. At the Van Tassel farm, where he's giving Katrina singing lessons, "Balt" tells him the story of Major André, creating another spooky walk home when he again sees the Horseman.

Brom stops up the schoolhouse chimney with a pumpkin, but an invitation to the Van Tassel's party arrives, buoying the pedagogue's spirits. Ichabod dances with Katrina since Brom isn't a dancer. Crane finally hears the story of Headless at the party and his suit for Katrina is rejected. The ride home is presented with horror stylings and an actual head is thrown at Crane through the covered bridge—Disney still maintains its pride of place. The next day a shattered jack-o'-lantern is found next to Ichabod's hat and Brom and Katrina wed in the spring. Two boys find one of Brom's horseshoes, which they think came from the Headless Horseman. They present it to the new schoolteacher, along with the legend. Like Irving, this version doesn't really develop either Brom or Katrina's characters. It's pretty obvious the two want to be together, though.

Stone Arch's goal is, like those of Shelley Duvall, the CBS Library, and *Ichabod!* the musical, to encourage reading. There's no real need to embellish the tale, but they do take it in a horror direction while leaving an explicit Halloween out of it. Apart from the jack-o'-lantern, the holiday, appropriate to the time, isn't mentioned. The same will be true for our next graphic tale. Pitched at a somewhat older readership, Zenescope Entertainment offers more fantasy-based fare. Zenescope's cover art for *Sleepy Hollow* features a jack-o'-lantern, but it doesn't show up in the story. Halloween's still in play, but it's not a major draw for these graphic tales.

Zenescope's Grimm Fairy Tales' graphic novel *Sleepy Hollow* also actually came out before the Fox series premiered, but in the same year, 2013. Written by Dan Wickline, penciled by AC Osorio, with colors by Erick Arciniega, this particular rendition plays on history repeating itself. The colonial era Headless Horseman isn't a mercenary, but John Marsters, a patriot betrayed by a loyalist Abraham Van Brant, for stealing his girlfriend Katrina. Van Brant and his associates, in a fit of extreme jealousy, behead Marsters. Generations later, Craig Marsters is a student at Tarrytown University. His roommate, Ty, is a basketball player who arranges academic help for his teammates by getting exam answers from smart students, like Craig. To do this a double-crossing scheme is arranged by Ty and his girlfriend Katie. They have Katie pose as Craig's girlfriend and when she suggests Ty rough him up to get the answers, he comes up with the idea of tying him to the railroad tracks with the help of his basketball buddies. They release him just before a train roars by. Convincing his friends it was a mistake, Ty knocks Craig onto the rails where he is then beheaded. At the exact same location, it turns out, where Craig's ancestor was decapitated. Dead Craig, channeling the betrayal of his ancestor, arises as the Headless Horseman and kills all the students in on the plot, wearing their heads on a grisly belt as he does so.

Here we have the love triangle involving a Kat(rina) but one that's intentionally deceptive. Katie and Ty only trick Craig (sounds a little like Crane) into thinking she's his girlfriend because he's smarter (like Crane). This graphic version introduces what will become a common theme, likely extrapolated from Burton, that the Horseman kills out of revenge. Other modern retellings take this horror element as fundamental. There is still some humor here, as there will be in the Fox series, but we're mostly now in the realm of graphic novel horror.

This particular treatment may be "race neutral" since the two main Black characters are opposites. Ty is drawn as African American, and he kills his roommate. Professor Sela Mathers of Terrytown University is also Black. She's the one who narrates the colonial-era history. She's rendered, however, in miniskirt with a very low-cut blouse that reveals her bra. Sleepy Hollow has become sexy. African Americans can be good or bad in this nightmare. A Black woman shares center stage in the next major adaptation, on television. Race has at last become important in Sleepy Hollow.

Race and Relevance in Sleepy Hollow

Let's go back to Knickerbocker for a moment. Slavery was a reality in Irving's lifetime. He lived in New York, a state that would eventually support abolition, but just as he put the Old Dutch Church into his tale for realism, he also included some African Americans. He doesn't explicitly call them slaves, but his treatment of them makes modern readers a bit uncomfortable. Consider when Ichabod receives his invitation to the Van Tassel's party. In Irving's own words: "It [school] was suddenly interrupted by the appearance of a negro in tow-cloth jacket and trowsers, a round-crowned fragment of a hat, like the cap of Mercury, and mounted on the back of a ragged, wild, half-broken colt, which he managed with a rope by way of halter. He came clattering up to the school door with an invitation to Ichabod to attend a merry-making or 'quilting-frolic,' to be held that evening at Mynheer Van Tassel's; and having delivered his message with that air of importance, and effort at fine language, which a negro is apt to display on petty embassies of the kind, he dashed over the brook, and was seen scampering away up the hollow, full of the importance and hurry of his mission."

The Van Tassel servant, notice, isn't in school with the other children. He's poorly dressed and considers himself important to have been sent on an errand to the school teacher. Irving is writing in a humorous vein here, of course, but the discomfort continues with the party itself. There we learn "The musician was an old gray-headed negro, who had been the itinerant orchestra of the neighborhood for more than half a century. His instrument was as old and battered as himself. The greater part of the time he scraped on two or three strings, accompanying every movement of the bow with a motion of the head; bowing almost to the ground, and stamping with his foot whenever a fresh couple were to start." One of the servile roles given to African Americans in this story is entertainment. This caricatured, nameless character plays for the benefit of the dancing Dutch. As we've seen, most adaptations of Sleepy Hollow change his race, avoiding the concern.

Again, all the characters in "The Legend" are treated as caricatures, but the only mentions of African Americans place them in obvious outsider roles. This is ironic since Irving may have learned the legend itself from an African American mill worker in Sleepy Hollow (see Chapter 5). We start to see why Fox's *Sleepy Hollow* hit the chord that it did. It was more than monsters appearing on a weekly basis. Placing an African American woman in a central role was radical for Sleepy Hollow. The police captain is also Black. Fox's version was asking us to look at America. Consider who we are. "The Legend of Sleepy Hollow" is America's ghost story as well as its myth.

For a myth to remain relevant, it must meet the needs of any given time. As the millennium continued to unfold a veritable explosion of Sleepy Hollow media appeared, confirming that a need was being addressed. Novels, graphic and text-based, poured out. Many of them bore distinct marks of the new vision Burton and Fox had brought into the labyrinth. And they would all be, in their own way, growing the myth.

This wasn't however, the first television version of Sleepy Hollow and its Headless Horseman, as we've seen. Most of the previous efforts tried to retell the tale without serializing it—it's a short story after all. Knickerbocker never attempted a sequel, nor really delved deeply into what might've happened to these characters after that fateful night. Traditions of headless horsemen went back centuries, even at the time of Irving. His creative development of the character of Ichabod Crane and putting him into an unlikely love triangle and setting it in Sleepy Hollow made a winning combination back then, but the story had unrealized potential.

According to Fox

Fox's 2013 reintroduction—or perhaps, reconstruction—of Sleepy Hollow was a surprise hit.* Maybe its success shouldn't have been that much of a surprise since primetime supernatural has had a strong track record since the days of the *Twilight Zone*. And "The Legend of Sleepy Hollow" has become a powerful myth. This series, taking the ubiquitous title *Sleepy Hollow*, was created by Phillip Iscove, Alex Kurtzman, and Roberto Orsi. It boasted an ensemble of both writers and directors. The coterie of writers—28 credited by the end of the series—under the guidance of 30 directors—made this a true group effort. It was a labyrinth within a labyrinth. Ultimately the series would lack coherence, however, and even the popular monster-of-the-week trope combined with fashionable *Hamilton*-era American history couldn't save it. There may have been a larger problem, however, when this team decided to write religion out of the script. But let's consider what they got right.

As in Burton's rendition, the writers and directors followed horror conventions for their *Sleepy Hollow*. Heads do roll, and yes, there is blood. Remember that in Irving's gentle story nobody gets seriously hurt. Ichabod's pride, maybe, but nobody loses a head. The truth of the existence of the ghost is left carefully undecided. Things trend very differently in modern day Sleepy Hollows. These current renditions reflect the times in which they're made and the myth as it's changed over time. Fox's *Sleepy Hollow* is horror but also keeps an Irvingesque level of humor, mostly from Crane's confusion at the modern world (perhaps inspired by the Burton-Depp collaboration *Dark Shadows*, which appeared in 2012). It definitely drew from Burton's *Sleepy Hollow*.

The Black Lives Matter movement began in July of 2013. Recall in Burton's *Sleepy Hollow* no African Americans appear. The same is true of Disney's version and several of those in-between. Ub Iwerk's first cartoon version had "Black" characters insensitively drawn. Edward Venturini's

---

* See, for example, *Entertainment Weekly*: https://ew.com/article/2013/12/04/crazy-ones-mom-sleepy-hollow-second-chance-reviews/, accessed 17 June 2024. The sources behind the Fox series discussion may be found in my article "Reading the Bible in Sleepy Hollow." For the other media discussed, the information was found by reading or watching the material.

first feature film also had African Americans appear. From Disney on, perhaps due to fear of controversy, the players mostly became all white. Taking racial history center screen, the Fox series put the dominant role—the one that knows modern rules—in the hands of a Black woman. Throughout the first season, she has an Asian-American colleague (Andy Brooks) and the precinct has a Black captain named Frank Irving. Long gone are the problematic descriptions by Irving (see Chapter 14). We've entered a century that dreams of being more equitable and of handling all people with inherent worth and dignity. This is mirrored in the television series. Foregrounded even, taking the myth in a new and necessary direction.

The Fox series has 62 episodes that can't all be summarized here. Like *The X-Files* the series had a central narrative but this is mixed with various monster-of-the-week episodes that don't necessarily advance the overall plot. This organizing myth of *Sleepy Hollow* is fairly intricate and veritably bursting with complexities. One of those elements, borrowed from Burton, is that religion is a driving factor in what's going on in Sleepy Hollow. Here's how it goes:

An ancient demon named Moloch has decided the time is right to begin the apocalypse. It will take place where one of his minions fell many years ago—Sleepy Hollow. Another of his minions was born there in the same era.

The present day Sleepy Hollow—presented as much larger than the actual current town (for religious reasons)—is the focal point for the end of the world. This Sleepy Hollow is shown as having a population 144,000. The number has significance because in Revelation 7 in the Bible, it's the number of those sealed by God for preservation during the coming time of trial—the apocalypse. The entire series revolved around the end times.

Tom Mison's Ichabod Crane is both Crane and Rip Van Winkle. Dead for 250 years, then resurrected in a most religious way, he finds himself reanimated in the bewildering twenty-first century. Presented as a former Oxford professor, Ichabod is an Englishman sympathetic to the American cause of independence. He was therefore also a captain in the U.S. continental army. As a captain, in military status he technically outranks a lieutenant. As a professor, he outsmarts most people. This is a Crane of a different feather. Not only that, he had married Katrina Van Tassel, the Horseman's former love, and she was both a Quaker and a witch (more Burton influence), as well as a nurse. As the man who beheaded him, Crane's in pretty serious trouble when the Horseman also shows up in Sleepy Hollow. But that's a little bit backwards—the Horseman's the driver here.

Although the Headless Horseman (whose head is restored in season 2) is actually Death—the fourth horseman of the apocalypse—before that he was Abraham Van Brunt (Brom Bones). Van Brunt signed himself to Moloch because Katrina decided to marry Ichabod while she was engaged to Brom. His love was such that he'd rather end the world than let her go. Crane was actually Brom's best friend in this telling. He too was deeply in love with Katrina. The love triangle survives. Both of her lovers were sincere and good men. At first.

Since the book of Revelation in the Christian Bible lists four horsemen—conquest, war, famine, and death—it makes sense for Crane to pay attention to George Washington's Bible, which was buried with him. These horsemen are being raised by the demon Moloch, and this is where the Mills sisters get implicated. Moloch was a "foreign god" in the Bible. Over time he morphed into a demon. His transformation was so complete that he became essentially synonymous with the Devil over time. And the Devil is always in the details. And in labyrinths (minotaurs and devils wear similar horns, after all). In order to bring about the end of time, he must raise the other three horsemen.

The year of Crane and the Horseman's death was 1781 (about a decade earlier than Irving had set the story). During a battle near Sleepy Hollow Crane had shot the masked Horseman, but he did not die. He arose and continued to approach Crane, whom he slashes with his axe. As Crane falls, he lops off the Horseman's head. Together they fall and their blood mingles as they die. They are magically interconnected. When one comes back to life, so does the other. Moloch has decided to begin the apocalypse in the twenty-first century and when the Horseman—one of the four horsemen of the apocalypse—is resurrected, so is Crane. The Horseman's now after his head again, naturally enough. If the Horseman hadn't been raised, Crane wouldn't have shown up. We're obviously in a labyrinth here.

This covers the male characters Irving provided. The main female role here is also where African American history enters the story. Although Sheriff's Lieutenant Abigail Mills (Nicole Beharie) is FBI material (a nod to the *X-Files* here), she decides to stay in Sleepy Hollow because of her own experience with Moloch and the death of her mentor. She and her sister Jenny (Lyndie Greenwood, who later takes the baton when Beharie left the show) encountered Moloch in the woods of Sleepy Hollow as children. They became delinquents. Abbie was taken under the wing of Sheriff August Corbin (Clancy Brown, someone we encountered in Shane Williams' *Night of the Headless Horseman*, in Chapter 8). Unbeknownst to Abbie, her sister was also being mentored by Corbin, even as she remained a delinquent. Abbie had decided to join the FBI after her application was successful. Corbin, however, was one of the Horseman's first victims and Abbie feels compelled to stay in Sleepy Hollow to take his work to completion after he dies. She then meets Ichabod. Jenny comes back into her life and assists in underground ways.

As an African American woman, Abbie seems an unlikely ally to the confused, patriarchal yet progressive Crane. She is, however, the one modern-day person willing to take a chance that he's telling the truth. When a spate of decapitations suddenly starts to occur, Abbie takes charge. She decides to cooperate with Ichabod to stop the carnage. Soon it becomes clear that this was an ancient supernatural plot.

Katrina's not gone entirely. She's in Purgatory. She's nearly displaced by Abbie Mills, but Katrina's being a witch complicates things. As season one progresses, another character, Henry Parish, is introduced as a "sin eater." By the end of the second season it's revealed that Parish is actually Ichabod's angry son Jeremy, although he's older than Crane. Crane died not knowing he had a son, but Jeremy's rage leads him to sign on as the second of the four horsemen, War. Katrina, who is eventually released from Purgatory, sides with Jeremy in the effort to bring back her coven. If you're lost in this labyrinth, you're not alone. It seems that with so many writers and directors a strong though-line is lacking. One thing is clear, however: religion is behind all of this.

For example, a magical priest, also over two centuries old, is decapitated by the Horseman in the present day in the first episode. His house of worship isn't the Old Dutch Church, but he's been making sure that the Horseman's head, buried in his graveyard, remains undetected. The priest,

Tom Mison as Ichabod Crane and Nicole Beharie as Abbie Mills in Fox's *Sleepy Hollow* pilot episode. Extras on the street are unnamed (© 2013 Twentieth Century-Fox Film Corporation, All Rights Reserved).

although killed in the pilot, signals that the end times are here. Along the way Ichabod and Abbie were identified as the two "witnesses," also from the book of Revelation. For the first two seasons the series focused on that biblical book.

Tying the Bible and occult closely together, the series also summons characters like George Washington, Thomas Jefferson, and Benjamin Franklin, drawing in American mythology. In fact, George Washington's Bible is central to the first season. Religion and American history, and a liberal use of monsters, hung on a frame constructed by Washington Irving, the series started out strong and suffered a slow decline. Clearly this plot is labyrinthine and not all of the paths joined up.

Abbie Mills and Crane worked, at times with Jenny, to prevent Moloch from raising the other horsemen of the apocalypse. Perhaps as a hint of original director/writer hopes and dreams, the pilot has Ichabod tell Abbie that there is a seven-year period for the two witnesses, during the apocalypse. By the way "apocalypse" is simply the Greek title for Revelation. Apocalypse means "unveiling," or "revealing"—in the standard phrase, "revelation." (That's why the book title, in English, is singular.) Seven years, however, proved just a dream.

The End of Sleepy Hollow

Notice that this series avoids mentioning "Washington Irving." Nods are given to him by naming the police captain Frank Irving and having a pretty major role for George Washington. No character refers directly to the story, or suggests "The Legend of Sleepy Hollow" is history. In fact, in this universe "The Legend of Sleepy Hollow" doesn't seem to exist. The characters are the retelling of Irving's tale, they don't need to ask Knickerbocker how it goes. Ichabod, the Headless Horseman/Brom Bones, and Katrina are presented as historical, but not fictional characters. They are all from the late eighteenth century and have been kept alive, or resurrected, through magical means. Notice also that this isn't a Halloween story. Irving never wrote a sequel, of course. He would barely recognize the myth he started.

Killing off the biblical demon Moloch was a fatal misstep. Fear of the apocalypse drove the first two seasons and when the danger was spent, a new one had to be conjured.* It's pretty hard to outdo the end of the world,

---

* After season two showrunner Mark Goffman left the series, which is likely the reason for the new direction the plot took. See Kimball, "*Sleepy Hollow*," https://tvseriesfinale.com/tv-show/sleepy-hollow-season-three-renewal-for-fox-tv-show-35946/, accessed 18 June 2024.

though. The writers tried to enlarge upon this but had to go rogue from the Bible to do so. Revelation does mention "tribulations," so Moloch was made into the first of seven tribulations. The second was less believable and not biblical at all. Mixing mythologies, Pandora became the second tribulation, but this Greek mythological character works for a Sumerian god, "the Hidden One." Instead of following a biblical script, now we're getting lost in a maze. Sumerian literature contains the oldest known mythology in the world, but they had no known stories about the end times. And Pandora, from many centuries later, wasn't really a bad person at all. Trying to make them biblical "tribulations" just didn't work.

Even the seven tribulations didn't play out. After Beharie left the series, Crane had to find a new second witness. Forsaking Sleepy Hollow (and this never works) he finds a candidate in Washington, D.C. Why he didn't end up with Jenny is a bit of a mystery. The third tribulation is a mortal named Malcolm Dreyfuss who wants to restart the apocalypse with the four horsemen again. To save the world Crane sells his soul and the series fizzles to an end after four seasons.

One thing the series got right was that religion makes a good driver for horror. It settles comfortably in Sleepy Hollow. The viewership began a steady decline from the start of the first season. Perhaps it's because Irving's special draw was being a short story. Perhaps it was because so many writers and directors were involved. This is a series beyond the control of a single Irving, or even Knickerbocker, a labyrinth with no exit.

The Horseman here is supernatural and complex. Although Crane claims he was never a man, as the series develops he's Brom Bones, not a Hessian mercenary. He joined himself to Moloch's cause and became immortal. The Horseman shows Burton's influence in being a denizen of Hell who rides the earth. Also in his being deliberately decapitated, not accidentally losing his head to a cannon. Crane here is also, in his own way, immortal. Katrina shares remarkable longevity as a witch. Irving's four main characters are all present, collapsed into three. The potential of expanding Irving's love triangle to include Mills was always there as long as she remained and worked closely with Crane.

This version of the tale took care to introduce strong women and African Americans into the plot. Attempting to redress some of the previous oversights in Sleepy Hollow, it offered a pluralistic vision of good that didn't focus solely on the white man. And there was a lot of history thrown in. *Sleepy Hollow* directly addressed America's perennial problems with racial and gender inequality in the strong figure of Abbie Mills. Nicole Beharie's leaving the show was its death sentence. Not only were we one witness down, but it was the Black woman who was answering the cultural need. She outlived the demise of the promising Four Horsemen plot that could've potentially kept the series going for seven years. Irving had dropped the reins on the story centuries ago with its caricatured Black servants. Washington Irving, the white man, moved into the background here. Racial equality would now be part of life in Sleepy Hollow. Other media, however, made skin color immaterial, at least in some respects. And some of this was again directed back at kids.

Blue Halloween

Given modern developments in horror—also in literature and cinema in general—adults are careful what they let their children experience. We still get bouts of book banning, for instance. And many parents thought Tim Burton's *The Nightmare Before Christmas* was too scary for children. But kids like scary stuff. The story of Sleepy Hollow, as presented by Irving, is safe for juvenile adaptation. No heads get chopped. Katrina is never bedded. The ghost may not even be real. It might helpfully serve as gateway horror. It all depends on at which stage of development you might be arrested. Not all versions are scary.

Perhaps the highest profile children's retelling in the maze so far this current millennium is *The Smurfs: The Legend of Smurfy Hollow* (also from 2013, directed by Stephan Franck). At 22 minutes long, it's classified as a short. Perhaps, given the very low age profile for its viewers, this one might eventually displace Disney as the first introduction to the story. How that affects the maze remains to be seen.

Three Smurfs around a campfire suggest telling ghost stories. This leads Narrator Smurf to offer the titular legend. Around Halloween (in the sixteenth century, well before Irving and long before modern Halloween), the Smurfs are carving pumpkins and preparing for the annual smurfberry hunt. Brainy Smurf has won the smurfberry picking contest for nine years running and this annoys Brawny Smurf. (Brains versus brawn is still here.) There is a covered bridge—a Disney innovation—that leads to the haunted Smurfy Hollow, where the Headless Horseman is said to dwell. Brainy's secret is that he doesn't believe in the Headless Horseman and smurfberries grow in profusion in Smurfy Hollow. Brawny follows him and decides to spook Brainy with a shadow puppet of the Headless Horseman.

The frightened Brainy gets caught in one of Gargamel's traps. When Brawny feels guilty about his prank, he and Smurfette go looking for Brainy only to get caught themselves. Just as Gargamel is about to do whatever he does with Smurfs, the real Headless Horseman appears. Everyone races for the bridge, but the Horseman throws a flaming jack-o'-lantern at Gargamel, dumping him in the river. In a strange twist, this is what is said to have happened to old Brouwer in Irving's original, not commonly shown in movie or television versions. Well, at least the being dumped in the creek part is in Irving. When all the Smurfs make up again, we learn that Papa Smurf's magic had turned a goat and a moth into the Headless Horseman, so there is no real ghost after all. And no Old Smurf Church.

The Smurfs (originally *Les Schtroumpfs*) were created in 1958 by the Belgian cartoonist Peyo. That means they are older than Johnny Depp. In another oddly appropriate twist, "Smurf" is the Dutch translation of "Schtroumpfs." "The Legend," remember, is set among the Dutch. Originally comic book characters in a series set in the sixteenth century, the Smurfs are plagued by a wizard named Gargamel. Although the Smurfs had some international fame earlier, they became unavoidable in America when Hanna-Barbera unleashed a Saturday-morning cartoon based on them in 1981. They continue to pop up in movies and the occasional short, such as *The Legend of Smurfy Hollow*.

Like most post–Disney retellings, this is a Halloween themed story. The Horseman, while a magical conjuring, as in *The New Misadventures of Ichabod Crane*, nevertheless carries a jack-o'-lantern for a head. Although Fox took Halloween out of the myth—necessary for a serial spanning years—for most Americans the myth of Sleepy Hollow is part of October's holiday.

Kids take longer to grow up these days. Childhood has been subdivided from infancy through tween years to proper teenager to young adult, and now even young professional. Each stage along the way is an opportunity to commodify Sleepy Hollow. As gentle horror, even some seniors don't mind it so much. At least it's an American classic—a myth for all ages. And the story continues.

In Puppets

The following year, the Handmade Puppet Dreams Film Series released an eight-minute short titled *Ichabod: Sketches from Sleepy Hollow*. The executive producer, Heather Henson, is a member of the famous puppeteering Henson family, responsible for the Muppets and much of *Sesame Street*. Directed and narrated by Hobey Ford, this is also a gentle retelling, focusing on Ichabod. The characters, as the series title implies, are puppets. And as with many such shorts, the story is told in very basic form.

Ichabod arrives in Sleepy Hollow and is first met by a boy, a dog, and Brom Bones. His love of ghost stories is emphasized and when he meets Katrina Van Tassel in the graveyard (presumably on a Sunday), Brom is looking out at them through the windows of the Old Dutch Church. At the party Ichabod proposes to Katrina and is refused before the stories begin. Brom frightens him off with the tale of the Headless Horseman and in the chase scene a flaming jack-o'-lantern is flung at his head. Crane is then seen leaving Sleepy Hollow on the ship that brought him, and interestingly, the narrator notes he lost the girl but gained the dog. Indeed, the dog is in nearly every scene and it isn't Brom's mongrel—Brom kicks the dog in frustration at the dance. At least Ichabod gets something.

Again, kid friendly, this Ibex Puppetry production was released in October of 2014, during the height of Fox's Sleepy Hollow craze. It's still a Halloween tale with its jack-o'-lantern and the Old Dutch Church is still there. Like Knickerbocker (and Disney), this telling has no dialogue. Younger readers eager for more, however, might also find new possibilities for this maze in the form of visual novels.

More Graphic Novelties

Since Sleepy Hollow graphic novels had begun to appear, serialization seemed natural enough. Boom! Studios adapted directly from the Fox series and published their version of Sleepy Hollow in book form in 2015, based on four individual comics that appeared the previous year. Written by Marguerite Bennet, illustrated by Jorge Coelho, and colored by Tamra Bonvillain, *Sleepy Hollow*, advertised as "From the Fox Series," features the Mison Crane, Abbie and Jenny Mills, and Frank Irving. It even manages to draw in Katrina and Henry Parrish (before he was revealed as Ichabod's son). The four-book series unfolds what could've been a typical episode in the television series, although one that never aired. Without going into too much detail, Colin Van Bilj, a madman genius musician, was hired by the Hessians. He composed a song, hidden in a puzzle box he invented, that would trap hearers into their own personal Hell. Moloch is implicated but not shown.

Crane and Abbie, with the help of Jenny and Frank, are drawn into Hell and have to destroy Van Bilj's monstrous music box to escape. It's very much like a series episode, tying humor in with horror. The book edition also includes some funny short stories by Noelle Stevenson. Boom! produced another series based on these characters subtitled *Providence*, and has experimented with other characters in the setting as well. Sleepy Hollow horror lives on in the graphic world.

Also missing here is Halloween. Has it gone forever from the story? No. Halloween is here to stay, but it steps out of the myth once in a while, and least in some parts of the maze. Traditional novels will bring it back.

Clearly, the Fox series, inspired by Burton, caught the imagination of a new generation. It rewrote the myth considerably, demonstrating that there was cultural relevance to this old legend. As the last chapter demonstrated, novels were experiencing a resurgence among young readers. Reinforced by Burton and Fox, the myth would continue to develop in long-form writing, and the stories would show just how the myth of Sleepy Hollow could be made to fit issues relevant to the twenty-first century.

12

Novel Mythologies

Ichabod Crane has a secret. The people of Sleepy Hollow would drive their teacher from town forever, if they knew. The pedagogue is in love with Katrina Van Tassel. Everyone knows that. The secret? Ichabod Crane is really a woman.

Novels for younger readers were making a comeback. Jessica Verday's series demonstrated that Sleepy Hollow was still fertile ground for youthful imaginations. Scattered between and after Tim Burton and the Fox adaptations of Sleepy Hollow, many novels, primarily appealing to the young adult and early professional demographics appeared. Sleepy Hollow remained culturally relevant as well as a source of cash for publishers.[*]

For our first example we need to step back a little in time, to 2005, before Fox. And also back in time to high school again.

High School Never Ends

Sleepy Hollow High, as we saw in Chapter 10, was an off-beat movie from 2000. There's also a book series by that name, initially published by Razor Bill, under the series title "The Hollow." Written for young adult readers, it consists of four books with the first, *Horseman*, produced in 2005. The other three volumes are *Drowned* (also 2005), *Mischief,* and *Enemies* (both 2006). Now branded as the "Sleepy Hollow High" series, they were written by Christopher Golden and Ford Lytle Gilmore. Currently only *Horseman* is still sold in print form with the other three volumes available as eBooks. We'll take a look at this first book to get a sense of the series.

---

[*] The novels read in the course of writing this chapter were really the only resources to cite. I did eventually come across Joe Nazare's article in his *Ultimate Annotated Edition* which also discusses, briefly, a few of these novels that I'd found on my own. Bringing these books together suggests the analysis here.

Horseman follows the adventures of Aimee and Shane Lancaster as they move to Sleepy Hollow with their father, following their mother's death. Just at the moment they arrive in town, mysterious events begin to happen. A large black dog is reported, which attacks humans. A strange tree that moves and whispers nasty things to people shows up in the woods. Pets attack owners. And, yes, a Headless Horseman rides and begins decapitating people. Aimee and Shane befriend Stasia, the hot girl of the high school, and the three of them—who believe in the supernatural—have to figure out how to stop this from getting out of hand.

The adults, including Aimee and Shane's father, don't believe in anything paranormal. The kids, however, are chased by the black dog, find the evil oak tree, and dodge the Headless Horseman. Stasia's family has been in Sleepy Hollow from the earliest days and her house is haunted. The house ghost, it turns out, is her ancestor and he has information about what's happening in the town. It all goes back to Ichabod Crane.

This novel, like several of the movies considered, treats Washington Irving as preserving a true tale in "The Legend." Shane discovers in the town archives that the beheading victims aren't random (paging Tim Burton). Indeed, they are all descendants of the town council from when Crane lived there. The ghost reveals that Crane was an occultist. In a deal to make Sleepy Hollow prosper, his magic had spawned several monsters, some of which are now reappearing in the town. He conjured the Headless Horseman to contain the monsters he raised, but he cheated the spell to do so. While he was supposed to offer himself as a sacrifice, instead he decapitated Baltus Van Tassel. The head of the village's wealthiest family thus becomes the Headless Horseman. But that's not quite right. A demonic entity called Acephelos ("headless") is the occult power with whom Crane deals. This is a demon, not a ghost. In any case, after creating the Horseman, Crane absconded with the money. Burton's influence is heavy here.

The town elders swore, with their lives as collateral, that no descendant of Ichabod Crane would ever return to Sleepy Hollow. Just the year before this first book appeared, Kyle Newman's movie *The Hollow* used a similar plot device. Also using high school students as the main characters, the circumstances and resolution are familiar. Crane's family had changed their name after leaving Sleepy Hollow and returned to the Horseman's wrath a couple centuries later, not knowing their own identities. Also, borrowing from Burton, the Horseman kills for revenge. This is a labyrinth that circles back on itself.

According to the novel, the Horseman will end his killing spree if his head is returned, also as in Burton's film. Stasia's ancestral ghost reveals Baltus Van Tassel's identity to her and Aimee, which leads to the climax in the cemetery with the Horseman attempting to kill the kids as they search for his head. And there's a love triangle, of sorts. Both Aimee and Shane fall for Stasia. Aimee in the sense that she's her new best friend and that will be ruined by Stasia becoming her brother's girlfriend. Shane and Stasia do have feelings for each other, but both know they can't jeopardize Aimee's need for friendship and sibling support by acting on their feelings. Nevertheless, two characters crave the affections of the girl everyone wants. True lesbian love will enter the maze a bit later.

We won't follow this labyrinth into all the books of the series, but there are a few important points to stress. One is that the genre is horror. Aimed at younger readers, but horror nevertheless. A second point is that the story has its resolution in the autumn, but it's not a Halloween story. It's also a secular tale with the Old Dutch Church mentioned a time or two but playing no actual role. The plot itself appears to draw from both Burton and Newman, and perhaps Summerfield's *Sleepy Hollow High*. The scare is here to stay, but other novels will also adapt the newer scenarios offered post–Burton, fitting the cultural interests of their time. Some are based on the Fox universe mythology.

Fox Novels

After the Fox series demonstrated a new market—and a virtually new mythology, a blend of horror and romance—novels based on Mison's Crane also appeared. We've seen a graphic example in the previous chapter, but two novels from 2014 also pick up the thread. *The Secret Journal of Ichabod Crane*, by Alex Irvine and *Sleepy Hollow: Children of the Revolution*, by Keith R.A. DeCandido. Both are copyrighted by Twentieth Century–Fox.

The Secret Journal of Ichabod Crane is as close to a novelization of the first season of Sleepy Hollow as we're likely to come. Framed, as the title suggests, as Crane's diary, it narrates the events in Sleepy Hollow as they become known to Crane. It doesn't really add new episodes to the mythology, but it codifies it.

In addition to following the first season fairly closely, this novelization includes asides that make for some additional fun. Crane's interaction, for example, with a modern day Tea Partier is amusing. The novelization format serves as a brief rendition of the new mythology of Sleepy Hollow, along with its monsters. More than that, as Fox's *Sleepy Hollow* has spun out its own mythology, this novel becomes a way of piecing it together without having to watch and rewatch all the first season episodes for clues. The story is complex, as most myths are, and the only way to get through such a labyrinth is with a map.

Making the novel a diary limits the point of view to Ichabod Crane, but it also reveals some of what was only subtly present on the screen. For example, the population of 144,000 for Sleepy Hollow is explicitly explained. And even the name Sleepy Hollow is described as a corruption of a "hallow"—a sacred place—where evil sleeps. All of this helps tie the emerging mythology into a system and provides a kind of roadmap through this particular part of the labyrinth. Although Abbie Mills is part of it, the narrative is that of the white man. The second example is a more typical novel.

Keith R.A. DeCandido had a long record of writing television tie-in novels before undertaking *Children of the Revolution*, and it shows. This reads like a horror/detective novel—fast paced and suspenseful. Wedged between the first season episodes "The Golem" and "The Vessel," like the Boom! Studios graphic novel this is another spin-off story involving Crane, the Mills sisters, and Frank Irving. Like the series it weaves Revolutionary Era history into a fantasy story. In this case the coven of Serilda of Abaddon, the witch destroyed in season one's "Blood Moon" episode, steals Revolutionary Era silver medals—inscribed with runes—in order to resurrect their fallen leader. The novel doesn't focus on any one of the ensemble cast for point of view, instead making the circuit as the various characters solve parts of the mystery.

There's plenty of supernatural work afoot, and even some horror novel moments. These are sprinkled with the characteristic humor of the television show's theme of Crane being out of place in the twenty-first century. Skillfully interwoven into the storyline of season one, it's actually set earlier than Irvine's *Secret Diary*. These two novels, along with the Boom! Studios graphic works demonstrated that, had the series kept up its energy, it could've added even more significantly to Irving's myth.

The television series had spun enough of its own mythology that readers knew who Serilda was, and even the brief references to Henry Parrish in the novel would've been caught. They would know that Crane didn't yet know that Henry was his son Jeremy, and like true fans, they'd know the backstory to all the main characters. Such a mythology has an established place in the legendary constellation that Diedrich Knickerbocker sketched, first found in 1820. And it also inspired others to write in similar universes, taking the story along new paths in the labyrinth. It stands to reason that we haven't seen the last of these Fox characters.

Published, Self or Not

Even before Fox's *Sleepy Hollow* finished its brief run, modern authors began to realize the potential for recasting the story in radically new ways.

Many of them were self-published. Do you look at the publisher of the book you're reading? For most of us it makes little difference. If the subject is interesting, or the writing compelling, we tend to read on. Besides, publishing is its own labyrinth. Knowing the publisher can be important, however. Part of America's nightmare is not knowing with whom you're dealing.

The internet has enabled easy self-publishing. This isn't always bad, but it comes with some limitations. You can call your self "publisher" anything you wish, as long as it's not a name already taken. Self-published books, however, haven't been vetted by an acquisitions editor. Many haven't been seen by a copyeditor. They can go straight from the keyboard to between the covers with nobody but the author checking them. You may have run into this on occasion. If you're reading a book that's really not good at all, glance at the copyright page and see if it's self-published. Nobody has checked it out for you. But it's right up there on Amazon with the rest of them.

Of course, self-published books can be good. Historically some famous authors started out by vanity publishing—paying to have their books printed and sold. It's very difficult to break into mainstream publishing because anyone can be an author these days. If you're dedicated, you can make a living from self-publishing eBooks on Amazon.

What does all of this have to do with Sleepy Hollow? Well, there's a current literal cottage industry in taking up the reins of the Headless Horseman and writing alternative visions of what "really happened" in Sleepy Hollow. Then self-publishing them. And if you're really into it you can write a series of books on it. Some will get picked up by mainstream publishers, but most will not. As we follow the trail of literary retellings of the new millennium, which spiked after Fox's television series led America back into the maze, we'll find some self-published and some produced the old fashioned way.

"The Legend of Sleepy Hollow," like any retold story, is subject to serious modification, as we've already seen. That's the nature of myth. The original is in the public domain—Washington Irving already wrote the story, why not use it? Remember, he had no children so there are no heirs to dispute anything. These modern modifications are necessary to keep the myth alive and relevant, and some of them have spun entirely new worlds from the short story Irving left behind. Let your imagination run wild.

Looking at the publisher of the book sometimes provides important information that, even in the internet age, may be difficult to come by. Some books are published under more than one title, or as part of a series and again outside of that series. Perhaps it's happened to you as well—such situations might cause you to buy the same book twice. Besides that, we're starved for choice. There are a ton of them out there. We'll limit ourselves to a few more creative retellings here, starting with a self-published set.

Sleepy Hollow Horrors

Austin Dragon clearly loves the Sleepy Hollow story. Instead of one large novel, he has written a two-volume series, "Sleepy Hollow Horrors," focused on defeating the Headless Horseman. Both were published in 2015. The thing is, most ghost stories leave the spirit at large at the end. As horror movies demonstrate, that allows for sequels. This rendition seems to be the end of the Horseman, who, as we'll learn, isn't really from Sleepy Hollow at all. Dragon self-publishes under the sobriquet of Well-Tailored Books.

While favoring creativity over historical veracity, Dragon entered the ring with his first "Hunt for the Foul Murderer of Ichabod Crane" book centered on Ichabod's nephew, Julian Crane. Of course, in Irving's version Ichabod has no family mentioned, but new approaches expand the labyrinth in fresh directions. This isn't the only version to introduce Crane's hidden family, as we saw on Fox. Set ten years after Irving's story, *Hollow Blood* introduces Julian's quest for the murderer. The people of Sleepy Hollow don't like him, but he pairs up with the local Marshal who claims that Crane is still alive and he knows where. There are broad hints that this Marshal isn't what he says he is. The Horseman isn't based in Sleepy Hollow, but is somewhere further upstate, way to the north. Up near the Canadian border. It's revealed that the Headless Horseman is indeed real and has been demanding sacrifices to keep the peace. The Marshal has been luring in victims to the Horseman for years, and murdering them. One of those victims was Ichabod. Why the Headless Horseman can't kill them himself isn't explained, but he does use weaponized pumpkins on his prey.

The series clearly draws on Knickerbocker's original, often borrowing significant wording from Irving. It also draws elements from Burton's retelling and the Fox television series. Re-envisioning new scenarios and roles for Irving's characters is a time-honored American tradition. Julian Crane survives his encounter with the Horseman and kills the evil Marshal.

The Devil's Patch, the second volume, introduces an ensemble cast. Various rogues and adventurers, each of whom has had an encounter with something supernatural, start the book off with several potential directions to take. Julian Crane, meanwhile, has returned to Sleepy Hollow to recover from his encounter with the Horseman before setting out to kill him. He decides to recruit a posse to help him in the task and the ensemble cast joins him. Brom Bones comes along too. They ride up near Canada and come to the Devil's Patch, the place where Julian had earlier encountered the Horseman, his actual lair. After a couple of Horseman attacks, Julian realizes that the land itself has to be destroyed to stop Headless. His crew helps with this and they return home victorious. Hans Van Ripper and Diedrich Knickerbocker (also a character in the story) venture back up to the Devil's Patch, find the Horseman's head, and destroy it so that he can never return.

As I mentioned earlier, this seems to be a version informed by the Burton movie and the Fox television series. It turns more into an adventure story than horror, as it goes along. Expanding the myth, rather like Anthony Ferrante's *Headless Horseman*, it removes the entity from the Hudson Valley. And it's not a Halloween story. It's unclear what the Headless Horseman really is, in Dragon's rendition. He's semi-corporeal, and his home isn't Sleepy Hollow. It's a little uncertain what he was ever doing so far south in the first place. He transforms people into animals and has magical abilities. He's stopped when his home is destroyed. End of story.

Isn't there something terribly disturbing about having the Headless Horseman destroyed? As we saw in Chapter 3, his role as a mythical monster requires his survival. He can't be defeated, otherwise all the stories back to Irving's collapse in on themselves like a house of cards. Care must be taken with our myths.

Let's now move on to novels that focus on the long overdue women's points of view. These also began to appear only in the new millennium. Verday's series, discussed in Chapter 10, was among the first. The women's novels tend to focus on relationships instead of monsters. Honestly, however, this is what Knickerbocker was doing in the first place. These interpretations also give a fresh take on the whole myth of Sleepy Hollow and address a large part of the American nightmare.

Through Women's Eyes

Published by the small, and focused, company of Vlya Publishing—which produces lesbian literature only—Andi Marquette offered *The Secret of Sleepy Hollow* in 2015. Set in modern times, it reincarnates the story among young women. Abby (Tabitha) Crane is a graduate student at the University of Connecticut. She has come to Sleepy Hollow to do research around Halloween. (I told you it'd be back!) She meets Katie, who is a Van Tassel descendant and a grad student at Binghamton University. Katie's a local, however, and the two become lovers. This lesbian take on the myth moves in a new path through the maze.

As Abby researches at the historical society, she finds clues that Katrina Van Tassel was truly in love with Ichabod Crane. Only Ichabod was really a woman named Elizabeth in disguise. While all of this is unfolding the two contemporary young women encounter the real Headless Horseman. In interpreting Irving's version, however, they work out that Katrina drove "Ichabod" out of town to protect him and to allow Elizabeth to appear. It's still a love triangle, but the man is actually a woman.

Not only is it a love triangle, it's also another retelling with Irving's "Legend" treated as factual. The main characters are descendants of the Crane and Van Tassel families, and there is a Headless Horseman. All the same, it's a gentle retelling. A gothic romance where nobody loses their head, and where love triumphs over jealousy. It's a hopeful message in the American labyrinth and it underscores the benefits of diversity and inclusion. The tale is mythic, but with no real role for the Old Dutch Church. Often the church represents outdated social mores.

In this novel the Halloween celebration in Sleepy Hollow is a major event. Indeed, it's the focal point for Horseman activity. Although many modern retellings start to branch away, Sleepy Hollow's sibling of Halloween is never far from view.

While likely not intentionally connecting the holidays, the story ends at Christmastime as the two young women once again get together on the semester break. In bringing the story to a conclusion here Marquette perhaps unwittingly underscores Halloween's kinship to Christmas. There is reference to Thanksgiving, but the Horseman appears only on the two holidays that are tied together in the American mythical imagination.

Myths stay alive by remaining relevant. Ours is a world where women should be treated equitably with men. Where gender and sexual orientation aren't fixed categories. Where "race" is recognized as an artificial construct that oppresses. Myths that can accommodate all of that will still maintain their draw. Told through women's eyes, the story loses nothing and gains a great deal.

Another recent offering in the female viewpoint realm is *The Spellbook of Katrina Van Tassel* by Alyssa Palombo, published in 2018. A first-person account told by Katrina, this retelling brings a fresh perspective to the Hollow. Ichabod Crane is described as young and courtly—tall and gangly, yes, but no cartoon. Katrina thinks him handsome. He plays guitar and initially boards with the Van Tassel family. It's Katrina who tells him the tale of the Headless Horseman. In this version it's Ichabod who makes Katrina jealous rather than the other way around.

The Old Dutch Church features in an early episode in the novel, as

Katrina takes Crane to the family pew and observes him jealously with the other ladies afterward, on his first public outing. The church also appears at the expected wedding and baptism scenes, but does not play a major role in this vision of Sleepy Hollow. Not caring for her childhood friend Brom Bones, Katrina falls fairly instantly in love with Crane. In fact, they start having sex before his teaching duties even begin.

Sex scenes are something Irving avoided—that wasn't the kind of literature he wanted to be associated with, in his day. D.H. Lawrence wouldn't even be born for another 65 years. In any case, in Palombo, the secret couple, firmly committed in this way, recoils at Baltus Van Tassel's insistence that Katrina take Brom's suit seriously. Baltus is dismissive of anyone who doesn't have means or who doesn't know how to run a large farm. We saw this concern expressed in Pierre Gang's movie rendition, and in Zoran Janjic's before that.

Also there is an introduced female character, Charlotte Jansen, whom Brom, in younger days, accused of being a witch. She has powers and so does Katrina, as Tim Burton suggested. Katrina and Charlotte are best friends. Charlotte helps Katrina in keeping her affair with Ichabod secret but also preventing conception, using herbal birth control remedies. They ultimately don't prevent a child, however.

Caught with Katrina in their romantic outdoor hideaway, Crane is challenged to a duel by Brom, which Ichabod survives, although shot. (Some *Hamilton* influence here.) Katrina, now early in pregnancy, learns that her father has rejected Ichabod's proposal and Crane then disappears on the now canonical Halloween night. Supposing that he's run off either from having his suit rejected or to avoid responsibility as the unborn child's parent, Katrina reluctantly marries Brom so that she can keep the child and hide its true father. Together with Charlotte, Katrina continues her search for Ichabod—his hat and a shattered pumpkin had been found near the bridge. They also practice white witchcraft to try to learn of his fate.

Brom tries to become an accommodating husband, and when Katrina's daughter is born, a good father. Still experimenting with herbal concoctions, Katrina learns the truth—Brom, drunk and outraged, murdered Ichabod on that Halloween night. He's been consumed with guilt ever since, but Katrina sends him away, drunk again. Then his headless body is found, implying that the Horseman is real and has avenged the murder of Crane.

This feminist version of the story gives voice to Katrina, who, in Irving's tale, is a cipher. A "coquette," she plays with the affections of men, but seems to prefer Brom all along. Palombo subverts that telling with a complex and emotional Katrina who becomes her own woman at the end.

She loves Ichabod and barely tolerates Brom. She's nevertheless caught up in the female dilemma of pregnancy before marriage, which, in that day, was an extremely serious situation. Due, I might add, to religious outlooks.

Palombo continues the Disney innovation of the Halloween party and Burton's declarations that the Horseman resides in Hell. Locating the monster there perhaps shifts his character from ghost to demon, as we've seen. Like Irving, however, Palombo leaves the existence of the Horseman ambiguous. The locals believe him to carry victims off to Hell, but there's no certainty that he's really there. The labyrinth becomes more complex. Ichabod actually dies.

Many more Sleepy Hollow novels exist. In addition to all of the media discussed here with Knickerbocker's characters, a host of retellings focus on the Hudson Valley and its hauntings without them. They're nevertheless greatly inspired by Irving's tales. For example, consider *World's End* by T.C. Boyle (discussed briefly in Chapter 8), *The Widow's House* by Carol Goodman, and *Ghosts of the Missing* by Kathleen Donohoe. These stories too build on the legacy left by Washington Irving while not directly taking on his characters. They're still part of the mythology because of location. Indeed, the haunted Hudson is one of the greatest draws to Irving's rendition of the story. Places can retain their ghosts forever.

We've seen examples of exporting the myth to other locations but such dislocation comes at a price. "The Legend of Sleepy Hollow" is a Hudson Valley story. And location can be everything for a myth. And some mazes are actual places.

13

The Haunted Hudson

Ichabod Crane jerks awake from his fever dream. Gasping, he grasps Katrina as he bolts upright in bed. As she soothes him he tells of how his father murdered his mother to save her soul. Upon reflection he decides it is the location that is haunted. "I should never have come to this place," he declares, "where my rational mind has been so controverted by the spirit world." It is the Hudson Valley that is haunted.

Aging and already a famous but ever anxious writer, Washington Irving settled in Tarrytown for his last years. The town of Sleepy Hollow would not exist without him. In a way, he gave the Hudson Valley permission to be haunted. Openly so. Because he made it famous with "The Legend of Sleepy Hollow" others felt no shame in exploiting its reputation. As will be discussed in Final Thoughts, he wrote an essay, "Sleepy Hollow," maintaining the "truth" of the myth he'd popularized. Not only was he responsible for the town's renaming in 1996, he was singlehandedly the one who promoted its eldritch image. Or was there more to it than that?

Writers appeal to a fairly small segment of the population that reads for pleasure. You, dear reader, are in rarified company! Granted, in the days before radio, television, or internet, entertainment options were fewer. And for many, their lives didn't offer much opportunity for leisure time. Books, in early days, were not cheap (kind of like your cable bill today). Writers succeeded by connecting to the common interests of readers. Washington Irving's style is folksy and friendly. There's fun involved. He appealed to the common person. "Sleepy Hollow" captures that appeal by being about ordinary people in an ordinary, if haunted, place. And setting is vital.

Location, Location, Location

The labyrinth for the Minotaur called the Headless Horseman is Sleepy Hollow. Washington Irving perhaps unwittingly unleashed its myth. Early America was a haunted place. It's difficult to keep in mind that "Indian attacks"—and that doleful story of the unfeeling theft of their land—still took place in Irving's lifetime. We think of New York City today and the idea of Indian attacks is as fabulous as Knickerbocker's *History*. The history of the Hudson Valley, however, which Irving never wrote, came to include its own collection of ghost stories. Irving was merely the first to press. These stories, however, cling to the mythic location not only of Sleepy Hollow, but also of the entire Hudson Valley. Irving had only peeled back the corner. Sometimes those hauntings appear to burst into reality, as is the way of haunted locations. Perhaps the myth made this possible?

"The Legend of Sleepy Hollow" is written in language anybody can understand. Perhaps it's a form of populism, but the story focuses on a specific location within a defined region. A small, somewhat isolated grove. Sleepy Hollow's not really even a town in Irving's tale, it's so small. It's insular and the locals have their own soporific way of life. They get by, but they're not wealthy. One area family, the Van Tassels, prospered. The rest seem content to accept the largesse of that successful clan while not expending too much energy. They're farmers and life is bucolic.

This could describe any number of small towns in America. Horror fans know that the country outside the city is a fraught place. The landscape holds secrets, fears, and threats. This could be anywhere, but it's not. Sleepy Hollow is the particular haunt of ghosts, a land of myth. Ghosts are generally tied to locations. These are local possessions, holdings of the supernatural and uncanny.* Mazes encompass specific locations. Over time it became clear that the Hudson Valley region was filled with oddities. They, like the myth, grew scarier as time passed. We'll watch it unfold in a time-lapse way as things grow stranger and stranger in that legendary region just north of New York City. Sleepy Hollow's only one small parcel on the haunted Hudson.

It's a mistake to think all places are the same. Scientists tell us that microclimates affect specific areas only. And varying compositions of soil and bedrock make a difference. Diverging amounts of light fall due to geographical features. Foliage differs by region. We should—we need to—take seriously what the locals say about their place. They live there. They may see things that others don't. If we refuse to listen, how will we learn?

The Hudson River, which carved out this valley over eons, defines the region this chapter explores. It expands the setting in which we've been wandering, demonstrating that myths never really hold still and mazes

---

* This observation is taken from the title of Judith Richardson's excellent book on the Hudson Valley, *Local Possessions*.

grow. The uncanny can happen anywhere, but the Hudson Valley is one of those regions that many enter with a nervous glance over their shoulder, a lingering look of possibility in their eyes. There's something strange here, and not all of it has to do with Washington Irving and his Headless Horseman.

Corridors of Strangeness

What is it that makes certain areas feel uncanny? There's no scientific way to measure such a subjective thing. A haunted location to me might feel completely prosaic to you. Even so, there are some places that a large number of people experience as strange, uncanny, or haunted. Such feelings may be dismissed by skeptics, yet they persist. In the current climate haunted places are sought out instead of avoided, and the Hudson Valley is one of them. Haunting has gained some measure of respectability. Like Sleepy Hollow, it becomes what we need it to be.

Long after Washington Irving another corridor of strangeness popularized this idea. Who hasn't heard of "the Bermuda Triangle"? Debunked countless times, it just won't go away. At the root, it's the idea that certain areas may somewhat reliably bring you into the uncanny. Although no scientist will accept it, there are even now many places referred to as, for example, "The Bridgewater Triangle," or the "Green Valley Triangle." The Hudson Valley is one such region, even if it doesn't resemble a tricorne. It's more of a corridor than a triangle. Even so, it has a long history as weird. The Valley, especially from New York City to Albany—perhaps because of the size of its population—has a disproportionate tally of high strangeness reports.

Irving may have heard locals discussing ghosts during his younger years in Tarrytown. Many people were, after all, dying of yellow fever in Manhattan and elsewhere when he was sent there as a child. And there had been Revolutionary War activity both in the City and the Hudson Valley as well as other epidemics in the past. Many people had died prematurely. Not to mention the treatment of the indigenous population. And African slaves. Here Irving situates the dreamy ways of the Dutch amid forests and footways of tragedy. Isolated and familiar with spirits, their lives reflect bygone eras. They reflect the landscape with its many pathways, some of which turn unexpectedly. Avoid Major André's tree, for example.

Nostalgia about "the old ways" can be quite powerful. Clearly it motivates voters who feel the world is changing too rapidly. People often believe their childhood was simpler, a time of less worry and stress. Looking at those Dutchmen lounging about, smoking their pipes and drinking their ale, letting others do the work, offers some enticing dreams. But that lifestyle is haunted by the ghosts of the woman in white, Major John André, and a headless Hessian, among others. André and the Hessian, at least, come from elsewhere and both died in the Hudson Valley. This land seems to trap and slay outsiders, like the secret chambers of King Minos in his labyrinth.

Henry Hudson and Major André

Way back before Washington Irving, even before the New Netherlands, the strange case of Henry Hudson unfolded. Little is known of Hudson's life beyond his explorations. Sent by the Dutch, then the English, to discover the "northwest passage"—a northern water route to south and east Asia from Europe—Hudson, in command of the ship *Half Moon*, explored estuaries along the east coast of North America. Eventually he sailed up a particular river, the one that now bears his name. He made it as far as what would become Albany. The Hudson itself originates in the Adirondacks and meanders some 300 miles southward to the Atlantic in New York City. In general terms it keeps a north-south orientation and is fairly wide up to Catskill. This voyage took place in 1609, and Hudson's trading with American Indians along the way established the basis for Dutch claims to the territory since the Netherlands had financed the voyage.*

The next year Hudson sailed from and for England in *Discovery*, again seeking the fabled northwest passage. In 1611—the same year the King James Bible was published—after becoming ice-bound in Hudson Bay, his crew mutinied. Hudson, his son, and seven men were set adrift in a small boat as *Discovery* eventually set sail for home. Hudson was never seen again.

Despite the lack of details about the man, Hudson became famous. Both the bay where he was set adrift and the river he'd explored two years earlier were named for him. There's a sense of haunting to this name that's bound to accompany being abandoned in the Arctic.† Indeed, the ghosts of Hendrik Hudson—his Dutch name—and his crew led Rip Van Winkle to his strange fate. Traditional tales see the river still haunted by the intrepid explorer and his crew.

---

* Much of the information on Hudson can be found in Shorto, *The Island at the Center of the World*.
† McCorristine, *The Spectral Arctic*, 22–24.

We're on more solid historical ground with Major John André. A British officer who, with the assistance of Benedict Arnold, carried the plans of how to take West Point in his boot during the Revolutionary War, he was stopped by three local patriots near Tarrytown. One of them wore a Hessian overcoat—the Hessians keep coming back—causing the 29-year-old André to mistake him for a loyalist. Remember, German mercenaries fought for the British. The conversation led to a search that revealed the hidden plans. Some historians state that had André not been apprehended the Revolutionary War might've ended with a British victory. Such thoughts only add to the mystique of place.

Tried and hanged, John André became an element in local haunting. His death took place in Tappan, not Sleepy Hollow. Still, many seem to have regretted the likable young man's death, caught, as he was, in a spate of ill luck. Regret is part of any honest national story and its afterlives. The event merits a mention in "The Legend of Sleepy Hollow" as Ichabod Crane is on his fateful ride, and "the great tree where the unfortunate Major André was taken" is said to be haunted by unearthly moans. The story of André was even written into a play (*André*) by William Dunlap and produced in New York City in 1798, two decades before Irving's tale. In keeping with the populist element here, Dunlap reused some of the material for a later play, *The Glory of Columbia, Her Yeomanry*.* Even James Fenimore Cooper seems to have integrated André's story into *The Spy*.† Suffice it to say, the story of John André still haunted America at the time Irving wrote. And specifically haunted the Hudson Valley.

Washington Irving emphasized the strangeness of this river valley that would continue to the present day. Even with the most populous metropolitan region in the country at its southern extremity, or perhaps because of it, people see strange things all along this corridor in upstate New York.

The Haunted Valley

Washington Irving wasn't writing "horror," and yet, in a way, he was. By singling out the Hudson Valley as a haunted location, populated with the Dutch, he was establishing a kind of horror of place. This land had been taken from others. Indeed, by the time of the tale, ownership had

---

* The information on stage shows of Major André can be found in Lachman, *The Villainous Stage*.
† Burstein, *Original Knickerbocker*, 240.

been snatched from the Dutch by the English after having been taken from the First Nations by the Dutch. Such things leave scars.

More than that, Irving was imbuing the story with a deep sense of location. Labyrinths are, by definition, places. And Sleepy Hollow is a magical, haunted kind of place. The story really couldn't have happened anywhere else, which is one of the reasons that Anthony Ferrante's *Headless Horseman* movie doesn't really work. The Hudson Valley plays a part in the narrative. It's almost a character in its own right.

"The Legend of Sleepy Hollow" involves a traditional tale—the Headless Horseman preceded Irving—that lays heavy emphasis on the local landscape. In today's urban dimensions Sleepy Hollow is only about 30 miles from New York City. It would've been further in Irving's day since New York has continued to grow and expand since then. Nevertheless, a valley of the uncanny so close to a large and sophisticated metropolitan area exerts a tremendous appeal. What secrets do these hills just outside the massive city hold?

Other parts of the country may also lay claim to headless horsemen, but there's something uncanny about the wider Hudson Valley itself. There's no answering the "why" question—some places are just like that. Books that spin their yarns of Empire State hauntings always seem to end up with a corridor along the Hudson particularly populated with ghosts and other supernatural beings.

On the southern end, New York City—despite its glassy towers and modern accoutrements—is a gothic place. Wander the streets of Manhattan before daylight and you'll see. Or look closely as you stroll past the juggernauts that now form its boney spine. It's not just that the Woolworth Building makes it onto lists of "most gothic" structures, it's the feel of the place as a whole. There's no way to quantify it scientifically. Everybody's somebody in New York. Everybody's also nobody in New York. That many people compressed in such a compact area, so many people living and dying in such a small space. Lives compressed together. There's something haunting about New York City, even with all the frenetic activity both day and night.

The haunting continues up that corridor carved out by the Hudson. From the state capital to its largest city, the uncanny has taken hold. Just a few examples will demonstrate its character. As with Sleepy Hollow novels, there are many accounts of the strangeness of the Hudson Valley. This is only a sampler.

One of the oddest celebrities of the turn of the twentieth century was Aleister Crowley. Crowley is well known in esoteric circles and it may be cheating to include him here since he was a world traveler, and yet even he felt a connection with the Hudson Valley. An Englishman, Crowley

13. The Haunted Hudson

styled himself as "the wickedest man on earth" and "the beast."* He developed magic and played a hand in the forming of Wicca. Now, esoterica gets pretty technical pretty fast, but Crowley spent a biblical-sounding 40 days and 40 nights on Esopus Island in 1918 on an esoteric retreat. Esopus Island is, of course, in the Hudson. Did Crowley, affecting his demonic stylings, realize that just about a century earlier Washington Irving gave the valley its original demon?

Also in the realm of esoterica, the famous nineteenth-century Spiritualist, Andrew Jackson Davis, even earlier than Crowley, was known in the region. As a clairvoyant he came to be known as "the Poughkeepsie seer." Famous as both a healer and visionary, he made his home in the Hudson Valley.

Or consider that sprawling fiction franchise of the sixties and seventies, *Dark Shadows*. A daily soap opera created by Dan Curtis—containing 1,225 episodes, the series spun off movies, novels, and games.† The centerpiece became the conflicted vampire Barnabas Collins. Although set in Maine, the action moves to the Hudson Valley in the penultimate novel written by Marylin Ross, *Barnabas, Quentin and the Hidden Tomb* (Paperback Library). The debt to Washington Irving is spelled out clearly in the story. It stresses the haunted nature of the Hudson, and this from the point of view of a vampire! The novels did not follow the plots—often quite literate—of the television series. During the 1840 sequence of the original daily broadcast, however, the headless Judah Zachary probably derives from the Headless Horseman. The first feature-length movie in the franchise, *House of Dark Shadows* (1970), was filmed at the Lyndhurst Estate in Tarrytown. The next year *Night of Dark Shadows* was also filmed there. Once more, a strangeness came to the maze that is this valley.

This weirdness sometimes bursts its banks and spills to other locations in the eastern part of the state. We might consider this as a key location of a twilight zone. Rod Serling, creator of *The Twilight Zone*, was also an upstater. Born in Syracuse, he grew up in Binghamton. Serling's sense of place often comes through his stories, even if he was from further west, not the Hudson Valley proper. He wrote many of the episodes for the five-year run of the *Twilight Zone* series himself. Among the many tales, at least one was set on the Hudson, revisiting ground cleared by Irving. Serling's "Dead Man's Chest," from one of his *Twilight Zone* story collections, focuses on the uncanny nature of the Hudson River Valley while the characters attempt to find Captain Kidd's treasure.‡

---

* Bogdan and Starr, *Aleister Crowley and Western Esotericism*.
† Thompson, *The Television Horrors of Dan Curtis*.
‡ Rod Serling's "Dead Man's Chest" may be found in *Chilling Stories from Rod Serling's The Twilight Zone*.

Geoffrey Crayon had even presaged the premise of seeking Kidd's treasure on the Hudson in the Money Diggers section of *Tales of a Traveller*, attributed to Diedrich Knickerbocker.* The place we're from has its hooks in us and those able to express it well raise a sense of nostalgia for a location perhaps we've never been. It seems that many who've wandered this labyrinth have come to the conclusion that the Hudson was somehow haunted, both by money and ghosts.

Serling may have written a story or two about the haunted Hudson, but this region was already its own twilight zone. Serling knew that bringing large and small together created a provocative setting. Juxtapositions such as the broad contrast between large city and rural countryside so close together set the stage for ghosts and other strangeness. Consider the crossing over between the spiritual and the physical. The ghost throws a physical pumpkin that unhorses a man. No, Toto, this isn't Kansas, no matter how much dust might be in the wind.

Maverick director Ed Wood has gained a cult following largely because his *Plan 9 from Outer Space* (1959) is often considered the worst movie of all time. Undeterred by minuscule budgets and lack of success, Wood directed several bad movies that have brought him posthumous fame.† Wood fits into our Hudson story by virtue of his birth in Poughkeepsie. But this unconventional director caught the attention of none other than Tim Burton whose 1994 film *Ed Wood* starred Johnny Depp. Depp would, of course, reappear in Burton's *Sleepy Hollow* five years later. The strangeness of this labyrinth runs deep. *Plan 9* famously includes flying saucers for which you can plainly see the strings. And the Hudson Valley continues to be haunted, sometimes from above.

Hudson Valley UFOs

"Keep watching the skies," Ned Scott warns at the end of *The Thing from Another World*. As befits a corridor of strangeness, UFOs can be found hovering above the Hudson Valley. A few famous UFO flaps captured the attention of astronomer J. Allen Hynek—who earned a cameo in Steven Spielberg's *Close Encounters of the Third Kind*. Hynek, the man who came up with the "close encounters" scale, began as an astronomy professor and UFO skeptic when he was assigned to work with Project Blue Book, the official Air Force investigation into aerial anomalies. After years of this work Hynek became skeptical of the skeptics and began

---

* See Burstein, Original Knickerbocker, 182–83.
† Grey, *Nightmare of Ecstasy*.

investigating earnestly. The last book he was involved with was *Night Siege*, an account of the 1983 to 1986 UFO flap centered on the Hudson Valley. This account was published by Ballantine Books. Was Hynek aware of Washington Irving's role in all of this? Of America's ghost story being set in the same region as all this unexplained aerial activity? Things were definitely getting strange in this labyrinth.

Even after the period outlined in *Night Siege*, a few intense years were experienced in the Pine Bush region of the Hudson Valley through the nineties. Almost nightly observations of strange lights in the sky took place in Pine Bush only to taper off in the new millennium. Local author Linda Zimmerman also chronicled sightings in the region, and others have addressed how this area is a corridor of high strangeness.* Interestingly, in "The Legend" Irving wrote, "stars shoot and meteors glare oftener across the valley than in any other part of the country." Coincidence?

Those interested in such things know to look to books on local oddities, of which there are plenty, to feed that hunger. Such guilty pleasure reads of the regional uncanny point to the many strange things said to happen in the area. While mostly focusing on ghosts they inevitably include the tales of cryptids down here and UFOs above. And many center along the Hudson.

Remember Whitley Strieber's 1987 book *Communion*? The cabin in upstate New York where many of the events occurred is near Kingston. By now it should be no surprise that Kingston abuts the Hudson River.

Wherever you might be in this labyrinth, it seems pretty clear that this particular corridor, regardless of Irving, has a reputation for unexplained things in the air. Although UFOs—literally as "unidentified" flying objects—have been reported throughout history, a resurgence of modern interest came during the Second World War and especially after. Oddly, it wasn't until the eighties that the Hudson Valley became a hot spot of this particular strangeness. Then the idea continued, intermittently, through the end of the millennium. Sleepy Hollow isn't known for this particular form of haunting, but UFOs have been seen and reported in New York City, at the southern end of the valley. Even John Lennon's "Nobody Told Me" mentions them. Lennon himself had a UFO encounter before being shot to death outside Rosemary's Bramford. Watching the skies may suggest unusual connections along the Hudson maze.

---

* Zimmermann, *In the Night Sky*.

Haunting of Place

Some evocative places capture the American imagination while others do not. This sampler has shown one strange success story. Other such odd places never come to prominence. Just an example: America's original oil country. No, not Texas. Rather, the economically depressed and easily overlooked northwestern part of Pennsylvania. After Texas, Pennsylvania still supplies the second-highest amount of fossils fuels to the U.S. energy industry.* Despite the names Pennzoil and Quaker State, few people realize that those people living modestly, many near poverty, in the Appalachian foothills around Titusville, Oil City, and Franklin, are what remains of the birth of the petroleum industry. Col. Edwin Drake struck oil near Titusville in August 1859, just as America was weaning itself from sperm oil. This was only a few months before Washington Irving died. The industrial revolution was about to start and oil would literally grease the wheels of heavy industry. Alas, the petroleum pools were shallow. Places named Petroleum Center and Pithole became ghost towns in the history of what has become one of the most lucrative industries of humankind. Tourism in the area is virtually nil. No writer has arisen to center it in the American imagination. Drake was, perhaps significantly, born in the Hudson Valley, during Irving's European years.

The Hudson Valley no doubt benefited from its early literary patron's attention. It caught America's imagination very early. Washington Irving didn't invent its strangeness, but he made it respectable to talk about it. The Valley had its ghost tales. Knickerbocker merely brought them out into the open. The idea that just outside the reach of sophistication and glamor rests a tired little village still haunted by its past is cause for wonder. The Hudson Valley would maintain its uncanniness through the developing of New York into a mega-city with the railroads that stream into it, one with stations at Albany, Poughkeepsie, and Tarrytown. From the time of Henry Hudson on, this river valley took on tales of strangeness.

And it played a role in the development of Christmas, the other Halloween. "A Visit from St. Nicholas" was written by Poughkeepsie resident Henry Livingstone, Jr. Perhaps appropriate for this valley of tricksters, it was later claimed by New Yorker Clement Clarke Moore.† Things are slippery here.

Although Manhattan was a much smaller place when Irving was born and raised there, he also managed to give it a sense of identity through his

---

* https://www.eia.gov/todayinenergy/detail.php?id=49356, accessed 19 June 2024.
† Foster, *Author Unknown*, shows pretty definitively that Clement Clarke Moore was not the author of "The Night Before Christmas."

writing (principally *A History of New York*). With fewer writers attempting to do so for the Hudson Valley, and even fewer for Sleepy Hollow, his impact in these areas was so much the greater. Beyond that, however, there must be some species of authenticity to the tales—something that speaks to readers who may have never been to Tarrytown. Something that suggests that it's a haunted corridor worthy of attention.

As time went on many novels were set along the Hudson's shores and movies have been filmed or set there, evoking its atmosphere. But Washington Irving got there first. As is true of many cultural phenomena, the first to give it successful expression can't really be displaced. What did happen, however, is that his tale, in an already uncanny setting, evolved into myth. Maybe it was the larger culture becoming more accepting of spooky things—the horror genre remains an outlier, but people don't faint at the sight of Boris Karloff in Frankenstein monster makeup anymore. And Sleepy Hollow embraced this vision. In the new millennium haunting actually became an attraction. The scare was here to stay.

This chapter opens with a scenario from Tim Burton's *Sleepy Hollow*. Ichabod Crane claims not that the ghost isn't real, but that his rational mind has been controverted by the spirit world. His choice of words is significant. "Controverted" implies that the spiritual world is real and it's his mind that only reluctantly accepts that reality. And that reality continues throughout time.

Irving would become the author American literary dreamers would follow. He established his reputation with *A History of New York*, but came to fame with his Hudson Valley stories. His reputation sagged until cinema and television began to pick up the thread, re-envisioning the Hudson Valley as a place where anything might happen. Sleepy Hollow would become a real place in this haunted corridor. In the right location a Headless Horseman can become a demon, a hero, or perhaps even a UFO.

14

Unseen Ghostly Characters

The master was cruel. He abused his servants so badly that one young lady, an indentured servant from Scotland, decided to run away. The master, his anger aroused at this affront, pursued her on horseback. Enraged when he finally found her, he tied her behind his horse as he rode home. The girl couldn't keep up. She began to stumble, pleading with the master to slow down. Unmoved, he kept pace. She fell. He rode on, dragging her all the way home. Horribly mangled, the girl died from her injuries. The people in Leeds, New York, claim that her ghost may still be seen on certain dark nights haunting the road where she was murdered.

Have you ever seen a ghost? If so you're not alone. Ghosts and their hunters are everywhere these days. Ghost hunting has become big business in many countries, and in America you can actually make a living at it. For a young nation we've got more than what seems our fair share of specters. In the labyrinthian history of the United States, we've left many dead in our passage through time. Ghosts are part of our national mythology. They reveal who we are. And they inhabit Sleepy Hollow.

Horror Story

The opening scene for this chapter is from a local ghost story set in Leeds, not quite a hundred miles north of Sleepy Hollow. Like most ghost stories it's allegedly true. The cruel master is named Ralph Sutherland, or sometimes Salisbury. The tale is set in the early 1700s, well before Irving's legend. It's difficult to say how old the narrative might be since such accounts often circulate in oral tradition long before they're written down.*

What kind of story is "The Legend of Sleepy Hollow" anyway? It's not

---

* For the Leeds ghost story, "Sutherland" is given by Farnsworth, *Haunted Hudson Valley*, 58, and "Salisbury" is used by Schlosser, *Spooky New York*, 258.

really scary by today's standards, and yet it has become an adjunct of Halloween, a horror tale. Now the story and movies based on it are promoted as horror. Part of the dilemma here is that Washington Irving was dabbling in gothic themes while writing a lighthearted tale of what was likely a prank to rid a Dutch community of an outsider. And yet there's scary content here. Because of ghosts.

Horror stories—or at least stories with monsters—are as old as written stories themselves. Perhaps 4,000 years old, the Epic of Gilgamesh has monsters. Other texts from ancient Mesopotamia also have ghosts.* Those would've been unknown to Irving, of course. Besides, he was consciously trying to write American literature. Charles Brockton Brown wrote earlier gothic novels, and Edgar Allan Poe was writing his haunted tales during Irving's lifetime. Horror is defined differently by different readers, but stories with ghostly chases on a dark night would seem to fit. Even if it wasn't horror in Irving's day it is in ours. Myths meet the needs of their time.

Clearly part of the problem lies in defining horror. As an intentional genre, horror emerged only in the twentieth century.† Booksellers and filmmakers promote genres so that customers can consume more of the kind of books or movies they like. Culturally, horror had (and still has) a bad reputation. Sleepy Hollow was first known as just literature. Poe came slightly later and, joined by others, the darker strains of some of his stories coalesced into their own type, or genre, that carried on from the gothic tale. Eventually what became known as "horror" would encompass "The Legend" as well as the early gothic literature—more recent works explore such themes more intentionally. Defining horror, as a genre, still remains difficult. Ghosts, however, bring a story into the genre, gently or violently.

As we've explored this ghostly tale we've come to see that it transforms from a comic story to horror over the centuries. It became a myth along the way. We often mistakenly assume that the meaning in a story rests with the author's intent. In actual fact, any influential story gains its importance from what the society that reads it requires. The future influences the past; our interpretation of the past becomes our present reality. Later interpretations are read back into the original—adaptations are lenses that sometimes obscure what historians of literature claim as the author's likely intent. We'll never know for sure, of course, what Irving was intending for his story, filtered as it was through Geoffrey Crayon, and Diedrich Knickerbocker, as well as our own minds. For us, at this historical moment, it's a ghost story.

Stories evolve over time, and some evolve into myths. We've heard

---

* Finkel, *The First Ghosts*.
† Goldstone, "Origins of the U.S. Genre-Fiction System," 203–33.

the story many times and repeatedly met its main characters. It's a story full of ghosts. Firstly the Headless Horseman. Secondly, Ichabod Crane. But there are other implied specters in the myth. As a story that reflects its time, as well as ours, let's look at the supporting cast of metaphorical ghosts.

Cast of Thousands

Ghosts, as discussed in this chapter, are metaphors. This has been in the background all the way along. Ghosts are metaphors for those who are oppressed by a society. Peoples oppressed until backed into positions of invisibility, whose only real strength is their ability to haunt. Sleepy Hollow became mythic by reflecting the cultural moment. Our current moment is one of awakening our awareness that people of the First Nations, African Americans, women of any ethnic heritage, and many others have been systemically suppressed. They've become America's ghosts.

The ghosts of this chapter are Irving's unseen cast. Like the Horseman on the night of the great chase scene, they may not be literal ghosts. Ghost stories, however, tell us a lot about who we are and who we imagine we are. Irving lived in an America too young to have many myths. He was consciously trying to invent an American literature. Although his story has a main cast of four, let's look at the metaphorical ghosts that populate it—and by which we're still haunted.

In Washington Irving's "The Legend of Sleepy Hollow" nobody dies, apart from the Hessian—and that was in the past. If the Horseman hadn't died, however, there would've been no story. Perhaps we can deal with our own death by considering somebody else's, and what happens next. Through ghosts. But maybe some of the ghosts are of our own making. Let's start with the most obvious.

We explored the Horseman in Chapter 2. He represents the things we fear most. The foreigner. A German in Dutch territory. Human but not human, he's a monster. As a ghost he can't be killed. The people of Sleepy Hollow fear him, and if it's not Brom Bones in disguise at the end, he's a spirit that can reach across into the physical world and harm the living. Crossing borders like that is what monsters do best. Each of these aspects build him into a mythic entity. Ghosts are outsiders.

Even today as we watch politicians try to make excuses for uncivil behavior it's clear that fear of the "outsider" is alive and well. Africans have been on this continent nearly as long as Europeans have. How can they any longer be considered "outsiders"? Women have been on the planet just as long as men. What qualifies them as "outsiders"? The Spaniards settled North America before the English, or even the Dutch, arrived. How do Hispanics not belong? And what of those who were already living on this continent thousands of years before Europeans arrived—how have they been made "outsiders"? Ghosts, it turns out, are incredibly common. A nation where the original owners have become outsiders is a maze indeed.

In Irving's day certain assumptions were unquestioned: men should run things, different races fell on a scale of superior to inferior, those who owned property should have more say in how things were run. We now recognize that these assumptions were misguided. They nevertheless created a number of unconventional ghosts for this myth. One set of ghosts was assigned by nation of origin. "Nation," understood, of course, as Europeans perceived it.

Ghosts of Race

"The Legend" employs stereotypical images of the few African Americans it mentions, all in subservient roles. Irving lived before emancipation. His comic treatment of African Americans is, however, of a piece with his comic treatment of pretty much all of the characters in this story. It's still uncomfortable.

It may be that Irving first heard of the Headless Horseman from an African American mill worker in Sleepy Hollow, as we saw in Chapter 5. This doesn't excuse Irving, but he, or Knickerbocker, treats everyone as a caricature in this tale. Crane is cartoonish in description. Katrina is flirty, flittering, and scheming. Brom is all brawn and a man of little brain. Nevertheless, the African Americans' role as literal outsiders is illustrated well on Ichabod's final night in Sleepy Hollow.

During the dance, Irving wrote: "He [Ichabod] was the admiration of all the negroes; who, having gathered, of all ages and sizes, from the farm and the neighborhood, stood forming a pyramid of shining black faces at every door and window, gazing with delight at the scene, rolling their white eyeballs, and showing grinning rows of ivory from ear to ear." Are you comfortable reading that? Ghosts.

The Black people admire the whites who are all dancing on land stolen from the indigenous Americans. The African Americans, excluded, stand outside. We need a Headless Horseman to correct us. Since Headless, the Galloping Hessian is a white man. Or is he? Benjamin Franklin once wrote (I know this is a long quote but please keep with it—it's important!):

And since Detachments of English from Britain sent to America, will have their Places at Home so soon supply'd and increase so largely here; why should the Palatine Boors [that is, Germans] be suffered to swarm into our Settlements, and by herding together establish their Language and Manners to the Exclusion of ours? Why should Pennsylvania, founded by the English, become a Colony of Aliens, who will shortly be so numerous as to Germanize us instead of our Anglifying them, and will never adopt our Language or Customs, any more than they can acquire our Complexion.

Which leads me to add one Remark: That the Number of purely white People in the World is proportionally very small. All Africa is black or tawny. Asia chiefly tawny. America (exclusive of the newcomers) wholly so. And in Europe, the Spaniards, Italians, French, Russians and Swedes, are generally of what we call a swarthy Complexion; as are the Germans also, the Saxons only excepted, who with the English, make the principal Body of White People on the Face of the Earth. I could wish their Numbers were increased.*

Squirming yet? That's right, even Aryans are swarthy to Franklin's eyes. And dark was inferior. How widely held this view was is difficult to assess, but modern-day white supremacists tend toward twentieth-century German ideas of Aryans as pure white. Even ghosts have ghosts.

Looking at our Hessian what do we see? He rides only in the dark. That which we fear most is simultaneously both an insider and an outsider. We can't see his face. We can't know what he's thinking. He's a ghost for hire, loyal to the highest bidder. He lost his own head to a cannonball. Since he's not after your head, his purpose is to scare you. Remind you. He just seems to be an angry white man who can't be banished. If only he had a head we might reason with him. And since he's only out at night we can't easily assess his race.

Take a moment to think of your typical American ghost. Although special effects have offered us an eerie greenish glow once in a while, the typical ghost is white, isn't it? All souls are white. It's bodies we have trouble with, and bodies are required to harm us physically. If the Horseman can't actually take your head all he can do is scare you to death. And notice, Knickerbocker said nothing about his being after anyone else's head.

It's difficult to assess Washington Irving's level of engagement with this particular borrowed character. He doesn't even use the word "mercenary." Without him there's no story, but as he appears at the end, he's likely Brom Bones in disguise. Did Irving consider his own ghostly character real? Was he able to tame the ghost he unleashed on the country? Is he just another angry white man in disguise?

---

* "Observations Concerning the Increasing of Mankind, Peopling of Countries, &c.," available at https://www.digitalhistory.uh.edu/disp_textbook.cfm?psid=85&smtID=3, accessed 19 June 2024.

Unlike Freddy Krueger or Jason Vorhees or Michael Myers, the Headless Horseman has no name. His lack of identity also renders him unknowable. He chases those caught out at night, for any head will do. He's the ultimate capitalist.

Interlopers and Mercenaries

Mythic outsiders constitute one of our most deeply rooted and also most embarrassing fears. We seem to be stuck at childhood level. As with those wearing a mask, or lacking a head, the intentions of outsiders are hidden. One that carries a sword—or a gun in modern society—declares him or herself to be a threat. Xenophobia has deep hooks in us and we have to make constant efforts to keep it at bay. The Hessian is neither American nor Dutch, but a lover of adventure in foreign lands. You don't want him in your neighborhood. Especially if you live in a maze.

Mercenaries are fighters for hire. They don't necessarily support the cause for which they fight and they can be outbid by the enemy. This fickleness makes the Headless Horseman a kind of Judas figure. He trades in cash. Keep in mind that Major John André—mentioned in Irving's story—was a British spy in the Revolutionary War. He was working with none other than Benedict Arnold; he was an outsider. Hanged in nearby Tappan, his ghost is also occasionally used in modern retellings such as Pierre Gang's 1999 television movie, as we've seen. A mercenary, like a traitor or spy, can't be trusted. The only safe person is a Dutchman. Appropriate to myth, all the characters are metaphors.

Consider Ichabod Crane again. His name marks him as likely English. An outsider, he is also ghostly. His description as gangly and flat-headed marks him as not like the stout, round-headed Dutch. As noted in the Chapter 1, hints of his ghostly nature are dropped throughout the legend. His preparations for the Van Tassel frolic include looking in a broken mirror (bad luck, he must surely know), and in cartoons, whitening himself with chalk dust. In the end the locals say he haunts the old schoolhouse. This white outsider isn't truly welcome either. Any outsider is a ghost. The Black people are excluded from the party, except the musician, and the indigenous Americans are mentioned only in passing as the locals cluelessly ponder why their land bears ghosts. Why so many ghosts?

Before Fox's *Sleepy Hollow* series began in 2013, African Americans held only a few servant roles in the tale, if they appeared at all. The young boy—not in school, note—who brings Ichabod his invitation is Black. He's portrayed this way in Edward Venturini's *The Headless Horseman*, grinning at the white schoolmaster's boon. The Van Tassels seem to be kindly masters, but the fiddle player is the only Black allowed inside for the party. "Entertain us," you can almost hear the landed gentry say.

Historians know that you can't blame people of the past for not holding modern views. We still find it hard to believe that they couldn't just open their eyes to see that "superior races" are only a way of guarding privilege. This idea, however, was strongly backed by that labyrinth-building institution—the church. Insisting that the tower of Babel myth means God wants races to be kept separate, and that those living in Africa were cursed by Noah when only eight people existed on the planet, those who read the Bible literally cast their vote with white supremacy. As with manifest destiny, who were the privileged to question their God-given good fortune? Mercenaries are brought in to police this privilege. And this privilege applies only to men.

Ghosts of Gender

As Ichabod whiles away his evenings with the old Dutch wives, he hears the story of the woman in white. Frozen to death while trapped outside at Raven Rock, she shrieks in storms. Nevertheless her story, like her voice, is drowned out by that of the Headless Horseman. Such is the fate of the women early in this myth, ghosts all.

The old Dutch wives, Knickerbocker suggests with a grin, are as credulous as Ichabod. They persist in their superstitious beliefs. The only woman who has an "active" role—and this is typical of Irving—isn't so active after all. Katrina Van Tassel is a prize to be fought over and won. Indeed, the other three main characters are all involved in just that struggle. This love triangle silences her voice, loses it in the wind. What does Katrina want? Does she even have a say? She's wanted as a possession. Ichabod sees her as ready cash. And Brom's motivation? Well, it's never really revealed, but ownership is the result. She'll be a ghost of her girlhood self.

Only in the twenty-first century would the myth of Sleepy Hollow really open up to women. Women would write novels featuring Katrina, and television would add strong female characters. Even at the point this book was published equal rights for women in America remain in doubt. Any society that makes ghosts of half its population will indeed be haunted.

Irving was a lifelong bachelor who claimed never to have understood women. Indeed, he seems to have come close—at least in his own mind—to marriage twice. But the world of Mary Wollstonecraft and her daughter Mary Shelley, was a world where women were ghosts. Men owned property. Men made political decisions. Whether women were even consulted was up to men. Even in America today, many men want the right to decide what happens to women's bodies. We continue to make ghosts. And if we listen closely, we can still hear them screaming before the storm. These are the building blocks of a gothic myth but they also have real life consequences.

Where Ghosts Lead Us

While we can't blame Irving for accepting the outlook that prevailed in the eighteenth and early nineteenth centuries, we can wonder why it took so long for a *Hamilto*n-esque artistic revisioning of race and gender in early America. No, *Hamilton* isn't history, but neither is Sleepy Hollow.

Of course, we have only four central characters. Only one is directly said to be a ghost. Two others may be as well. As we attempt to find our way out of this morass, the nature of ghosts might offer some guidance. We all end up dead. Until then we wander around in a maze of our own making. Why not recognize that everyone is trying to get by and that we all should have a fair chance to try? Even Ichabod Crane couldn't tell anything about the Headless Horseman at first sight except he was large and ill-proportioned. Perhaps we can learn something from this ghost. Katrina should have a say regarding what happens to her, otherwise she too becomes a ghost.

The stories we tell make us who we are. America has grown to have so many ghosts that one reality television show alone can't contain them all. Certain it is, the Headless Horseman wasn't the only American ghost of its day. Irving wasn't even living in America at the time he wrote Sleepy Hollow. Yes, it was a young nation, but it had already begun the processes of genocide and slavery and male entitlement. The oppression of others always leaves ghosts. And ghost stories. It leads to narratives that we can't help telling and retelling. Dressed in humor, "The Legend of Sleepy Hollow" somehow makes this easier while still lending its story to, if not inventing, a spooky autumn myth. Although written with a smile, there were nonetheless serious ghosts waiting to be encountered in this maze. Horror was just waiting to happen. In fact, it already had.

Irving, unlike many of America's other early writers, relatively prospered in his lifetime. Not truly wealthy, he was well-off. Interest in his most famous story has waxed and waned in social consciousness, but when it ascends it bears the "made in America" label. Mythic, and perhaps best known now in moving picture form, it was among the early tales selected for cinematic treatment. A legend endlessly remade, becoming more famous with each retelling. America's ghost story. Those ghosts aren't always who we think they are.

Ghosts can be leaders. They help us think through our actions without requiring us to accuse ourselves. Knickerbocker wasn't known for social commentary that addressed race except that, as a descendent of the English who took New Amsterdam from the Dutch, he gently chides that "other race." He does so from afar and perhaps he realized that his own people could receive the same treatment. Perhaps he was suggesting we follow the lead of ghosts. And the most prominent ghost in Sleepy Hollow doesn't have a head.

The myth continues to revisit Sleepy Hollow in new forms. Now as we start thinking about exiting this labyrinth, it's time to consider the most recent of adaptations. Sleepy Hollow continues to have importance for understanding equity and inclusion in the post–Fox world.

Final Thoughts

There's a monster in the woods of Sleepy Hollow. Its shape is ever-shifting, smoky even. It chops heads. It kills children. It's not the Headless Horseman. No, the monster is Ichabod Crane.

This book has been a mere sketch of Sleepy Hollow and its labyrinthine influence. Much more could've been written. Apart from new annotated editions, Sleepy Hollow has been more or less ignored in book-length treatments. It is my hope that this effort opens some conversation on it.

Washington Irving was, and always considered himself, an American first. How do Americans write myths? They engage religious ideas. And they stay relevant. Using Halloween's a good idea. We have seen how Sleepy Hollow adapted to changing outlooks on youth, race, and gender. We're reluctant to let this myth go because it still speaks to us. And it's speaking still.

Into the 2020s

Moving into the second decade of the third century of the tale—remember, "The Legend of Sleepy Hollow" was published in 1820—a renewed spate of afterlives has begun. Entertainment continues to shift to accommodate streaming and media produced by streaming companies and internet platforms—such as YouTube—providing even more venues for content. Besides all of this the older, continuing technologies of novels, movies, and television haven't ceased to retell Irving's myth. New versions of "Sleepy Hollow" range widely, with some, however, remain mostly faithful to the original.

The decade following Fox's successful series so far has seen many new presentations of the legend. Jonathan Kruk, for example, is a well-known local storyteller in Tarrytown. He has written a book on local folklore and his one-man retelling of "The Legend" was filmed, significantly, in the Old

Dutch Church. This autumnal repeat event was filmed for release in October 2020, the bicentennial of "Sleepy Hollow." It was directed by Guido Jiménez-Cruz and aired under the title *The Misadventures of Ichabod Crane*. We've seen "Misadventures of Ichabod Crane" before in this maze.* At 21 minutes this rendition is ideal for internet viewing. Produced in part by Historic Hudson Valley, it's a one-man show, often close to Irving's actual wording. The only part filmed outside the church is the chase scene. Otherwise, the Old Dutch Church reclaims its prominence here. Even as we become less religious we still find ourselves inside church walls. This is a gothic labyrinth.

Noteworthy here, apart from the atmospheric candlelight, the minimal, tasteful guitar music, and the dramatic retelling by Kruk himself, is that the only special effects—those of the chase scene—involve a flaming jack-o'-lantern thrown at Ichabod's head. It seems difficult to get back beyond Disney's major innovation, making this a Halloween tale (even though Fox moved away from that), making every day Halloween. Elizabeth L. Bradley, whose annotated editions of the *Sketch Book* and *History of New York* are published by Penguin, served as the screenplay advisor. The production values largely reflect those of an intimate personal reenactment.

Speaking of Kruk, he also wrote the foreword to a 2021 horror novel, *The Unhallowed Horseman* by filmmaker Jude S. Walko. Walko published his novel through Blue Falcon Productions LLC, his privately owned small business for filmmaking. Set in the present day, this is a horror novel through and through. It's clearly influenced by Burton and Fox. And it goes beyond them. With explicit sex and drugs, this is adult fare. Walko understands dysfunction and puts it on every page. There's even a corn maze for labyrinth fans.

Vincent Douglass was a neglected child, now thoroughly medicated and in high school. Lorraine (Rayne) Constance, the best-looking, but innocent, girl in Sleepy Hollow, finds him attractive. The sheriff is a descendent of Brom Bones and there's an Unhallowed Horseman on the loose. People are killed and Vincent, known to be unstable, is a suspect. As the tale unfolds the backstory of the Horseman is revealed; shot by a cannon hidden by some Revolutionary War patriots, he returns once the moon is right to seek his revenge on the descendants of those who killed him. The revenge theme, as we've seen, derives from Tim Burton.

Vincent is a fan of the Horseman, but his emotional troubles mean he's medicated out of his mind. (He's another ghost.) The police don't like

---

* The other "Misadventures of Ichabod Crane" was the television cartoon by Vic Atkinson in 1979; see chapter seven.

him and although Rayne finds him attractive, she's also a bit afraid of him.

The Horseman appears and the killing starts. Clearly supernatural, he shows up in several of the places Vincent is, pursuing him. Then, on Halloween night, which Sleepy Hollow really celebrates, the killing spree begins in earnest. It only ends when Vincent is shot since apparently he's been the murderer all along, or somehow linked to the Horseman. Very gritty and nihilistic, this version of the story again treats Irving's tale as past fact, but acted out in the modern period. And back on Halloween.

Horror is the only appropriate genre for this self-published rendition of the tale. It's difficult seeing any treatment for adults, after Burton, taking it out of the genre completely. Comedy isn't completely out of the running, however, as we'll see shortly.

Christina Henry, who is known for retelling fairy tales and classic stories, published her take on "The Legend," also in 2021. *Horseman: A Tale of Sleepy Hollow* is set two generations after Ichabod Crane and Brom Bones and Katrina Van Tassel, but they all appear in the narrative. According to Irving's story—and this is often presented in cinematographic treatments—Brom and Katrina wed. The narrator of this tale is Ben, who in today's terms would be considered transgender. He (his preferred pronoun) is the grandchild of Brom and Katrina.

Brom and Katrina's son, Bendix, was killed by a monster in the woods. Bendix's son, Benite, was raised by Katrina and Brom since his mother had also died (of disease). Several years later, the monster is again active in the woods. Benite, simply called Ben by everyone, is the monster hunter. And he's also hunted by the monster. Supernatural forces are never fully explained in Henry's continuation of the story, but she reinforces the uncanny atmosphere of the Hudson Valley. The woods are magical, literally. This is something that those who live there already know.

Henry is a master of magic realism. There really is something in the woods of Sleepy Hollow and it's taking children's heads. Some influence from Tim Burton's film version is found here, but the story has its own trajectory and inner logic. While out in the forest with a friend one day, Ben learns that a boy has lost his head in the Sleepy Hollow woods. Nothing like this has happened for about 14 years, so the villagers are quite upset. A monster has returned. It's not the Horseman, however. As Henry tends to do in her re-envisioned tales, she upsets expectations of how the characters act, as well as their motivations. The story is moved along by Ben's solving a mystery while avoiding the suspicions of the villagers for his unconventional behavior.

Ben actually sees the monster, but nobody will believe him. Not until it's too late. The one person who does believe is Katrina, Ben's grandmother. She, however, wants Ben to act like a girl because he was born biologically female. Katrina wants him to stay home and learn sewing and cooking. Ben's hero, however, is Brom. He's a good man, if rowdy. He married Katrina for love, not wealth. Ichabod Crane does appear, later in the story, but he's no protagonist. A cloudy, devious entity of the forest, he is the monster that has been haunting the woods, out for revenge on the Van Brunt family. Once again, revenge.

There are a couple of evil entities in Sleepy Hollow, including another introduced character named Schuler de Jaager. He and Ichabod are both entities that represent hatred and jealousy while the Headless Horseman remains an elusive supporter of balance in these supernatural woods. The mysterious evil also leads to Katrina's death, as well as the destruction of the Van Brunt home. De Jaager had transformed Ichabod into some kind of demon after Brom, disguised as the Horseman, scared him off.

Unlike many of the other adaptations we've seen, Henry's could be fit as a sequel after Irving's story without really changing anything in the original. It comes from a different point of view, but it doesn't contradict Irving. It's Knickerbocker-plus. From the beginning Brom outshines Ichabod, reminding readers that this was a love triangle story, and, in fact, Bones wins. We're accustomed to Ichabod's chase, his fear. We are the person on horseback, the interloper being run from this tight-knit community with its ghosts and beguiling lovers. Whether or not Irving's Horseman was Brom, Bones marries Katrina in the end.

Some renditions, as we've seen, shift this around so that Crane wins out. He becomes Katrina's spouse—this is implied in Henning Schellerup's television version and in Burton's retelling. Between the strange figure cut by Crane, the "coquette" Katrina, and the ghostly Horseman, Bones often gets short shrift. Henry makes him a rather more heroic figure in her reimagining of the tale, and it's worth considering the man who actually won—if he ever really lost—Katrina's heart.

Rewind back to Disney for a moment. Remember, nobody has any speaking roles. Crane croons and laughs, and the Headless Horseman also laughs (in a much more sinister key). Katrina and Brom say nothing, apart from his musical number about the Horseman. Disney's Brom prefers punching. Although he wins in the end, Bones is a dupe to the antics of the more sophisticated Ichabod. The myth continues.

The Schellerup television version, following on from Disney's non-vocal, giving-dogs-and-horses-alcohol Brom, presents Dick Butkus as an oafish Van Brunt. He brags about his orneriness and surliness. He's no catch. Although in the end, at least he's a man, but not for Katrina. Moving down the generations, the issues shift. The myth maintains its relevance by introducing a transgender protagonist. Sleepy Hollow's maze accommodates all who want to be part of America's ghost story.

What if—as Henry asks, as did Pierre Gang and Rick Ramage—Brom was the wronged man? He has loved Katrina from the beginning, but she sees the advantages to using Crane to make him jealous. Having Katrina's best interests at heart, *Horseman* suggests, Bones had purer motives than Crane. Even in Irving's version Ichabod saw the relationship in terms of his own personal gains. It's important to hear Brom's voice. And that of his offspring.

Henry's retelling of the story continues the long tradition of making the afterlives of Sleepy Hollow relevant to contemporary America. It speaks to where we are. Not only should female voices be heard, but trans voices as well. There's a place for everyone in Sleepy Hollow. And Henry lays out new paths in this labyrinth. Not all nightmare monsters are what they seem. Learning to accept "outsiders" instead of caving in to our fears when not all people are the same is one way to wake from this nightmare. It may be the only thread Ariadne left, leading out of this labyrinth.

The New Diabolic

In October of 2022 Global Asylum released an 84-minute movie *Headless Horseman*. The poster suggests an updated Sleepy Hollow—flaming jack-o'-lantern held by a "horseman" on a motorcycle—but the story isn't connected. Except by Disney magic. If we're still counting feature-length treatments this is number ten, maybe.

So this story is about Brandon and Sophia, two young people in love in Los Angeles. She has a past, a drug-dealer boyfriend named Angel. Angel kills Brandon, but Brandon makes a deal with the Devil as he's dying to sell his soul for a chance to get Sophia free. He's given a magical Freddy Krueger glove and a flaming pumpkin head, because, well, it happens on Halloween. He fails to free his girl by the deadline. Sophia, kidnapped, is being sent to Mexico on a drug deal, and sells her soul to the Devil in exchange for Brandon. When Angel and his goons are all killed, she ends up shot and the restored Brandon asks to make yet another deal with the Devil. In exchange for Sophia's life, he'll ride around pumpkin-headed and Krueger-gloved to harvest souls for Satan.

Okay, we get it. "Angel" is really a demonic character and the Devil isn't such a bad guy. That's about the limit of sophistication here. Yet even so, this story hasn't escaped Disney's version of the Legend. It is, however, horror. And it has a twisted love triangle.

What of the Disney magic remains in this low-budget film by Jose

Prendes? To lure viewers in the movie takes Disney's flaming jack-o'-lantern head, the rider on a "steel horse" (with apologies to Bon Jovi) image, and the title *Headless Horseman*. In as far as it resembles anything, it's *Ghost Rider*, but the story is thin, even so. Our cultural expectations keep us coming back for more, even if it's just false advertising. This is an American maze, after all.

One thing this horror flick has going for it is religion being dead center. It's supernatural horror with repeated deals made with the Devil, a priest who attempts to block the dark lord, and it also uses holy ground. The evil can't operate on church property, but this isn't of course, the Old Dutch Church. Even though this isn't our Headless Horseman, the film demonstrates that religion and horror work together, even if for cheap. And it shows how horror has assimilated the concept of "headless horseman" as a stock monster, which can be completely divorced from Sleepy Hollow. But at a price. It's almost funny. And the stories in this maze keep coming.

A Final Novel Approach

On the literary front in autumn 2022, Serena Valentino's *Raising the Horseman* galloped off the presses. This particular press was Disney Hyperion, continuing Disney's oversight of Irving. It feels like we're coming full circle. Irving's story's in the public domain, but Disney has been involved with it for many decades now. Valentino has been writing a Villain series, many of the volumes taking on the point of view of someone other than the typical protagonist in folkloric or fairy tale settings. In this respect, she's using a similar approach to Christina Henry, but pitched at younger readers. Like Henry's *Horseman*, Valentino's *Raising the Horseman* focuses on a biologically female descendent of Katrina Van Tassel and retells the story from a woman's point of view. A young woman, in this case.

In Valentino's Sleepy Hollow, set in the modern day, all the first female descendants of Katrina Van Tassel keep this name and inherit the substantial estate the original Katrina inherited from her father. Kat—the current Katrina—is a high schooler attempting to negotiate being a strong-willed young woman shackled to an ancient tradition where she holds an expected role. Her situation resembles that of the first Katrina, as she learns from reading her diary. Their lives follow a similar pattern as Kat's boyfriend Blake faces a rival in a relative of Ichabod Crane. Isadore Crow (renamed as in the Kyle Newman movie and "The Hollow" novel series), the young Crane returned to Sleepy Hollow, makes for an interesting twist on the love triangle as she and Kat discover a special connection. And it shows how ghosts speak.

There's clearly influence from the Disney, Gang, Burton, Newman, and Henry adaptations of the legend. Some of the scenes use the Disney embellishments, such as the frogs croaking "Ichabod" and the wind through the reeds. Gang first played on the idea that Katrina overheard Ichabod dismissing her dreams, and Burton gave the story a tree that bleeds when cut. Henry offered a descendant of Katrina, but one battling an Ichabod who was far from a protagonist. Still, Valentino's story is told with a great deal of originality and heart. It is very definitely a Halloween-based rendition, even going to the point of explaining some of the customs of the holiday. It's a blending of much that has gone on in this maze before. There are new paths yet to discover.

Valetino's story is a mix of romance and horror. Now that Sleepy Hollow has made its myth horror, it's also moving in other directions to blend with the genres of the time. After all, young adult literature has been blending horror and romance since Stephenie Meyer offered young readers *Twilight*. And even earlier in Marylin Ross's *Dark Shadows* series. Valetino's is a different kind of twilight zone, where unexpected mixes make the story what we need it to be at this point in time.

At the time of this writing, we know that Lindsey Beer is slated to direct a new Sleepy Hollow reboot. According to IMDb a horror film *Ichabod Crane* is also in development. The labyrinth and the nightmare that fuel it never end. And the mythology continues to grow. And it can still make us laugh.

The New Comedic

Many adaptations of Sleepy Hollow have laid out new pathways in the maze during the first two centuries of its life. Cartoons and after school specials gave way to serious drama with bloodshed and some unexpectedly scary monsters. Streaming has grown to a point that internet media could bypass television and the big screen altogether.

In 2022, starting in August, Shipwrecked Comedy ran a ten-episode mini-web-series titled *Headless: A Sleepy Hollow Story*. A YouTube comedy troupe initiated by Sinéad Persaud, Shipwrecked began with a Poe-themed sketch and has moved on to larger productions. *Headless* is a web series that was crowdsourced with a Kickstarter campaign and posted on YouTube. Directed by William J. Stribling, it envisions Ichabod Crane as a young professional coming to Sleepy Hollow to start his life over and ending up roommates with the Headless Horseman. And more. Brom Bones and Katrina Van Tassel are also there. As an obvious spoof, it's not a "serious" contender for the way the story "actually goes," but the set-up is highly original and shows how horror still blends well with comedy in America's myth. And remains relevant by addressing our ghosts. It also invites Rip Van Winkle back in.

Crane (Sean Persaud, also the co-creator and writer of the series) is the new middle school science teacher in Sleepy Hollow. His rent ends up becoming more than he can afford with his landlord, Douffe Martling (Joanna Sotomura), adding on extra charges and fees, so he puts up posters for a roommate. Missing posters are also displayed for Rip Van Winkle, who was attacked in the opening sequence. We don't see his assailant. Crane meets Katrina Van Tassel (Mary Kate Wiles) at a bar/drug store but she's catty about giving him any information. She goes by "Kat." Her friend and co-employee Matilda Bishop (co-creator Sinead Persaud) is a witch. Since he's been invited to the mayor's autumnal gathering, Crane attends only to learn that Baltus Van Tassel already knows who he is. He also meets Geoffrey Crayon, the town doctor and husband of Douffe. The names of these characters are borrowed from both Irving himself and some of the retellings over the years. Remember, Geoffrey Crayon was the pen name Irving used for *The Sketch Book*. Doffue Martling is one of the minor characters in that story and "Doffue Van Tassel" narrated Shelley Duvall's version.

Brom Bones (Gabe Greenspan), the gym teacher, watches him attentively as Crane learns that Kat is Baltus' daughter. Jealous as always, Brom tells Crane about the Headless Horseman, but Ichabod doesn't believe

Sean Persaud as Ichabod Crane in William J. Stribling's *Headless: A Sleepy Hollow Story* (© 2022 Shipwrecked Comedy, All Rights Reserved).

him. Being a science teacher he's naturally skeptical. Starting with Schellerup, and made mythic by Burton, the skeptical Crane fits the current millennium well. Brom attempts to scare Ichabod on his way home from the party by wearing a cheesy costume with a pumpkin head and charging him, but the real Horseman rides up. Crane and Brom cower as he holds out Crane's flyer for a roommate. So runs episode one.

Narrated by Diedrich Knickerbocker (Jon Cozart), accompanied by his ukulele, the series features a witch (Matilda) and several other quirky characters. It's not explicitly a Halloween tale, although there is a scene that provides a Halloween setting. And it utilizes several horror film references, including *Ringu* (1998). Both Diedrich and Matilda have larger roles in the plot. There are several recurring characters and most of them play a part in the resolution of the story.

Following the initial episode, the story goes in a completely different direction from Irving, of course. The missing Rip Van Winkle, we learn, was the previous science teacher. The Headless Horseman magically changes into the person whose head he wears (with Matilda's help), leading to unexpected scenarios that fuel the comedy and solve the mystery. Ichabod has, naturally, fallen for Kat. She seems to reciprocate but Crane learns that her father murdered his own former assistant. Along the way we also learn that the Headless Horseman was around long before the Revolutionary War, originating in the seventeenth century. A witch, who was Crane's direct ancestor, created the Horseman from Henrietta Hudson, wife of explorer Henry and founder of Tarrytown. As in Burton, there are multiple witches in Sleepy Hollow's history. Henrietta was, according to the plot, written out of history and now reclaims her place in it.

It turns out that Rip had decided to run for mayor the previous year. Baltus, rather than face a popular rival, tried to poison him but Kat accidentally drank his glass. Matilda, Kat's best friend and friend of the family, was able to keep Kat alive for a year by using a soul substitute—none other than Rip. He's been kept asleep for a year and Kat, who's technically dead, needs a new soul. Ichabod. Matilda, thinking she might be able to keep Kat alive and end the headless hauntings, returns Henrietta's head, but this means Kat is truly dead. Hudson congratulates Crane on being a noble descendant of her seventeenth-century friend. Knickerbocker, who was killed in the melee, becomes a new town ghost, and Crane gets a bike that he names Gunpowder.

There's a ton of development in this charming new version. Based initially on a story by Sinead Persaud, it's very inclusive and very internet savvy. The Horseman is a Horsewoman. Many cast characters are of Asian and African descent. Rip becomes the new mayor after Baltus is exposed, and he is Black. This is like Fox's *Sleepy Hollow*, only reverted to comedy.

And the real villain is Baltus Van Tassel, as Burton's Crane falsely surmised. The Sleepy Hollow myth is what we need it to be at any given time. Ghosts are finally having their say.

Full of references to current internet culture, the series neatly fits Sleepy Hollow into a contemporary setting. It is a completely secular rendition, with no Old Dutch Church—really, no religion at all. During a play telling the history of Sleepy Hollow, it's clear that *Headless* is nevertheless one of the better researched adaptations regarding local history. And that it also feels free to make up some of that history.

Although nobody is likely to suppose that this is a faithful telling of Irving's tale, this series has entered the pastiche of America's myth. Indeed, it has laid out its own new maze. Like other twenty-first-century entries into the growing Sleepy Hollow mythology, it demonstrates how current the ideas still are. They can be crowdsourced and posted for free on the internet and come out amazingly fresh. This creative retelling is perhaps the closest to the spirit of Irving among modern adaptations. Nobody mentions Irving since this is a re-enactment, as well as a re-envisioning of the legend.

The perfect comedic timing makes this ten-episode version fun and it brings Irving's two best known stories together again. Perhaps the Fox series inspired this, or perhaps it goes back to Zoran Janjic and even before. These two supernatural tales amid Crayon's mostly prosaic sketches, showed their kinship early on. Both claimed Knickerbocker authorship. Both had ghosts. And both were fun to tell and retell.

Headless is a satire of a satire. It reminds us that although spooky, Sleepy Hollow was written for fun. And if you're not enjoying yourself, why are you here? Sleepy Hollow's mythic draw includes smiles as well as shivers.

All the episodes of *Headless* together run for just over two hours and 22 minutes. Like Fox's *Sleepy Hollow*, they demonstrate that Irving's tale can be serialized and taken into unexpected territory. *Sleepy Hollow* took the story into television horror territory. *Headless* made it web-based and moved it back toward comedy. This tug-of-war between comedy and horror has been going on since Burton and others envisioned Sleepy Hollow as actual horror, beginning in 1999. Scary elements had been part of the legend from the beginning, but so had humor. The story is now see-sawing between them.

The Myth of Sleepy Hollow

In 1839, nearly 20 years after "The Legend of Sleepy Hollow" was published, Irving submitted an essay called "Sleepy Hollow" to *Knickerbocker Magazine* under the pen name Geoffrey Crayon, as mentioned a couple of times above. *Knickerbocker* was started by Irving's friend, Charles Fenno Hoffman, not Irving himself. By this point in his life, Irving had published ten books, one of them in four volumes. It was becoming clear to him by now that Sleepy Hollow would be his legacy. Sixteen years later part of this "Sleepy Hollow" essay was repurposed in *Wolfert's Roost*, his penultimate book and final collection of sketches. By 1855 he may have hoped his last book, the five-volume *Life of George Washington* (his namesake) would be his landmark. Nevertheless, by including his own Sleepy Hollow mythology in "Wolfert's Roost: Chronicle III" he may have been admitting something to himself. One of his earliest pieces was his best. Notice also that he never wrote such a reminiscence for Rip Van Winkle.

The essay "Sleepy Hollow" shows Irving consciously building his own mythology around the story. Writing as Geoffrey Crayon, he again takes up his fictionalized persona of Diedrich Knickerbocker as part of his recollections. He reflects on his boyhood time in Sleepy Hollow—not yet a town, remember—and how an African American mill worker first told him of the Headless Horseman. Some half-century on, the memory might be unreliable. Still, if the first telling really made an impression on him—we can all remember who told us our first scary stories—this may well be accurate. In any case, he realized its mythic potential, its reflective properties. In "Wolfert's Roost," he makes this a reminiscence of Diedrich Knickerbocker, stating that the story of Ichabod Crane and the Headless Horseman is true.

Irving understood the value of maintaining his fiction, rather like horror movies that claim to be based on true events. He admitted learning the story from others, but never denied it was true. This technique remains widely used in horror today. The story may have been enhanced as he gained experience. Traveling around Europe as a younger man, he collected folk stories, some of which he adapted into sketches. He made Sleepy Hollow an essential American tale.

"The Legend of Sleepy Hollow" has indeed become an integral American myth. California, Illinois, and Wyoming each have a small town named Sleepy Hollow. Ichabod Crane, in a Halloween *Saturday Night Live* sketch, encounters the Headless Horseman and immediately begins asking about the potential of using his decapitated head for oral sex. The webcomic *The Adventures of Dr. McNinja* has an episode where Benjamin Franklin turns into a headless horseman. Chris Ebert's short story, "A Hollow Sleep," takes the Horseman's headless point of view.* The list of brief Sleepy Hollow references and asides is vast.

---

* Chris Ebert's story is found in *Ophelia and Other Weird Tales*. Ironically, the Horseman dresses as a clergyman; religion remains part of this maze. For the Headless Horseman episode in Dr. McNinja see *Operation Dracula! from Outer Space*, pp. 107–139.

The draw of the name has even grown to the point that invoking "Sleepy Hollow" is enough to lure viewers in. For example, in 2021 Amazon Prime streamed a series titled *Legends of Sleepy Hollow*, which had nothing to do with the Washington Irving story. A series of shorts, based on "urban legends"—few that some of us had even heard before—it was a horror series with no connecting thread. It had, however, name brand power. Another television series, *Sleepy Hollow Theater*, which ran from 2008 through 2015, hosted horror movies, again, on a different path than we've been on here.

Now that we've watched a bunch of movies—comedies, horror, children's—and some television—and read a ton of novels, and even glimpsed Sleepy Hollow on the web, what do we really know about the story? What have we learned about this maze? How did Sleepy Hollow become one of America's most prominent myths?

Myths are a form of religion. Sleepy Hollow has tapped into that vein and has grown from it. It remained minor throughout the twentieth century, but at the cusp of the millennium, all of that shifted. Now Sleepy Hollow keeps reappearing, often supercharged with religious ideas. And the Headless Horseman has become central to the story. We want to understand this demon who bursts from Hell to drag us back with him. Or who wants to begin the apocalypse. Crane and Mills will thumb through the Bible to try to understand what this Horseman really wants.

Sleepy Hollow is a distinctly American tale. This book has been an appreciation of Knickerbocker's legend and many of its mythic afterlives. What it's come to mean. Perhaps what it will come to mean. The point of a labyrinth isn't to solve it, but to get out of it alive and to learn something along the way. I've tried to unspool Ariadne's red thread, or green ribbon, as we've explored some of the complexities of this apparently simple story. Some, like Jack Torrence, freeze to death lost in a maze. But what is this labyrinth? It's the American mythic tradition.

That mythic tradition still struggles with the nightmare of racism and sexism. It repeatedly tells the story, reminding us of the work we still have to do. At the same time it reminds us of a day when the illusion of "all is well" could prevail. It grew up with Halloween, when we all wear masks. Only there's a Headless Horseman afoot. We should never forget that.

The purpose of this book hasn't been to evaluate Irving as a writer. He was definitely an early American pioneer in that regard whose star, to return to an earlier metaphor, has risen in popular culture but has stayed steady to low among academics. Not many books are written about Irving. Those that are tend to be indulgent, or even condescending. Irving had no roadmap to follow through the maze as he tried to make a living by writing. We, in our turn, will be judged by future standards, if we survive this nightmare. Irving's cultural star has most definitely benefited from the internet.

Disney gave the world a canonical version of "The Legend." Tim Burton's movie brought Sleepy Hollow back to life for many adults. The internet was in its infancy then. Although it was short lived, the Fox television series led the now fully established internet to take the idea and run with it. Irving makes only occasional cameo appearances in his story because the myth has moved beyond him. Sleepy Hollow has become part of America's Halloween, and not always kid-friendly while still appealing to the young. It has spawned wikis and fan clubs. No doubt, future renditions will keep this kind of appreciation coming. Such is the way with genuine myths.

This labyrinthian book is the story of how Americans become aware of Sleepy Hollow as a children's story and how many continue to follow it into adult horror. They find meaning along the way. They learn to listen to ghosts. Children's versions continue to appear. Adult versions as well. And now, especially, young adult. It has many media faces. Faces perhaps without a head. And through it all, religion has become entangled in its myth. This book is a reflection of what it means to be an American in all its complexity and diversity.

Useful Reading

Adhyanggono, Gerardus Majella, and Fransiska Linda Marcelina. "The Gothic Elements in Tim Burton's (1999) *Sleepy Hollow the Headless Horseman*: A Literary and Cinematic Aspect Analysis," *Celt* 13, no. 2 (December 2013): 239–254.
Allen, Frederick D. "Contributions to the New England Vocabulary," *Dialect Notes* 1 (1896): 18–20.
Allen, Janie Couch, and Elinor Griffith. *The Old Dutch Church of Sleepy Hollow: Legends and Lore: The Oldest Church in New York*. The Friends of the Old Dutch Church and Burial Grounds, 2017.
Anderson, Gary Clayton. *Will Rogers and His America*. University of Oklahoma Press, 2023.
Asma, Stephen T. *On Monsters: An Unnatural History of Our Worst Fears*. Oxford University Press, 2009.
Aveni, Anthony F. *The Book of the Year: A Brief History of Our Seasonal Holidays*. Oxford University Press, 2003.
Bacon, Edgar Mayhew. *Chronicles of Tarrytown and Sleepy Hollow*. HVA Press, 2018.
Baker, Emerson W. *A Storm of Witchcraft: The Salem Trials and the American Experience*. Oxford University Press, 2015.
Ball, Philip. *The Modern Myths: Adventures in the Machinery of the Popular Imagination*. University of Chicago Press, 2021.
Balserak, Jon. *Calvinism: A Very Short Introduction*. Oxford University Press, 2016.
Bannatyne, Lesley Pratt. *Halloween: An American Holiday, an American History*. Pelican, 1998.
Bannatyne, Lesley Pratt. *Halloween Nation: Behind the Scenes of America's Fright Night*. Pelican, 2011.
Barnard, Philip, Hilary Emmett, and Stephen Shapiro, eds. *The Oxford Handbook of Charles Brockden Brown*. Oxford University Press, 2019.
Barrier, Michael. *Hollywood Cartoons: American Animation in Its Golden Age*. Oxford University Press, 2003.
Beal, Timothy K. *Religion and Its Monsters*. Routledge, 2002.
Bennett, Marguerite, Jorge Coelho, Tamra Bonvillain, Jim Campbell, and Noelle Stevenson. Sleepy Hollow: *From the Fox Series*. Boom! Studios, 2015.
Bogdan, Henrik, and Martin P. Starr, eds. *Aleister Crowley and Western Esotericism*. Oxford University Press, 2012.
Bone, Robert A. "Irving's Headless Hessian: Prosperity and the Inner Life," *American Quarterly* 15, no. 2 (Summer 1963): 167–175.
Bowden, Mary Weatherspoon. *Washington Irving*. Twayne, 1981.
Boyle, T.C. *World's End*. Penguin, 1988.
Bradbury, Ray. *Something Wicked This Way Comes*. Avon, 1997.
Bradley, Elizabeth L. *Knickerbocker: The Myth Behind New York*. Rivergate Books, 2009.
Brandes, Stanley. *Skulls to the Living, Bread to the Dead: The Day of the Dead in Mexico and Beyond*. Wiley-Blackwell, 2007.

Useful Reading

Butler, Jon. *Awash in a Sea of Faith: Christianizing the American People*. Harvard University Press, 1990.
Butler, Jon. *New World Faiths: Religion in Colonial America*. Oxford University Press, 2008.
Clarke, Roger. *Ghosts, A Natural History: 500 Years of Searching for Proof*. St. Martin's Press, 2012.
Coleman, Robin R. Means. *Horror Noire: Blacks in American Horror Films from the 1890s to Present*. Routledge, 2011.
Conradt, Stacy. "11 Hair-Raising Facts About Disney's The Legend of Sleepy Hollow." *Mental Floss*, October 27, 2016, https://www.mentalfloss.com/article/87938/11-hair-raising-facts-about-disneys-legend-sleepy-hollow, accessed January 7, 2024.
Cowan, Douglas E. *America's Dark Theologian: The Religious Imagination of Stephen King*. NYU Press, 2018.
Cowan, Douglas E. *Sacred Terror: Religion and Horror on the Silver Screen*. Baylor University Press, 2008.
Davis, Kenneth C. *A Nation Rising: Untold Tales from America's Hidden History*. Harper, 2010.
Dawidziak, Mark. *A Mystery of Mysteries: The Death and Life of Edgar Allan Poe*. St. Martin's Press, 2023.
DeCandido, Keith R.A. *Sleepy Hollow: Children of the Revolution*. Broadway Books, 2014.
Denis, Gary. *Sleepy Hollow: Birth of the Legend*. Gary Denis, 2015.
de Villeneuve, Gabrielle-Suzanne Barbot. *Madame de Villeneuve's Original Beauty and the Beast*. Pook Press, n. d.
Dickey, Colin. *Ghostland: An American History in Haunted Places*. Viking, 2016.
Dragon, Austin. *The Devil's Patch: The Hunt for the Foul Murderer of Ichabod Crane*. Well-Tailored Books, 2015.
Dragon, Austin. *Hollow Blood: The Hunt for the Foul Murderer of Ichabod Crane*. Well-Tailored Books, 2015.
Dumas, Alexandre. *The Woman with the Velvet Necklace*. Fredonia Books, 2002.
Earle, Alice Morse. *Customs and Fashions in Old New England*. Charles Scribner's Sons, 1893.
Ebert, Chris. *Ophelia and Other Weird Tales*. Chris Ebert, 2009.
EW Staff. "Capsule TV Reviews: Give These Shows a Second Chance." *Entertainment Weekly* December 4, 2013, https://ew.com/article/2013/12/04/crazy-ones-mom-sleepy-hollow-second-chance-reviews/, accessed 17 June 2024.
Farnsworth, Cheri. *Haunted Hudson Valley: Ghosts and Strange Phenomena of New York's Sleep Hollow Country*. Stackpole Books, 2010.
Finkel, Irving. *The First Ghosts: Most Ancient of Legacies*. Hodder, 2021.
Forbes, Bruce David. *America's Favorite Holidays: Candid Histories*. University of California Press, 2015.
Foster, Don. *Author Unknown: Tales of a Literary Detective*. Owl Books, 2000.
Franklin, Benjamin. "Observations Concerning the Increasing of Mankind, Peopling of Countries, &c." Boston: Printed by S. Kneeland, 1755.
Gibson, Walter B., adapter. *Rod Serling's The Twilight Zone*. Wings Books, 1983.
Goldberg, Aaron H. *The Disney Story: Chronicling the Man, the Mouse and the Parks*. Quaker Scribe, 2016.
Golden, Christopher, and Ford Lytle Gilmore. *The Hollow: Book 1, Horseman*. Penguin, 2005.
Goldstone, Andrew. "Origins of the US Genre-Fiction System, 1890–1956," *Book History* 26, no. 1 (2023): 203–233.
Gottschall, Jonathan. *The Storytelling Animal: How Stories Make Us Human*. Mariner Books, 2013.
Grafius, Brandon R. *Lurking Under the Surface: Horror, Religion, and the Questions That Haunt Us*. Broadleaf Books, 2022.
Grafius, Brandon. *The Witch*. Devil's Advocates. Auteur, 2020.
Grey, Rudolph. *Nightmare of Ecstasy: The Life and Art of Edward D. Wood, Jr*. Feral House, 1994.

Useful Reading

Hanna, William, and Tom Ito. *A Cast of Friends*. Taylor, 1996.
Hastings, Christopher. *Operation Dracula! from Outer Space*. Inked by Kent Archer. Topatoco Books, 2009.
The Headless Horseman: A Retelling of Washington Irving's "The Legend of Sleepy Hollow." Illustrated by Emma Harding. Henry Holt, 1995.
Hedges, William L. *Washington Irving: An American Study, 1802–1832*. Johns Hopkins University Press, 1965.
Hellystia, Devi, and Heikal Hasan. "Narrative Functions in Burton's Sleepy Hollow Movie," *Vivid: Journal of Language and Literature* 10, no. 1 (2021): 31–40.
Henry, Christina. *Horseman: A Tale of Sleepy Hollow*. Berkley Books, 2021.
Hill, Frances. *A Delusion of Satan: The Full Story of the Salem Witch Trials*. Doubleday, 1995.
The Historical Society, Inc. *Images of America: Tarrytown and Sleepy Hollow*. Arcadia, 1997.
"History of Jack-o'-the-Lantern," *Dublin Penny Journal* 3–4 (1835): 229.
Hoena, Blake A., and Tod Smith. *Washington Irving's The Legend of Sleepy Hollow*. Stone Arch Books, 2014.
Hoffman, Daniel. "Irving's Use of American Folklore in 'The Legend of Sleepy Hollow,'" *Proceedings of the Modern Language Association* 68, no. 3 (June 1953): 425–435.
Horowitz, Mitch. *Occult America: White House Séances, Ouija Circles, Masons, and the Secret Mystic History of Our Nation*. Bantam, 2010.
Horowitz, Mitch. *Uncertain Places: Essays on Occult & Outsider Experiences*. Inner Traditions, 2022.
Hutton, Ronald. *The Stations of the Sun*. Oxford University Press, 1996.
Hynek, J. Allen, and Philip J. Imbrogno. *Night Siege: The Hudson Valley UFO Sightings*. Ballantine Books, 1987.
Ingebretsen, Edward J., S.J. *Maps of Heaven and Hell: Religious Terror as Memory from the Puritans to Stephen King*. M.E. Sharpe, 1996.
Introvigne, Massimo. *The Plymouth Brethren*. Oxford University Press, 2018.
Irvine, Alex. *The Secret Journal of Ichabod Crane*. Titan Books, 2014.
Irving, Washington. "The Adventure of the German Student." *Tales of a Traveller*. The Library of America, 1991: 418–24.
Irving, Washington. *The Historically Annotated Legend of Sleepy Hollow: Historical Annotations by Henry John Steiner*. Milestone Productions, 2014.
Irving, Washington. *A History of New York*. Penguin, 2008.
Irving, Washington. *The Legend of Sleepy Hollow and Other Stories*. Introduction and notes by Elizabeth L. Bradley. Penguin, 2014.
Irving, Washington. *The Legend of Sleepy Hollow and Other Stories: Or, The Sketch Book of Geoffrey Crayon, Gent*. Introduction by Alice Hoffman. The Modern Library, 2001.
Irving, Washington. *Rip Van Winkle & The Legend of Sleepy Hollow: With an Afterword by Clifton Fadiman*. Macmillan, 1963.
Irving, Washington. *The Sketch Book of Geoffrey Crayon, Gent*. A.L. Burt, 1820.
Irving, Washington. *The Sketch Book of Geoffrey Crayon, Gent*. Edited with an Introduction and notes by Susan Manning. Oxford University Press, 2009.
Irving, Washington. "Sleepy Hollow," *The Knickerbocker* 13, no. 5 (May 1839): 404–11.
Irving, Washington. *Wolfert's Roost, and Other Papers, Now First Collected*. Putnam, 1855, reprinted in Leopold Classic Library.
Iwerks, Leslie, and John Kenworthy. *The Hand behind the Mouse: An Intimate Biography of Ub Iwerks, the Man Walt Disney Called "the Greatest Animator in the World."* Disney Editions, 2001.
Janes, Regina. *Losing Our Heads: Beheadings in Literature and Culture*. New York University Press, 2005.
Jensen, Kelly. "'The Girl With the Green Ribbon': A Tale of Many Lives." https://bookriot.com/the-girl-with-the-green-ribbon/, accessed November 20, 2022.
Jones, Brian Jay. *Washington Irving: The Definitive Biography of America's First Bestselling Author*. Arcade, 2011.

Useful Reading

Kaplan, Stuart R., and William G. Miller. *The Game of Authors Compendium*. U.S. Games System, 2021.
Karlsen, Carol F. *The Devil in the Shape of a Woman: Witchcraft in Colonial New England*. Vintage, 1987.
Keller, Allan. *Life Along the Hudson*. Sleepy Hollow Restorations, 1976.
Kimball, Trevor. "*Sleepy Hollow*: Season Three Renewal for FOX TV Show." TV Season Finale, March 18, 2015, https://tvseriesfinale.com/tv-show/sleepy-hollow-season-three-renewal-for-fox-tv-show-35946/, accessed 18 June 2024.
Korkis, Jim. "Disney's 'The Legend of Sleepy Hollow' (1949)," *Cartoon Research*, October 30, 2020, https://cartoonresearch.com/index.php/disneys-the-legend-of-sleepy-hollow-1949/, accessed 7 January 2024.
Kornhaber, Donna. *Silent Film: A Very Short Introduction*. Oxford University Press, 2020.
Kruk, Jonathan. *Legends and Lore of Sleepy Hollow and the Hudson Valley*. History Press, 2011.
Lachman, Marvin. *The Villainous Stage: Crime Plays on Broadway and in the West End*. McFarland, 2014.
Laycock, Joseph, and Eric Harrelson. *The Exorcist Effect: Horror, Religion, and Demonic Belief*. Oxford University Press, 2023.
Lerangis, Peter. *Sleepy Hollow*. Archway, 1999.
Littlefield, Daniel F., Jr. "Washington Irving and the American Indian," *American Indian Quarterly* 5, no. 2 (May 1979): 135–154.
Machado, Carmen Maria. "The Husband Stitch." In *Her Body and Other Parties*. Graywolf Press, 2017, pp. 3–31.
Maltin, Leonard. "The Adventures of Ichabod and Mr. Toad." *The Disney Films*, fourth edition. Disney Editions, 2000: 89–92.
Maltin, Leonard. "The Rest of the Story." *The Disney Films,* fourth edition. Disney Editions, 2000: 283–324.
Marchese, Allison Guertin. *Hudson Valley Curiosities: The Sinking of the Steamship Swallow, the Poughkeepsie Seer, the UFOs of the Celtic Stone Chambers and More*. History Press, 2017.
Marquette, Andi. *The Secret of Sleepy Hollow*. Ylva, 2015.
Martin, Terence. "Rip, Ichabod, and the American Imagination," *American Literature* 31, no. 2 (May 1959): 137–149.
McCloud, Henry J. *Clerical Dress and Insignia of the Roman Catholic Church*. The Bruce Publishing Company, 1948.
McCorristine, Shane. *The Spectral Arctic: A History of Dreams and Ghosts in Polar Exploration*. UCL Press, 2018.
McGee, Mark Thomas. *Fast and Furious: The Story of American International Pictures*. McFarland, 1984.
McGinn, Colin. *The Power of Movies: How Screen and Mind Interact*. Vintage, 2005.
McGovern, Ann. *Ghostly Fun*. Scholastic, 1970.
Mengeling, Marvin E. "The Crass Humor of Irving's Diedrich Knickerbocker," *Studies in American Humor* 1, no. 2 (1974): 66–72.
Morton, Lisa. *Ghosts: A Haunted History*. Reaktion Books, 2015.
Morton, Lisa. *A Halloween Anthology: Literary and Historical Writings Over the Centuries*. McFarland, 2008.
Morton, Lisa. *Trick or Treat: A History of Halloween*. Reaktion, 2012.
Nazare, Joe. *The Legend of Sleepy Hollow: Ultimate Annotated Edition*. Kindle, 2020.
Nazare, Joe. "The Literature of Sleepy Hollow," https://joenazare.com/2020/10/26/the-literature-of-sleepy-hollow/, October 26, 2020, accessed July 7, 2022.
Neibaur, James. *The Monster Movies of Universal Studios*. Rowman & Littlefield, 2017.
Neuman, Robert. "Disney's Final Package Film: The Making and Marketing of *The Adventures of Ichabod and Mr. Toad* (1949)," *Animation, an Interdisciplinary Journal* 14, no. 2 (2019): 149–163.
Nowell-Smith, Geoffrey. *The History of Cinema: A Very Short Introduction*. Oxford University Press, 2017.

O'Neill, Tim. "Is Halloween Pagan?" *History for Atheists*, October 17, 2021, https://historyforatheists.com/2021/10/is-halloween-pagan/?fbclid=IwAR2boVmdjb0lSAguEWVmv7afqx-8xPU0QfJ5jiSpdPCB8tMBkdh1vxVmT78, accessed October 31, 2022.

Owens, Susan. *The Ghost: A Cultural History*. Tate, 2017.

Palombo, Alyssa. *The Spellbook of Katrina Van Tassel*. St. Martin's Griffin, 2018.

Paul, Howard. "Recollections of Edgar Allen [sic] Poe," *Munsey's Magazine* VII, no. 5 (August 1892): 554–558.

Petersen, Randy. *The Printer and the Preacher: Ben Franklin, George Whitefield, and the Surprising Friendship that Invented America*. Thomas Nelson, 2015.

Phillips, Kendall R. *A Place of Darkness: The Rhetoric of Horror in Early American Cinema*. University of Texas Press, 2018.

Phillips, Kendall R. *Projected Fears: Horror Films and American Culture*. Praeger, 2005.

Plate, S. Brent. *Religion and Film: Cinema and the Re-creation of the World*. Short Cuts. Columbia University Press, 2009.

Polise, Vincent. *The Pine Bush Phenomenon*. Trafford, 2005.

Poole, W. Scott. *Dark Carnivals: Modern Horror and the Origins of American Empire*. Counterpoint, 2022.

Poole, W. Scott. *Monsters in America: Our Historical Obsession with the Hideous and the Haunting*. Baylor University Press, 2011.

Popple, Simon, and Joe Kember. *Early Cinema: From Factory Gate to Dream Factory*. Short Cuts. Wallflower, 2004.

Restad, Penne L. *Christmas in America: A History*. Oxford University Press, 1995.

Rhodes, Gary D. *The Birth of the American Horror Film*. Edinburgh University Press, 2018.

Richardson, Judith. *Possessions: The History and Uses of Haunting in the Hudson Valley*. Harvard University Press, 2003.

Rogers, Nicholas. *Halloween: From Pagan Ritual to Party Night*. Oxford University Press, 2002.

Ross, Marilyn. *Barnabas, Quentin and the Hidden Tomb*. Paperback Library, 1971.

Rossing, Barbara R. *The Rapture Exposed: The Message of Hope in the Book of Revelation*. Basic Books, 2005.

Roth, Martin. *Comedy and America: The Lost World of Washington Irving*. Kennikat Press, 1976.

Rubin-Dorsky, Jeffrey. *Adrift in the Old World: The Psychological Pilgrimage of Washington Irving*. University of Chicago Press, 1988.

Salisbury, Mark, ed. *Burton on Burton*. Revised edition. Farrar, Straus and Giroux, 2006.

Sayad, Cecilia. *The Ghost in the Image: Technology and Reality in the Horror Genre*. Oxford University Press, 2021.

Schiff, Stacy. *The Witches: Salem, 1692*. Little, Brown, 2015.

Schlosser, S.E. *Spooky New York: Tales of Hauntings, Strange Happenings, and Other Local Lore*. Globe Pequot, 2019.

Schwartz, Alvin. *In a Dark, Dark Room and Other Scary Stories*. Harper, 2017.

Segal, Robert A. *Myth: A Very Short Introduction*. Oxford University Press, 2015.

Serling, Anne. *As I Knew Him: My Dad, Rod Serling*. Citadel Press, 2013.

Shorto, Russell. *The Island at the Center of the World: The Epic Story of Dutch Manhattan and the Forgotten Colony that Shaped America*. Vintage, 2004.

Silver, Carole G. *Strange and Secret Peoples*. Oxford University Press, 1999.

Skal, David J. *Death Makes a Holiday: A Cultural History of Halloween*. Bloomsbury, 2002.

Skal, David J. *The Monster Show: A Cultural History of Horror*. Faber & Faber, 1993.

Skinner, Charles M. *Myths and Legends of Our Own Land*. J.B. Lippincott, 1896.

Sojak, Notary. *G. Washington Slept Here: A Sleepy Hollow Local History*. Notary Sojak, 2021.

Squire, Walter. "The Pleasure and Pains of Texts: Kenneth Grahame, Washington Irving, and *The Adventures of Ichabod and Mr. Toad*." *Walt Disney, from Reader to Storyteller: Essays on the Literary Inspirations*, ed. Kathy Merlock Jackson and Mark I. West. McFarland, 2014: 80–91.

Stamper, J.B. *Tales for the Midnight Hour*. Scholastic, 1977.

Standiford, Les. *The Man Who Invented Christmas: How Charles Dickens's A Christmas Carol Rescued His Career and Revived Our Holiday Spirits.* Crown, 2008.
Straub, Peter. *Ghost Story.* Pocket Books, 1979.
Strieber, Whitley. *Communion: A True Story.* HarperCollins, 1987.
Strohl, Matthew. *Why It's OK to Love Bad Movies.* Routledge, 2022.
Sutton, Matthew Avery. *American Apocalypse: A History of Modern Evangelicalism.* Belknap Press, 2017.
Thompson, Jeff. *The Television Horrors of Dan Curtis: Dark Shadows, The Night Stalker and Other Productions.* McFarland, 2019.
Tudor, Andrew. *Monsters and Mad Scientists: A Cultural History of the Horror Movie.* Basil Blackwell, 1989.
Verday, Jessica. *The Haunted.* Simon Pulse, 2010.
Verday, Jessica. *The Hidden.* Simon Pulse, 2011.
Verday, Jessica. *The Hollow.* Simon Pulse, 2009.
von Behr, H.A. *Ghosts in Residence: Stories from Haunted Hudson Valley.* North Country Books, 2023.
Walko, Jude S. *The Unhallowed Horseman.* Blue Falcon Publications, 2021.
Weinraub, Bernard. "At the Movies," *New York Times*, 19 November 1999: section E, p. 20.
Wickline, Dan, A.C. Osorio, and Erick Arciniega. *Grimm Fairy Tales Presents: Sleepy Hollow.* Zenescope, 2013.
Wiggins, Steve A. *Holy Horror: The Bible and Fear in Movies.* McFarland, 2018.
Wiggins, Steve A. "Reading the Bible in Sleepy Hollow," *The Journal of Religion and Popular Culture* 28, no. 2–3 (2016): 187–198.
Yorinks, Arthur, and Richard Egielski. *It Happened in Pinsk.* Sunburst, 1987.
Zimmermann, Linda. *Hudson Valley UFOs: Startling Eyewitness Accounts from 1909 to the Present.* Eagle Press, 2014.
Zimmermann, Linda. *In the Night Sky: Hudson Valley UFO Sightings from the 1930s to the Present.* Eagle Press, 2013.

Index

Note: Only actors playing the four principal characters are listed.
Fictional characters are listed by first rather than last name.

Abbey Browning 155
ABC 100, 146
Abigail Mills 157, 163–66, 169, 174
"The Adventure of the German Student" 32
African American 43, 77, 120, 144, 146, 151–53, 160–62, 164, 166, 194–95, 197, 211
Albany 183, 184, 190
American Indian 13, 19, 107, 116, 184
American International Pictures 102
The Amityville Horror 49, 103, 107
Anderson, Leroy 90
Anderson, Nathan 150
apocalypse 6, 36, 136, 162–63, 165, 167, 212
Arciniega, Erick 158
Ariadne 5, 116, 205, 212
Aristocats 104
Arnaud, Étienne 61, 72, 75
Atkinson, Vic 103, 202, 146
Auberjonois, Rene 102

Baltus Van Tassel 20, 108, 109, 112, 119, 121, 124, 128–30, 132–33, 135, 146, 150–51, 158, 172, 178–79, 208–10
Beauty and the Beast 4, 179–81
Beer, Lindsey 9, 207
Begley, Ed, Jr. 6, 112, 115
Beharie, Nicole 163, 165, 166
Bennet, Marguerite 169
Bible 6, 19, 40, 47, 52, 54, 120, 128, 130–33, 136, 138, 161, 162–63, 165–66, 184, 198, 212
Black Lives Matter 161
Black Sabbath 94
blacksmith 118, 121, 151, 158
Bonvillain, Tamra 169

Boyd, Guy 102
Boyle, T.C. 116, 180
Bradbury, Ray 90, 91
Bradley, Elizabeth L. 202
Brown, Clancy 122, 163
Brown, Pamela 102
Butkus, Dick 107, 204

The Cabinet of Dr. Caligari 57
Calvin Montgomery 152
Calvinism 42, 46, 52, 85
Carpenter, John 92–93
Carradine, John 98
Carrere, Tia 122
Carter, Angela 79
Carter, Nick 147
Carver, Brent 118–19
CBS 101, 103, 158
cemetery 54, 71, 76, 114, 172
Charlotte Jansen 179
Christmas 4, 6, 15, 34–35, 81, 83–85, 87–93, 110, 167, 178, 190
"Christmas Dinner" 89
Church of Satan 48
Civil War 31, 152
Clancy, Carl Stearns 63, 66
Clash of the Titans 12
Close, Glenn 116
Coelho, Jorge 169
Cooper, Alice 105
Cooper, James Fenimore 11, 100, 185
Corman, Roger 102, 104, 106
Cox, Neil 102
Crosby, Bing 6, 9, 75, 77
cross 102, 114–15, 133, 138, 152
Crowley, Aleister 186–87
Cuoco, Kaley 147

221

Index

Daedalus 6, 7, 27, 148
daguerreotype 55
Dame Martling 76, 77
D'Angelo, Beverly 112
Darby, John Nelson 136
Daredevil 22, 29, 114, 116, 119
Dark Shadows 105, 161, 187, 207
Davis, Andrew Jackson 187
DeCandido, Keith R.A. 173, 174
Deliverance 152, 153
demon 23, 36, 49, 50, 52, 125, 129, 130, 138, 162, 163, 165, 172, 180, 187, 191, 204, 212
de Paul, Gene 28, 77
Depp, Johnny 3, 6, 9, 99, 106, 115, 117, 123, 124, 126, 127, 134, 154, 157, 168, 188
de Villeneuve, Gabrielle-Suzanne Barbot 79–80
Día de los Muertos 81, 92
Dickens, Charles 83, 88–89
Disney, Walt 70–1, 77, 78
Doffue Van Tassel 112–15, 208
Donohoe, Kathleen 180
Dracula 48, 63, 69, 71, 103, 211
Dragon, Austin 176
Dumas, Alexandre 33
Duvall, Shelley 74, 111, 112, 114, 115, 119, 158, 208

Ebert, Chris 211
Edward Scissorhands 134
Edwards, Jonathan 44
Eggers, Robert 2, 42
The Exorcist 48, 115, 117, 123, 136

Fadiman, Clifton 80–81, 95
Ferrante, Anthony C. 152, 153, 177, 186
Ford, Hobey 168
Foster, Meg 107
Fox 1, 9, 30, 36, 40, 52, 59, 77, 111, 117, 121, 122, 134, 141, 145, 146, 152, 153, 156, 157–62, 164, 168, 169, 170, 171, 173, 174, 175, 176, 197, 200, 201, 202, 209, 210, 213
Francis, Alec B. 61
Franck, Stephan 167
Frank Irving 162, 165, 169, 174
Frankenstein 11, 47, 48, 56, 71, 76, 191
Franklin, Benjamin 44, 165, 195–96, 211
Fritz Vanderhoof 107–09
Frost, Cy 150
Furth, George 96

Gang, Pierre 111, 114, 117–19, 147, 151, 158, 179, 197, 205, 207, 212
Genesis 52
Geronimi, Clyde 72, 77
Ghost Rider 206

Gilmore, Ford Lytle 171
Goldblum, Jeff 6, 106, 112, 158
Golden, Christopher 171
Goodman, Carol 180
Grahame, Kenneth 74, 105
Greek (mythology) 10, 12, 40, 52, 108, 166
Greenspan, Gabe 208
Greenwood, Lyndie 163
Griles, Edd 112, 113
Gunpowder 22–3, 25, 46, 70, 77, 115, 119, 209
Guy Fawkes Day 86, 91

Halloween (movie) 82, 93
Hamill, Mark 122
Hamilton 161, 179, 199
Handmade Puppet Dreams Film Series 168
Hanna-Barbera 96, 98, 168
Hans Van Ripper 23, 46, 121, 122, 147, 148, 177
Hawthorne, Nathaniel 11, 24, 67
Häxan 63
Hell 16, 36, 50, 52, 66, 114, 115, 121, 123, 129, 132, 134, 136, 138, 152–53, 166, 169, 180, 212
Hendricks, Ben, Jr. 65
Henry, Christina 203–05, 206, 207
Hercules 10, 12
Heredity 27
Historic Hudson Valley 202
A History of New York 7, 14, 15, 16, 17, 18, 19, 21, 26, 62, 65, 78, 86, 88, 191, 202
Hoena, Blake A. 158
horserace 25, 114, 119
House of Dark Shadows 187
Hudson, Henry 4, 41, 50, 184–85, 190, 209
The Hunchback of Notre Dame 80
Hydra 152, 153
Hynek, J. Allen 188–89

Irvine, Alex 173, 174
Iscove, Phillip 161
Iwerks, Ub 70–74, 76, 77, 141

jack-o-lantern 28, 61, 72, 75, 82, 86–7, 88, 90, 93, 97, 98, 102, 105, 107, 110, 114, 115, 116, 120, 121, 122, 130, 135, 145, 148, 149, 152, 158, 167, 168, 169, 202, 205, 206
Jackson, Shirley 8, 59
James, Henry 8, 101
James, M.R. 8, 89
Janjic, Zoran 96, 98, 103, 105, 113, 114, 115, 179, 210
Jiménez-Cruz, Guido 202
Jones, Jeffrey 128, 129

Index

Jones, Stephen Graham 107
Jonson, Ben 114
Judas 197
Julian Crane 176–77

King, Stephen 48, 58, 59
Kinnye, Jack 72, 77
Kirkland, John 98
Kolchak: The Night Stalker 100, 132
Kreskin 103
Kruk, Jonathan 32, 201–02
Kurtzman, Alex 161

Lawrence, D.H. 179
Lefevre, Rachelle 119
Lemelin, Paul 118
Lerangis, Peter 140
lesbian 173, 177, 178
Levin, Ira 48, 178
Lord Byron 78, 115

Machado, Carmen Maria 34, 35
Macy, William H. 122
Major André 23, 28, 50, 118, 121, 158, 185–85, 197
Manhattan 1, 7, 10, 14, 18, 73, 78, 183, 186, 190
Marquette, Andi 177, 178
Mather, Cotton 20, 49, 65, 115, 119
McGovern, Ann 33–34
McNutt, Robert 116
mercenary 21, 27, 28, 35, 36, 113, 119, 121, 128, 144, 145, 158, 166, 196, 197
Meredith, Lois 65
Meyer, Stephenie 154, 207
Millie Cooper 150
Minotaur 6, 24, 26, 27–30, 35, 181
Mischief Night 91
Mison, Tom 3, 158, 162, 164, 169, 173
Moloch 36, 162, 163, 165, 166, 169
More, Thomas 78
multiplane camera 71

Nathaniel Wiley 145
New Amsterdam 26, 200
Newman, Kyle 146, 147, 148, 149, 172, 173, 207
Night of Dark Shadows 187
Night of the Living Dead 48, 103
The Nightmare Before Christmas 81, 88, 167
A Nightmare on Elm Street 99, 124
Noah 198
Nosferatu 57, 63

Oktoberfest 150
Old Brouwer 46, 97, 168

Olson, Doug 150
O'Meara, Peter 149, 150
The Omen 27, 48, 136
Orsi, Roberto 161
Osorio, AC 158

Palombo, Alyssa 79, 178–79, 180
Pandora 166
Parish, Mitchell 90
Pecknold, Robin 34
Perry, Luke 122
Persaud, Sean 208
Persaud, Sinéad 207, 208, 209
Peyo 168
Philipse, Frederick 42, 128
Pierce, Marcus 1
Poe, Edgar Allan 11, 13, 24, 31, 32, 43, 47, 54, 55, 56, 58, 102, 104, 105, 126, 144, 145, 193, 207
Pola, Edward 88
Polidori, John 115
Poltergeist 49
PorchLight Entertainment 146
postage stamps 4, 100
Prendes, Jose 206
Price, Vincent 101, 102, 103, 134
Purcell, Henry 97
Purgatory 50, 164

A Quiet Place 26

Rabbit Ears 116
Ramage, Rick 149, 150, 151, 205
Raye, Don 28, 77
Reid, Thomas Mayne 31
Revelation 153, 162, 163, 165, 166
Revolutionary Era/War 7, 75, 118, 128, 145, 174, 183, 185, 197, 202, 209
Rice, Anne 154
Ricci, Christina 127
Richardson, Miranda 125
Ringu 209
Rip Van Winkle 8, 10, 11, 16, 18, 50, 59, 60, 74, 78, 80, 95, 96, 1103, 104, 162, 184, 208, 209, 211
Rogers, Will 6, 8, 63, 64, 75, 99
Room 237 107
Rosemary's Baby 48, 51, 103, 136, 189
Ross, Marylin 187, 207
Rowling, J.K. 154

Saint Nicholas Society 88
Saint Paul 40
Salem 9, 20, 41, 67, 128
Salmagundi 18, 19, 86
Samhain 84–5, 92

Satan 48, 129, 205
Saturday Night Live 211
Schellerup, Henning 99, 105, 106, 107, 108, 109, 111, 112, 113, 114, 119, 120, 121, 125, 147, 148, 151, 204
Schwartz, Alvin 34
Serilda of Abaddon 174
Serling, Rod 187, 188
shades 155
Shakespeare, William 89
Shelley, Mary 11, 198
The Shining 107, 112
Shipwrecked Comedy 207, 208
Showtime 112
Shrek 2 2
Skeleton Dance 71, 73
Smith, Tod 158
Smurfs 167–68
Snow White and the Seven Dwarves 73
Spongebob Squarepants 96, 122
Stamper, J.B. (Judith Bauer) 34
Stevenson, Robert Louis 91
Stewart, Charisse 150
Stigmata 49, 149
Straub, Peter 89, 101
Stribling, William J. 207, 208
Strieber, Whitley 189
Summerfield, Kevin 142, 144, 173
sword 28, 70, 76, 100, 111, 129, 139, 144, 146, 148, 149, 152, 197
SyFy 152

The Texas Chainsaw Massacre 152
The Thing from Another World 93, 188
Thomerson, Tim 113
transgender 203, 205
The Twilight Zone 33, 50, 105, 161, 187, 188, 207

Valentino, Serena 206–07
vampire 9, 26, 68, 115, 154, 156, 187
Van Dien, Casper 127
Velma Van Dam 104

Venturini, Edward 28, 54, 63, 64, 65, 66, 68, 70, 73, 76, 77, 83, 99, 108, 113, 161, 196
Verday, Jessica 154, 155, 171, 177
Vincent Douglass 202
Vsadnik bez golovy 31

Walken, Christopher 134
Walker, Andrew Kevin 115, 124, 140
Walko, Jude S. 202
Walpole, Horace 11, 47
Washington, George 6, 40, 41, 157, 163, 165, 211
wassail 89, 90
Weinrib, Lennie 97
Weiss, Sam 98
Whitefield, George 43–44
Wicca 131, 187
Wickline, Dan 158
Wiles, Mary Kate 208
will-o'-wisps 86
Williams, Shane 36, 111, 120, 121, 122, 129, 147, 163
windmill 76, 121, 148
Winthrop Palmer 108–09
witch 41, 42, 54, 67, 89, 91, 104, 121, 127, 128, 129, 130–32, 133, 140, 162, 164, 166, 174, 179, 208, 209
Wolfert's Roost 13, 16, 78, 211
Wood, Ed 144, 188
Wyle, George 88

The X-Files 9, 162, 163

Y2K 136
Yagher, Kevin 124, 140
Yankee 19, 21, 62, 64, 65, 75, 82, 94
Yorinks, Arthur 35
YouTube 98, 201, 207

Zegers, Kevin 147
Zenescope's Grimm Fairy Tales 158
Zeven, Vong 145

www.ingramcontent.com/pod-product-compliance
Lightning Source LLC
Chambersburg PA
CBHW032040300426
44117CB00009B/1135